Familienunternehmen und KMU

Edited by

A. Hack, Berne
A. Calabrò, Witten/Herdecke
H. Frank, Vienna
F. W. Kellermanns, Tennessee
T. Zellweger, St. Gallen

Both Family Firms and Small and Medium Sized Enterprises (SME) feature a number of distinct behaviors and characteristics which could provide them with a competitive advantage in the market but could also lead to certain risks. The scientific series at hand presents research which provides an empirical and theoretical contribution to the investigation on these specific characteristics and their impact on business practice. The overall aim of this series is to advance the development of theory in the areas of family firm and SME management.

Thomas Pijanowski

Lending Behavior toward Family Firms

With a foreword by Prof. Dr. Andreas Hack

Springer Gabler

Thomas Pijanowski
Witten/Herdecke, Germany

Dissertation Witten/Herdecke University, 2013

ISBN 978-3-658-06682-6 ISBN 978-3-658-06683-3 (eBook)
DOI 10.1007/978-3-658-06683-3

The Deutsche Nationalbibliothek lists this publication in the Deutsche Nationalbibliografie; detailed bibliographic data are available in the Internet at http://dnb.d-nb.de.

Library of Congress Control Number: 2014945235

Springer Gabler

Printed on acid-free paper

Springer Gabler is a brand of Springer DE.
Springer DE is part of Springer Science+Business Media.
www.springer-gabler.de

Dedication

"If I have seen a little further it is by standing on the shoulders of giants."
(Newton, 1676)

This dissertation is dedicated to my parents, Janosch and Barbara Pijanowski. Thank you for letting me stand on your shoulders. You are the best parents I can imagine.
Unfortunately, my dad is not able to see this dissertation finished and to celebrate it with us. He died in 2011. I deeply hope that I was able to bring the same amount of joy, happiness and inspiration to his life as he did to mine. *I will always miss you, Dad.*
The remaining space is left blank in memory of my father.

Foreword

What do you think when you hear the term "family business" or "family firm"? Do you already have a picture in mind? Most people do. They make generic associations with firms that they perceive as family firms. In addition, many family firms explicitly use such references to their family background in their marketing and communication efforts – probably in order to elicit specific associations made with the term "family firm" and to influence stakeholders' behavior. But does it work? In recent years, researchers have started to investigate whether the organizational form of "family firms" has become a positively loaded category itself and whether the communication of family involvement influences the behavior of stakeholders such as customers or job seekers. For those two groups, research has shown that the communication of family involvement does indeed influence the behavior of customers and job seekers.

Another interesting and important group of stakeholders are lenders since financing represents one of the main challenges for family firms. Sufficient capital is the basic requirement necessary to operate the business, to fund innovation, to drive growth and to successfully hand over the business to next generations. Difficulties in raising enough funds might jeopardize the company's ability to survive. Hence the question: Does the communication of family involvement positively influence the company's ability to raise financing? This is the key issue examined by Thomas Pijanowski, who uncovers new facets on how changes in the communication of family involvement impact the lending behavior of bank loan officers within the lending process. Building upon sound theoretical approaches (Socioemotional Wealth, Agency Theory, and Resource-Based View) Thomas Pijanowski formulates a strong theoretical model on the impact of family firm involvement on bank loan officers' behavior. In addition, he manages to overcome most of the empirical weaknesses of other studies on lending behavior toward family firms by applying a powerful method, i.e. conjoint-analysis. He uses a unique sample of 90 loan officers making the results extremely valuable and enhancing their credibility.

Results indicate that loan officers are influenced by information on the type and level of family involvement within the company of a prospective borrower. The study shows that loan officers react positively to family-related information. Furthermore, Thomas Pijanowski shows that loan officers are susceptible to the similarity bias in that they prefer family firms that are more similar to themselves with respect to their socioemotional wealth orientation, indicating that different loan officers treat different types of family firms heterogeneously as a result of behavioral biases.

Thereby, the present study makes an exceptional contribution to research in that it applies new theoretical concepts to the research question, starts to examine differences in lending behavior toward varying types of family firms and consequently addressing the issue of heterogeneity of family firms and finally employs an experimental approach in order to supplement the currently available studies.

In addition, it is a valuable piece of work for practitioners, especially for family firm executives who are concerned with raising funds and wondering whether to promote the company's familiness in this context. Overall, Thomas Pijanowski's dissertation exceeds common expectations for a doctoral thesis and therefore deserves a broad readership in both academia and management practice.

Prof. Dr. Andreas Hack

Acknowledgements

The film director Guy Ritchie once said: "I'm not under too much of an illusion of how smart or un-smart I am because filmmaking ultimately is about teamwork." The same applies to me and this dissertation. Though it is an individual work, I know that it would not have been possible without the help, support, guidance and efforts of a lot of people. Therefore, I would like to take the opportunity to explicitly thank all of those people who contributed to it.

First, I would like to express my deepest gratitude to my advisor, Prof. Dr. Andreas Hack, for his excellent guidance, encouragement and patience. I have been amazingly fortunate to have an advisor who gave me the freedom to explore on my own and at the same time the guidance and structure to progress and not lose track along the way. He provided me with an excellent atmosphere for doing and completing this research project.

I would also like to explicitly thank Prof. Dr. Arist von Schlippe for giving me the opportunity to conduct a research project in collaboration with the Wittner Insitute for Family Businesses (WIFU). I was delighted to interact with him as he always managed to open up my horizon showing me new perspectives on things. I really enjoyed our numerous conversations.

Next, I would like to thank my parents, Barbara and Janosch Pijanowski, for working so hard to provide for my education and for their unconditional love, support and encouragement. This project would have been so much harder without you. Thank you for everything you did for me.

Furthermore, I am grateful to all of the loan officers who supported this research project by taking the time and participating in the experiment. When you read this, you probably received this dissertation as a little gift for your help.

I would also like to thank Prof. Dr. Elliott Parker, Prof. Dr. Andrea Calabrò, Prof. Dr. Franz Kellermanns, Dr. Nils Kraicy, Dr. Hannes Hauswald, Vanessa Schlüter, Julia Scheller, Katlin Zimmer and Sabrina Matenaar who have provided useful comments, feedback, camaraderie and support along the way. In addition, I would like to thank all of the other doctoral students at the Wittner Insitute for Family Businesses who conducted their research projects during the same time. It was always a pleasure to critically discuss ideas with you in our colloquia.

I am also thankful to all of my friends who dragged me away from the laptop and got me to move and workout. It's only because of them that my back didn't hurt all the time from the endless hours of sitting in front of my computer. Overall, I would like to thank all of my friends for supporting me during this time.

Finally, I would like to thank Dr. Joann Schoen for putting in so much work and proofreading the dissertation in such a detail. I really appreciated it and hope to be able to return this favor in the near future one way or another.

Well, that's it. I hope that I mentioned every person who contributed to this dissertation one way or the other. However, if you do not find yourself in the text in the way you were expecting it, I am sorry for that. In this case, feel free to drop by and complain to me about that. I will welcome you with a drink or two and you can help me to remember the good times.

Thomas Pijanowski

Table of Contents

List of Figures

List of Tables

List of Abbreviations

AIC	Akaike Information Criterion
AIMR	Association for Investment Management and Research
BIC	Bayesian Information Criterion
BSE	Breast Self-Examination
e.g.	exemplī grātiā (for example)
EFA	Exploratory Factor Analysis
EUR	Euros
HLM	Hierarchical Linear Model
i.e.	id es (that is, that means, in other words)
IPE	Investor Protection Environment
KMO	Kaiser-Meyer-Olkin
NSSBF	National Survey of Small Business Finance
OLS	Ordinary Least Squares
PCA	Principal Component Analysis
PSE	Proactive Stakeholder Engagement
R&D	Research and Development
RBV	Resource-Based View
SCA	Sustained Competitive Advantage
SD	Standard Deviation
SEW	Socioemotional Wealth
VRIN	Valuable, Rare, Inimitable and Non-Substitutable

1 Introduction

1.1 Problem Outline and Research Question

Family firms play an important role within society and represent a predominant organizational form of businesses within the world's economic landscape. Depending on the country in focus and the particular definition of the term family firm that underlie individual studies, literature estimates that family firms represent about 50-96% of all businesses (International Family Enterprise Research Academy, 2003). Additionally, numerous scholars regularly point out to the significant role of family firms within our economic system and the need to scientifically investigate this form of organization (Anderson & Reeb, 2003; Morck & Yeung, 2004; Chrisman et al., 2005; Chrisman et al., 2007). As a consequence, research on family firms has grown rapidly during the last two decades (Gomez-Mejia et al., 2011).

A large part of family business research focuses mainly on internal aspects of the family firm (Botero & Blombäck, 2010). It tries to identify unique characteristics within the company or between the company and the family which separate them from other non-family firms or mark differences between different types of family firms like e.g. governance structures, succession performance or dynamics between family members and the business (see e.g. Fiegener et al., 1996; Gomez-Mejia et al., 2001; Randoy & Goel, 2003 or see Sharma, 2004; Chrisman et al., 2010 for a review of important research streams in family business research). In comparison to that and despite their importance, relatively little attention has been paid to stakeholders and especially to the effect of family firms on external stakeholders (Debicki et al., 2009). But it seems that a recent trend in family business research has evolved. A growing number of scholars start to investigate the impact of family firms or more specifically the impact of family involvement within a company on external stakeholders. So Craig et al. (2008), Carrigan & Buckley (2008) and Blombäck (2009) investigate the effect of family involvement on customers, Covin (1994) analyses the influence of family engagement on potential employees and Salvato & Moores (2010) and Trotman & Trotman (2010) discuss potential research on the effect of family firms on auditors. Besides those groups, another group of external stakeholders, which is of significant interest to both scholars and practitioners, are lenders as debt represents a major source of capital for family firms. According to pecking order theory, firms typically prefer internal to external financing. But in case of insufficient internal financial resources, firms favor debt over new external equity due to lower information costs (Myers, 1984). This proves to be especially true for family firms as control is an important factor for this type of business (Coleman & Carsky, 1999; Croci et al., 2011; Erikson et al., 2003; Morck & Yeung, 2003; Poutziouris, 2001; Romano et al., 2001; Gomez-Mejia et al., 2007; Berrone et al., 2012). In addition, scholars note that funding represents one of the main challenges for family firms (Coleman & Carsky, 1999; de Visscher et al., 1995). They argue that sufficient capital is a basic requirement to operate the business, to finance innovation, to push growth and to successfully transfer the business to next generations. Difficulties in raising enough funds might negatively influence the firms' competitive position and consequently threaten its survivability. In this context, de Visscher et al. (1995) point out to the fact that "Many family businesses die because capital or liquidity problems prevent them from surviving generational, strategic or ownership transitions" (p. 4), which underlines the importance of a good access to external financial resources. Therefore, it would be essential to know whether family involvement or the communication of it has an impact on the behavior of lenders – the group of external stakeholders that plays such a crucial role for family firms.

In general, companies can use various types of debt, which can be roughly categorized in e.g. (1) private versus public debt, (2) bank versus other debt and (3) syndicated versus bilateral debt (Brigham & Ehrhardt, 2011; Quiry et al., 2011; Sinkey, 2002; Greenbaum & Thakor, 1995). Coleman & Carsky (1999) and Achleitner et al. (2011) found that family firms primarily use private bank debt. When viewed from the perspective of lending banks and additionally taking into account the overwhelming importance and large number of family firms within the economic system, it becomes clear that family firms represent an essential client base for banks, as those will be the primary customers for business loans. Because of its importance for both family firms and banks, this study focuses on this type of debt, i.e. private bank debt and asks whether the communication of family involvement has an impact on family firms' access and conditions to private bank debt financing. Answering this question is important as (1) this type of debt is a significant way to secure resources to operate the business from the family firms' perspective and (2) the business with family firms represents an important source of revenues from the perspective of lending banks so that inadvertent variations of behavior might have detrimental consequences.

Besides the traditional investigation of differences between family and non-family firms, scholars underline the importance of studying differences between family firms in order to account for the high degree of heterogeneity within this group of businesses (see e.g. García-Álvarez & López-Sintas, 2001 and Chrisman et al., 2003). Those scholars basically state that family firms are not a homogeneous group of businesses but differ significantly from each other. Some even claim that differences between various types of family firms might be greater and of higher relevance than differences between family and non-family firms (Chua et al., 2012; Chrisman & Patel, 2012; Bennedsen et al., 2010). As a consequence, the leading research question of the present study is: Do lenders of private bank debt deal differently with different kinds of family firms? Or to put it differently: Are lenders of private bank debt influenced by information regarding the form and degree of family involvement within the company of a prospective borrower?

1.2 Status Quo of Related Research

Starting by reviewing the general literature regarding the topic of lending, it was found that scholars typically use either (1) neoclassical approaches, (2) agency theory and/or (3) the behavioral economics framework to examine and explain lending behavior in general. All of these approaches provide varying perspectives on the question of whether and why lenders deal differently with individual borrowers. Whereas neoclassical approaches argue from a strict rationality-based perspective stating that loan officers will differentiate between borrowers only because of objective differences among these companies (Greenbaum & Thakor, 1995; Panagopoulos & Spiliotis, 1998), agency theory examines the question from a contractual perspective and basically asserts that differences in lending behavior occur because of problems that are related to information asymmetry and goal divergence which are adverse selection and moral hazard (Jensen & Meckling, 1976; Stiglitz & Weiss, 1981). Finally, scholars that use the behavioral economics framework assume that lenders are not fully rational decision makers, thereby make decision using simple judgment and decision mechanism and are thus subject to decision biases which cause differences in lending behavior (see e.g. Biggs et al., 1985; Beaulieu, 1994 and Lipshitz & Shulimovitz, 2007).

When reviewing the literature in the field of family business research on the topic of whether and why lenders deal differently with family firms, it can be noticed that scholars that address this topic majorly rely only upon agency theoretical perspective by arguing that family firms represent a whole set of opposing forces that both alleviate or intensify agency conflicts causing family firms to either benefit or suffer regarding credit availability and/or contract terms (see e.g. Anderson et al., 2003 and Niskanen et al., 2010). One stream of research argues, for instance, that family firms have longer investment horizons as a consequence of the family members' substantial investments in the company which causes them to act more risk-averse and which ultimately lowers the risk of moral hazard problems and thus leads to a beneficial treatment on the side of the lenders regarding those companies (see e.g. Kang, 2000, McConaugby et al., 2001; Le Breton-Miller & Miller, 2006). On the other hand, an opposing stream of research asserts that family firms are characterized by a higher risk of agency conflicts and are thus discriminated by lenders. Those scholars argue e.g. that a higher degree of family involvement leads to concentrated power which makes it easier for those firms to pursue unfavorable policies from the lenders perspective (Chua et al., 2011; Gomez-Mejia et al., 2001; Mueller & Inderst, 1999). When reviewing the empirical evidence with respect to those views, it can be found that the generated empirical data of the existing studies report highly ambiguous results and are not sufficient to answer the main research question in focus adequately, i.e. whether lenders deal differently with family firms or more specifically with different kinds of family firms (see e.g. Bopaiah, 1998 and Anderson et al., 2003 for evidence of a positive relationship and Niskanen et al., 2010 and Steijvers & Voordeckers, 2009b for evidence on the negative impact). In addition and as said before, it can be found that all of the currently available studies that address this question solely rely on an agency theoretical perspective, completely ignoring other potentially relevant theoretical frameworks that might provide interesting insights (e.g. behavioral economics). Those approaches have proved to be useful for the analysis of lending behavior on a general level (see above) and thus might turn out to be useful concepts for answering the question in focus in the context of family firm research. On top of these issues, current research focuses mainly on differences in lending behavior toward family and non-family firms while completely neglecting the heterogeneity within the group of family firms which is said to be of even greater importance and is frequently emphasized by various scholars (Chua et al., 2012; Chrisman & Patel, 2012; Bennedsen et al., 2010). Moreover, the review of the empirical papers reveals potential methodological problems that might have partly caused the high degree of ambiguity within the empirical results. A further problem might lie in the methodological monotony of the currently available literature as these typically use regression analytical techniques and ex-post data sets while ignoring other approaches like e.g. experiments (see section 2.2 for a detailed review on this issue).

Reviewing the general family business research literature, it can be noted that scholars in this research area typically rely on the agency perspective, the Resource-Based View (RBV) and most recently the socioemotional wealth (SEW) approach to explain the unique characteristics of family firms (Siebels & Knyphausen-Aufseß, 2012; Chrisman et al., 2010; Berrone et al., 2012). However, when again considering that scholars who examined lending behavior toward family firms mostly relied only upon agency theoretical arguments while neglecting other potentially relevant theoretical perspectives (the RBV and the SEW concept), additional gaps within the currently available literature start to unveil. All of these aspects underline the relevance of examining the leading research question with additional studies.

Summing up the status quo, it can be said that though the currently available literature addresses the previously set main research question of whether and why lenders deal differently with family firms, it is also characterized by significant research gaps which make it impossible to answer the question adequately solely on the basis of the currently available literature. In particular the main research gaps are (1) the lack of theoretical diversity, (2) a failure to acknowledge the heterogeneity of family firms, (3) the insufficient analysis of the impact of context parameters, (4) the risk of methodological flaws and (5) methodological monotony.

Please note that this section gave only a brief overview of the currently available literature in order to introduce the topic and raise awareness toward the existing research gaps, making it easier for the reader to understand the rationale behind the present study. The actual literature review is part of the body of this thesis and will therefore be discussed later in detail.

1.3 Purpose and Scope of the Research Project

The main goal of this thesis is to contribute to answering the leading research question of whether and why lenders deal differently with family firms or more specifically with different kinds of family firms. As described in the preceding section of the introduction, the currently available literature on this topic is characterized by some significant gaps in research. This study aims to address some of those research gaps in order to enhance our understanding of the effect family involvement or the communication of it has on lenders. In particular, the current study intends to contribute to the discussion in four ways.

First, this dissertation attempts to expand the theoretical spectrum that is being used to answer the main research question by applying new theoretical perspectives that are typically used within the study of lending behavior in general and in the field of family business research but have been neglected within the study of lending behavior toward family firms. Unlike currently available literature, the present study will adopt a behavioral economics perspective to the research question by focusing on the loan officers' judgment and decision making processes which are typically investigated using concepts from psychology. In addition, the study seeks to complement this perspective by insights from the SEW approach and the RBV. However, it is to be said that an exhaustive application of all potential sub-constructs of the behavioral economics framework would not be feasible due to the enormous amount of these sub-constructs encompassing concepts like e.g. the self-serving bias (Campbell & Sedikides, 1999; Heider, 1958), anchoring (Tversky & Kahneman, 1974; Einhorn & Hogarth, 1986) or the endowment effect (Kahneman, 1991; Russo et al., 1996). As a consequence and besides using behavioral economics as an overall framework, this study plans to apply two specific behavioral concepts to the research question, namely the similarity bias (Lazarsfeld & Merton, 1954; Byrne, 1971) and the idea of the framing effect (Tversky & Kahneman, 1981).

The second goal of the dissertation is to broaden the literature regarding the question of whether and why lenders deal differently with family firms by specifically investigating the effect of different types of family firms on the loan officers' lending decisions, i.e. whether lenders deal differently with firms that display distinct forms and levels of family involvement. Pursuing this goal will in particular contribute to the literature in the field of family business research as numerous scholars have pointed out to the significance and need of studies that examine family firm heterogeneity (Chua et al., 2012; Chrisman & Patel, 2012; Bennedsen et al., 2010). As described previously, current research regarding lending behavior toward family firms has completely ignored this topic, which indicates the novelty of this attempt.

Moreover, the status quo within the currently available literature reveals that scholars missed to intensively investigate the impact of contextual factors as potential explanations for variations in the loan officers' judgment and decision making toward family firms. Thus, the present study aims to contribute to the discussion by specifically investigating the impact of an additional contextual factor, namely the condition of the general economic environment. The corresponding finding might also explain part of the ambiguity of the currently available empirical studies and thus provide some clarity with respect to these mixed findings.

The fourth goal of the present research project is to break down the methodological monotony within the currently available literature by applying an experimental method. Experiments are said to be especially useful to make valid causal claims (Antonakis et al., 2010). Because the empirical results that are available at the moment have produced such ambiguous conclusions, which might be partly caused by methodological problems, it is advisable to apply a diversity of methodological approaches and instruments to rule out the risk of those issues and make more profound inferences. Consequently, this study aims to contribute to the discussion by providing empirical evidence on the question of whether and why lenders deal differently with family firms using an alternative methodological approach which in case of this dissertation is a conjoint experiment.

Summing up, the current study wants to contribute to the discussion by (1) applying new theoretical perspectives to the research question, (2) starting to examine the differences in lending behavior toward varying types of family firms and thereby addressing the issue of heterogeneity of family firms, (3) analyzing the impact of an additional contextual factor and (4) employing an experimental approach to generate empirical data in order to supplement the generated and currently available data sets. Thus, the main goal of this study is to investigate different facets of the influence of varying levels of family involvement on loan officers' judgment and decision making. However, it has to be noted that the present study will focus on the investigation of some selected aspects of lending behavior toward family firms as an extensive and adequate examination of all facets of the research topic would be beyond the scope of just one doctoral research project. In particular, two major foci have been set and will be discussed in the following.

In general, lending behavior consists of two major decisions: (1) the credit availability decision and (2) the loan contract term decisions. This study will focus on the investigation of the loan officers' credit availability decision. It is the central decisions loan officers have to make. The contract term decisions are, though important and strongly interrelated with the credit availability decision, secondary to the latter. Nevertheless, the decision whether or not to lend money will always depend on the specific loan contract terms. Completely excluding them would thus be inappropriate. Instead, it was assumed that those aspects are given and equal across all borrowers. Thereby, it was possible to focus exclusively on the loan officers' credit availability decision while at the same time not neglecting important factors of influence. In addition and as stated previously, family firms' main challenge is to secure access to sufficient funds that are needed to finance the business which underlines the importance for understanding differences in the loan granting behavior toward those firms. As a consequence, the present study focuses on the examination of the loan officers' credit availability decision.

In addition, the empirical part of the study will focus on lending behavior toward true family firms, i.e. company's where at least one generational transfer has already occurred. Founder-run entities and first-generation family firms will be intentionally excluded from this research project. Many scholars argue that the generational dimension is what actually defines family firms and distinguishes them from e.g. entrepreneurs (see e.g. Daily & Thompson, 1994; Ward, 1987). Adopting this view automatically dismisses founder-run entities and first-generation firms from the scope of this study as those will not be defined as family businesses. In this context, literature points out that founder-run and first-generation firms fundamentally differ from true family firms in aspects like e.g. their risk-taking behavior and their overall priority setting (see e.g. Stockmans et al., 2010 or Miller et al., 2007), which further questions whether those firms can be put on a level with true family firms. On top of those issues, banks often assign specialized loan officers to service the needs of entrepreneurs and small businesses and employ alternative lending policies. Including those types of business would bias the results. Thus, in order to not lose focus and due to the given constraints in resources for this project, the present study will focus on lending behavior toward true family firms.

1.4 Research Approach

In order to answer the research question and to achieve the above described goals, this study pursues a deductive research approach as it starts to derive testable hypotheses on the basis of various theoretical general frameworks which are operationalized and then subjected to a detailed empirical examination to verify respectively falsify the previously developed hypotheses. On the basis of the findings that have been gathered by this approach, the researchers will make inferences regarding the underlying theoretical model of the loan officers' judgment and decision making towards different types of family firms. This latter step will involve an inductive procedure rather than a deductive one.

Within the empirical part, this study will use an experimental methodology as its research instrument. As stated previously, the currently available literature has produced highly ambiguous results regarding the question of whether lenders deal differently with family firms. This could be partly attributed to the lack of methodological diversity across the currently available studies that all used regression analytical technics on ex-post data sets. Therefore, this study aims to introduce a different methodological approach to the investigation of the topic in focus which is why it uses an experimental avenue. In particular, conjoint-experiments were conducted as those are particularly useful to study humans' judgment and decision making (Louviere, 1988; Green & Srinivasan, 1990; Shepherd & Zacharakis, 1999). Actually, conjoint analysis has been developed for this reason, i.e. the study of humans' judgment and decision making process (Luce & Tukey, 1964; Louviere, 1988). It enables researchers to examine a participant's underlying preference structure with respect to a number of attributes of a decision task and thus uncover the actual decision rules participants use (Shepherd & Zacharakis, 1999). The conjoint experiment within the current study will investigate the effect of eight decision attributes using a fractional factorial design. More specifically, an 8_{IV}^{8-4}-design was employed in order to minimize the necessary profiles loan officers had to assess without compromising on the ability to test all of the defined hypotheses adequately (Box et al., 2005).

Within this analytical part of this thesis, a hierarchical linear model (HLM) approach will be implemented in order to evaluate the data adequately form a statistical point of view. Because the generated data points of conjoint experiments are not independent from each other as the decisions are nested within individuals and/or other entities and these might differ from other individuals' decisions as those might hold different experiences, values and/or mental models, it is likely that the generated data is characterized by autocorrelation, i.e. individual-level variance (Patzelt et al., 2011; Raudenbush & Bryk, 2002), which makes it difficult to apply standard ordinary least squares (OLS) regression as proposed by Shepherd & Zacharakis (1999). As a consequence, scholars that currently conduct conjoint experiments tend to use HLM to analyze the generated data sets. This approach allows for an appropriate assessment of data that is subject to autocorrelation and to some extent heteroscedasticity, i.e. differences in variability between different individuals (see e.g. Bruns et al., 2008; Shepherd, 1999 or Patzelt & Shepherd, 2009). In addition, scholars note that this approach is currently the state-of-the-art method for the evaluation of conjoint data (Patzelt et al., 2011). Hence, the current study will use HLM to analyze the gathered data.

1.5 Structure

This section aims to briefly outline the structure of the dissertation at hand and explicate the underlying rationale behind it. The overall structure is visualized in Figure 1 (please note that the size of the circles within the illustration indicates the length of the respective chapter).

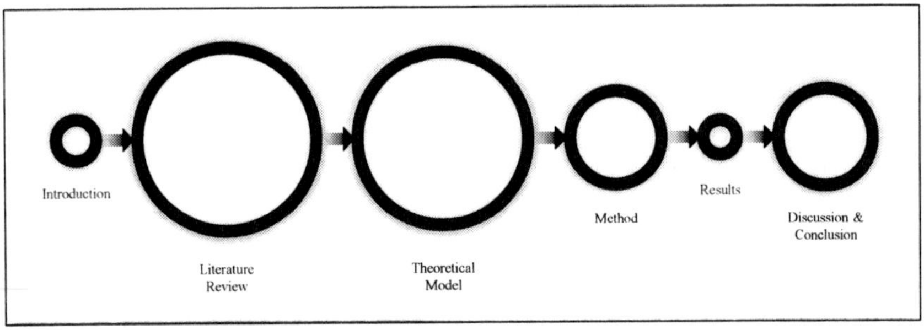

Figure 1: Overview of the Dissertation's Structure

In a first step, I review the extant existing literature in order to take stock of what is already known with respect to the previously presented leading research question, to consequently examine which facets of the problem have not yet been answered adequately and to finally develop a theoretical foundation for the consecutive theoretical and empirical part of this dissertation. Therefore, this review section will start by reviewing the literature on lending behavior in general with the aim to identify significant theoretical frameworks that explain differences in lending behavior toward borrowers in general. It will also include a presentation of the empirical evidence that has been generated in this rather general context. This will serve as a basis for the subsequent part. The following section focuses on lending behavior toward family firms and represents the core of the review. It will first review the theoretical arguments and then present and integrate the empirical studies, which compare debt financing access and loan contract terms of family and non-family firms. Moreover, it will critically assess the currently available studies, identify research gaps and develop ideas for future research directions regarding this topic. Finally, the author will review literature regarding two additional theoretical concepts within the field of family business research that will enhance the argument of this study, namely the SEW concept and the RBV. This chapter will be closed by drawing an interim conclusion with the key findings of the literature review that will pave the way for the subsequent part.

The third chapter of this elaboration focuses on the development of testable theoretical hypothesis on the basis of the previously reviewed literature in order to lay the foundation for the empirical examination of the influence of family involvement on loan officers' credit availability decisions. This step is crucial for the present study as it pursues a deductive research approach where the derived theoretical model forms the foundation of the subsequent empirical part of the study. The micro structure of this chapter is based upon the type of proposed effects, i.e. (1) main effects, (2) moderating effects and (3) interaction effects. This structure will also be used within the results section in order to facilitate the readers' reading process.

The fourth chapter outlines the study's research methodology that is used to test the previously described hypotheses. After an explanation of the used methods on a general level, the particular method and the individual parameters of the experimental conjoint approach are described. Besides an elaboration about the used experimental methods, this chapter will include a discussion about the econometrical strategy for analyzing the data that has been gathered with the help of the preceding experiment and thereby test the hypotheses of the theoretical model.

The upcoming chapter (chapter five) presents the empirical results of the previously described conjoint-experiment on the basis of the econometrical strategy that has also been outlined in the preceding chapter. However, it has to be noted that this chapter focuses only on results that relate to the leading research question and the to-be-tested hypotheses in order to ensure clarity and to not lose the plot of this study.

In the final chapter, the findings of the present study will be critically discussed in the context of the currently available literature. This discussion will also include an examination regarding the limitations of this particular study, how to possibly enhance or expand it in the context of future research and a dispute of how the study contributes both to the theoretical literature and to practitioners. This chapter closes by drawing a final conclusion that relates back to the aim and purpose of this study. Figure 2 illustrates the structure of this dissertation in more detail.

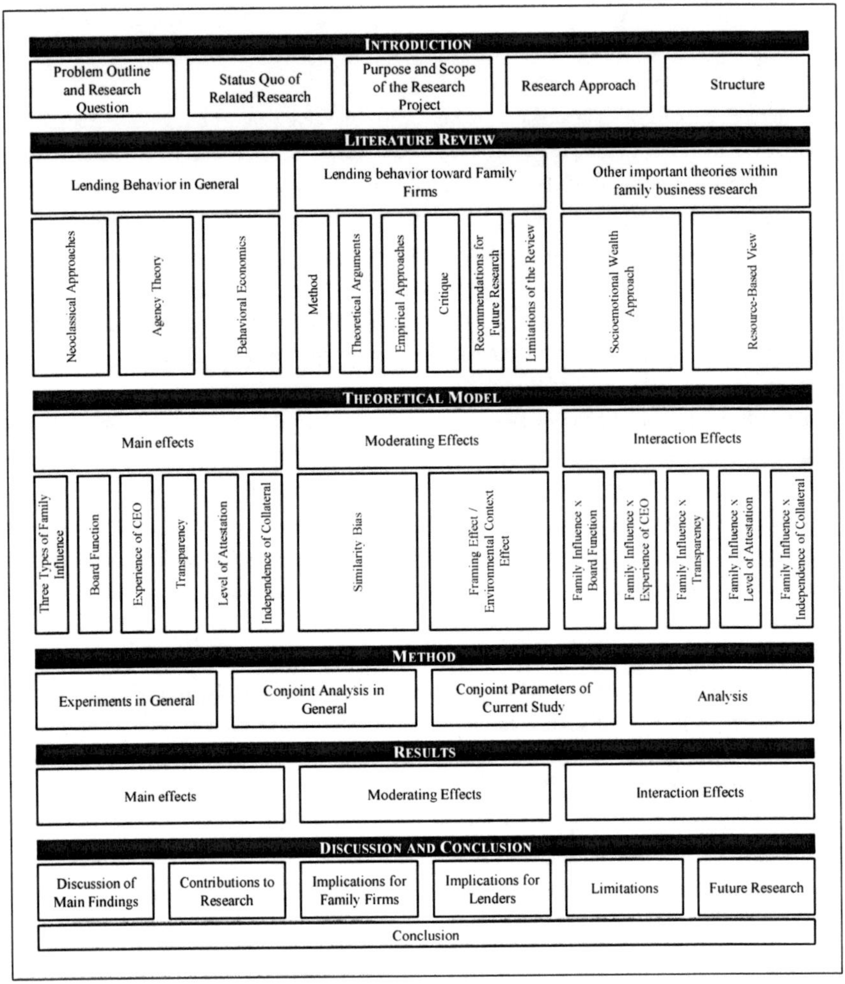

Figure 2: Detailed Structure of the Dissertation

2 Literature Review

This chapter presents an overview of the currently available literature that is relevant for this research project. In particular, this literature review pursues four goals. It aims to (1) give an overview of what is already known with regards to the research question in focus, (2) identify considerable research gaps which also provide additional arguments for the relevance of this study, (3) make propositions for future research of which some are pursued by this study and (4) establish a theoretical basis for the development of the present study's theoretical model.
In order to achieve those goals, this chapter has been structured as follows: First, the extant literature on lending behavior will be reviewed with the aim to identify significant theoretical frameworks that explain differences in lending behavior toward borrowers in general. This part will also include an outline of the empirical evidence that has been generated in this context. Knowing what has been examined with respect to lending behavior in general is necessary to be able to adequately and critically assess research on lending behavior toward family firms and thereby identify potential research gaps. This step will serve as a basis for the subsequent review of research regarding lending behavior toward family firms. After presenting the method for identifying and synthesizing available literature, this part of the thesis will first review theoretical arguments and then present and integrate empirical studies, which compare debt financing access and loan contract terms of family and non-family firms. At this point is has to be noted that the currently available literature does not provide any material regarding the loan officers behavior toward different kinds of family firms. As a consequence, the review is forced to focus on literature that discusses differences in lending behavior toward family and non-family firms. However, the generated insights can be used as a valuable starting point. In this context, non-family firms can be defined as firms with no influence of the family and thus might be interpreted as an approximation to family firms that are characterized by a very low level of family involvement. Before concluding and discussing potential limitations of the review regarding the existing literature on lending behavior toward family firms, the available studies will be critically assessed, research gaps identified and ideas for future research directions regarding this topic developed. At this point it has to be noted that this dissertation's review of the extant literature is selective rather than exhaustive. Furthermore, the reader should be aware that this review focuses on aspects of individual judgment and decision making. In the next step of this chapter, two important theories in the field of family business research are reviewed which have been ignored by currently available studies that examined lending behavior toward family firms but promise to be useful for this topic and will be used within this study. In particular, the SEW and the RBV are discussed. Finally, this chapter will be finished by summing up the generated insights of this review and presenting substantial consequences for the subsequent study.

2.1 Research Regarding Lending Behavior in General

Lending behavior in this study is defined as the total of all processes which are undertaken in order to make two main decisions: (1) the credit availability decision i.e. whether to lend money or not and (2) the loan contract term decisions i.e. what terms to include in a specific credit contract. When elaborating on the second decision category, literature typically discusses five specific contract terms which are debt maturity, debt amount, interest rate / fee design, collateral requirements and covenants (Greenbaum & Thakor, 1995; Sinkey, 2002). In the following, lending behavior will generally be discussed in regards to those two main decision categories. Nevertheless, it has to be clear that those two types of decisions cannot be separated in reality as they inevitably affect each other. The decision whether to lend money or not always depends on the specific loan contract terms. Scholars ignoring this interdependence will not be able to draw correct conclusions.

When reviewing the extant literature on the question of whether and why lenders deal differently with borrowers, three major research streams have been identified that propose varying perspectives on this topic by revealing different explanations, namely (1) neoclassical models, (2) agency theory and (3) behavioral economics. The remainder of this section will further elaborate on those research streams as they will help reviewing and critically evaluating research on differences in lending behavior toward family businesses.

2.1.1 Neoclassical Approach

Within neoclassical models, lenders are assumed to act perfectly rational on the basis of fully available information. Accepting those assumptions, lending behavior becomes a pure function of risk and return, which will be optimized depending on the banks' preferences using portfolio-modeling approaches (Greenbaum & Thakor, 1995; Panagopoulos & Spiliotis, 1998). An essential part of the risk term is the borrowers risk or the risk of default. This type of risk arises from unique characteristics or resources of a borrower like its profitability, leverage, cash-flow volatility, credit history, industry characteristics or location-based factors. Differences in lending behavior can only occur because of objective differences between borrowers' characteristics. Hence, lenders will, ceteris paribus, make the same loan availability and loan contract term decisions when faced with various borrowers having identical characteristics. A borrower with a higher degree of default risk has to pay a higher price in comparison to a low-risk borrower or will be rejected and vice versa. So, all else equal, neoclassical models basically assume that every borrower is associated with some kind of default risk as a result of the companies' characteristics or resources. As a consequence, the lender, who has full information about those aspects, can calculate an optimal behavior for every borrower (here in the sense of an optimal price, which functions as a clearing mechanism), so that credit rationing should not be a problem.

From a practitioners' perspective, firm specific characteristics play an important role as they are an integral part of the lending decision (see e.g. the requirements in the context of the Basel II accords). Nevertheless, pure neoclassical models are not appropriate when trying to describe or explain real lending behavior because they make two inadequate assumptions about reality which are critical and thus lead to systematic deviations between reality and neoclassical models. First, they assume the decision maker to have fully available information, which proves to be utopian in reality. Second, a central assumption of neoclassical models in general is perfect rationality. From this perspective lenders always compute the correct decision. However, research within behavioral economics has shown that people's decisions cannot be described or predicted with those models. They systematically deviate from neoclassical theory. Lenders do not use all available information, weight and interpret them differently in changing contexts and are highly susceptible to a variety of factors. This demonstrates how inappropriate such theories are for describing actual behavior which makes it necessary to consider agency and behavioral concepts when explaining lending behavior.

Even though neoclassical models are not appropriate to describe and predict lending behavior in reality, they reveal one essential source of potential differences in lending behavior: lenders deal differently with borrowers in terms of credit availability and loan contract terms because of objective differences between the borrowers' specific characteristics. At this point, it has to be noted that those refer to characteristics which are not associated with agency, but rather to firm specific resources where differences can be explained with approaches like the RBV.

2.1.2 Agency Theory

Currently, the majority of research on debt availability and loan contract terms is based on agency theory (see e.g. Jensen & Meckling, 1976; Stiglitz & Weiss, 1981). In general, agency theory focuses on conflicts that arise from information asymmetries and goal divergence between a principal and an agent who is supposed to act on behalf of the principal (Ross, 1973; Eisenhardt, 1989). Assuming that the agent has more information about himself, potential future actions and/or decision variables than the principal, pursues different interests and always acts selfish, two main agency problems emerge: adverse selection and moral hazard (Eisenhardt, 1989; Akerlof, 1970). Adverse selection refers to the situation prior to choosing an agent. Because the principal does not have as much information about the agent as the agent itself, two possible errors can be made: rejecting good agents (type I error of agency) or accepting bad agents (type II error of agency). Moral hazard problems arise from the possibility that the agent might carry out negative activities after being contracted in combination with the inability of the principal to monitor the agents' behavior. Agency theory is particularly concerned with resolving those problems using a variety of mechanisms, which are not costless. In that sense, the term of agency costs refers to the total costs associated directly with the agency relationship (risk of adverse selection and moral hazard) and the costs associated with using agency mitigating mechanisms.

In the wake of the above considerations a number of authors have applied those principles to the lending behavior of debtholders (e.g. Jensen & Meckling, 1976; Stiglitz & Weiss, 1981;

Leland & Pyle, 1977; Kreps & Wilson, 1982; Myers, 1977; Smith & Jensen, 2000; Smith & Warner, 1979). From this perspective lenders are concerned with choosing suboptimal borrowers (adverse selection) and the risk of wealth expropriation by shareholders as those might shift to risk-seeking behavior once the credit has been granted (moral hazard). In the latter case, lenders on the one hand bear most of the increased risk of default, but on the other hand do not participate in additional profits. In general, lenders have three options – they can (1) accept the risks associated with agency, which would not be optimal and is not an option within agency theory, (2) ration credit (see Stiglitz & Weiss, 1981 or De Meza & Webb, 1987 for an opposite view) and/or (3) implement processes that mitigate those agency problems. As agency theory is concerned with resolving agency problems, a key branch of research in this field investigates a variety of agency mitigating mechanisms. Typically, literature divides those mechanisms into four main categories: screening, signaling, monitoring and incentives (sometimes scholars refer to self-selection as a distinct category – see e.g. Picot et al., 2005; Hutzschenreuter, 2009; Wernick, 2007). Screening and signaling can be used to reduce agency costs regarding adverse selection, whereas monitoring and incentives are mechanisms mitigating moral hazard issues. In regards to the question that this study is interested in, agency theory suggests that potential differences in lending behavior toward borrowers might be caused and explained by differences in the agency costs associated with every borrower – either directly or by agency mitigating tools.

In order to mitigate costs directly associated with adverse selection lenders can screen potential borrowers. They try to find out more about potential borrowers in order to reduce informational asymmetries. Besides acquiring information from the borrower or third-parties, some authors include self-selection in the screening category (as mentioned previously some authors regard self-selection as a category of its own or as a signaling respectively screening mechanism; see e.g. Padilla, 2002 or Spence, 1973). Self-selection occurs when lenders offer different types of contracts which are only optimal for specific types of borrowers. So, e.g. bad borrowers will more likely choose a loan with low levels of personal collateral but higher interest rates (Bester, 1985; Comeig et al., 2010). A popular research area in this regard is the role of relationships in acquiring information about the borrower, so that asymmetries of information are retrenched over the duration of the relationship as the lender gains valuable information regarding payment and risk-taking behavior (see Boot, 2000 for a review). Whereas screening is initiated by the lender, signaling refers to actions of the borrower. In order not to suffer from credit rationing and unfavorable debt conditions, borrowers try to credibly signal their creditworthiness. In this context scholars mainly discuss the effect of different types of collateral, third-party guarantees and disclosure of private information (Stiglitz & Weiss, 1981; Leland & Pyle, 1977; Steijvers & Voordeckers, 2009a). Risks of moral hazard can be reduced by monitoring and incentives. Monitoring in lending relationships refers to the information gathering initiatives of the lender during the lending relationship. Here, covenants and loan maturity are usually discussed as the major mechanisms that perform this specific function (Berlin & Mester, 1992; Park, 2000; Rajan & Winton, 1995; Ortiz-Molina & Penas, 2004). Lastly, incentivizing is a further way to potentially reduce agency costs, which either establish a reward or a punishment in case of a particular behavior. Collateral is probably the most discusses incentives in the context of lending (scholars also refer to collateral as a tool to reduce informational asymmetries; in addition, see Coco, 2000 or Steijvers & Voordeckers, 2009a for a review on the use of collateral).

Besides the presented theoretical discussion in regards to agency mitigating mechanisms, a number of empirical studies examined the effect of those tools in solving this problem. In this context, scholars particularly used different firm characteristics as a moderator variable to account for potential variations in regards to inherent agency risks of specific groups. Unfortunately, the empirical results are highly ambiguous which was already emphasized by other authors (see e.g. Boot, 2000; Coco, 2000; Steijvers & Voordeckers, 2009a). In the following, this ambiguity will be illustrated using the examples of collateral and relationships as potential agency mitigating tools.

Using a regression model, Hernández-Cánovas & Martínez-Solano (2006) demonstrated that high risk borrowers have to provide more personal guarantees. Similarly, Menkhoff et al. (2006) and Brick & Palia (2007) found that firms which are associated with higher credit risk seem to pledge more collateral. However, Cressy & Toivanen (2001) and Machauer & Weber (1998) found no evidence for a relationship between risk and pledging collateral when incorporating risk degree and loan duration into the model. Additionally, Lehmann & Neuberger (2001) concluded from their empirical findings that high risk borrowers even seem to pledge less collateral. These finding emphasize the ambiguity among empirical evidence of studies arguing on the basis of agency theory. Expanding on the issue of collateral and presenting more controversies, Leeth & Scott (1989) found that older firms have to pledge collateral less often, which is confirmed by Degryse & van Cayseele (2000) who corroborated that smaller and younger firms seem to pledge collateral more often. In contrast, Voordeckers & Steijvers (2006) found that larger and older firms suffer from higher collateral requirements (see Steijvers & Voordeckers, 2009a for a more complete review of recent empirical evidence on collateral and credit rationing).

Including another example, a number of scholars tested the influence of the relationship duration on interest rates as agency theoretical considerations imply that the lender-borrower relationship helps to reduce informational asymmetries. Again the results are mixed. Whereas Berger & Udell (1995) and Degryse & van Cayseele (2000) found that the length of the relationship reduces the explicit interest rate, Petersen & Rajan (1995) and Elsas & Krahnen (1998) could not confirm any significant positive relation.

As described above, lenders and scholars designed a variety of tools to reduce agency costs, usually performing at least one of the following functions: screening, signaling, monitoring or incentivizing. Recently, scholars began to investigate interrelations between these contractual features, demonstrating that some contract elements can act as substitutes to others. Employing a simultaneous system of equations, Brick & Palia (2007) found evidence for the interrelation between explicit interest rate, collateral and fees in the context of relationship lending. Additionally, Ortiz-Molina & Penas (2004) report results arguing that loan maturities are used as substitutes for covenants in small firms. Jiménez et al. (2011) present further evidence on the interchangeability of collateral and the lender-borrower-relationship. All this evidence points to the conclusion that empirical studies in this field have to incorporate a variety of contract features and pay attention to substituting effects in order to be able to draw correct conclusions from their results. Scholars reviewing literature should pay attention to this fact as it represents an essential methodological quality criterion. Steijvers & Voordeckers (2009a) argued that researchers may benefit from including those interrelating effects as they might also explain discrepancies of empirical results.

Unfortunately and just like purely neoclassical approaches, scholars using solely agency theoretical models will not be able to explain lending behavior adequately from a descriptive perspective as it holds two main problems: (1) Agency theory does only concentrate on one part of the lending problem. It is just concerned with the risks arising from asymmetric information and goal divergence, so that other sources of differences like the previously discussed borrowers risk of default will be neglected. Agency theory is not helpful in explaining how lenders deal with those aspects of the lending decision. (2) Agency theory adopts one central assumption of traditional neoclassical models i.e. fully rational and selfish agents, making decisions on the basis of objective, although noisy and not fully verifiable information. Lenders are assumed to always compute the correct decision under the presented constrains. As previously argued, this assumption does not hold true in reality, which also might be one reason why agency theory focused studies generate such ambiguous results. This leads us to the next category.

2.1.3 Behavioral Economics

As mentioned, agency theory holds the potential of not explaining lending behavior adequately. In this context, Simon (1991) points out that "the attempts of the new institutional economics to explain […] behavior solely in terms of agency, asymmetric information, transaction costs, opportunism, and other concepts drawn from neoclassical economics ignore key […] mechanisms […], and hence are seriously incomplete" (p. 42). Therefore, the theoretical basis of this study will be expanded by including behavioral concepts in the review. But as this type of research has become such a wide and interdisciplinary field, employing concepts from economics, psychology and other areas, it is impossible to provide an extensive review of this research program within just one section of a thesis (other authors like Keren & Teigen, 2007 also realized this challenge – for this reason see e.g. Abelson & Levi, 1985; Einhorn & Hogarth, 1981; Kahneman et al., 1982; Gilovich et al., 2002 and Slovic et al., 1977 for reviews of behavioral decision research that offer different time spans, varying levels of depth and alternative foci in order to get a more detailed view on this topic). As a consequence, this section only outlines major topics within behavioral economics. In addition, it focuses on experimental findings rather than on an excessive description of underlying psychological theories. Therefore, this section will give a short and general introduction to behavioral economics and the general questions scholars are trying to answer in regards to lending behavior.

Unlike standard economic research, the main goal of behavioral decision research is to understand human judgment and decision making without assuming that people are rational. A majority of research in this field typically investigates what kinds of decision strategies people use when making judgments or decisions and how those deviate from traditional economic theories. In this context, current literature suggests that people use simple judgment and decision mechanism when faced with complex tasks and incomplete information (often referred to as heuristics or intuition) which lead to systematic errors in a neoclassical sense (often called biases). As a consequence, scholars have defined a variety of heuristics and potential anomalies in behavior (see e.g. Carter et al., 2007a for a review and categorization of decision biases). Most of those research attempts theoretically argue from a cognitive perspective and aim to complement traditional theories that are based on the assumption of the homo oeconomicus, a calculating, unemotional and utility maximizing agent (see the previously mentioned reviews within this research field). And even though numerous authors criticize the used arguments and findings, this stream of research offers valuable insights in regards to this dissertation's questions. So, behavioral research found out that people use only a fraction of available information, do not know their exact preference or utility function, are susceptible to emotions, respond differently to framing variations of a problem and are cognitively not able to fully analyze complex problems quickly. This lets us suppose behavioral aspects to represent a further source of explanation for the existence of differences in lending behavior toward different borrowers.

Besides other areas like marketing or law, a number of scholars applied the theoretical concepts and findings of behavioral research to the context of lending behavior in order to find out how lenders and especially bankers make judgments and decisions (this refers to both the decision process and the final decision outcome) and what kinds of factors influence their behavior. Reviewing the literature, six categories were identified that influence the loan decision and/or the underlying processes and which are usually investigated by scholars using the behavioral economics framework: (1) task characteristics (Biggs et al., 1985), (2) characteristics of the loan officer (Beaulieu, 1994; Bruns et al., 2008), (3) borrower characteristics (McNamara & Bromiley, 1997; Wright & Davidson, 2000; Wilson et al., 2007), (4) organizational characteristics of the lender (McNamara & Bromiley, 1997), (5) external information and opinions (Schneider & Church, 2008) and (6) emotions (Lipshitz & Shulimovitz, 2007; Kida et al., 2001). In the following some of the related empirical evidence will be presented. However, this demonstrates how susceptible loan officers are when making decisions about credit availability and loan contract terms. In addition, it can be expected that this type of research can be extremely useful when investigating differences in lending behavior toward family and non-family firms or different types of family firms, especially when considering that borrower characteristics are found to have significant influence on judgments and decisions of loan officers.

In the following, selected empirical evidence for the importance of behavioral research in studying lending behavior will be presented as judgment and decision making in this context is influenced by systematic biases in regards to the use of information and underlying processes which are inconsistent with neoclassical theories. This section is structured according to the categories of influence which have been defined previously. In addition, studies will be presented, which investigate the relative importance of various influence factors. This part of the thesis will focus on studies that were thought of having the potential to inspire scholars to generate ideas about how to apply those concepts to the question whether lenders deal differently with family and non-family firms or different kinds of family firms.

Using process tracing methods, Biggs et al. (1985) showed that bank loan officers adopt non-compensatory decision strategies with increasing task complexity. For this reason the authors varied the number of applicants (borrowing companies) and the number of cues available to analyze the loan and found that loan officers tended to acquire less information in relative terms with increasing complexity and eliminate alternatives quickly that do not meet a criterion level at any dimension.

Characteristics of the loan officer also influence judgment and decision making. So, Rodgers (1999) found that novices (here: MBA students) are prone to use only financial information in making lending decisions whereas experienced loan officers also incorporate management information like e.g. information about managers' experience. Additionally, Andersson (2004) asserts that experienced loan officers search for significantly more cues when making decisions than inexperienced loan officers. However, he finds no evidence that experts show a high level of agreement in their final decision. Similarly, Bruns et al. (2008) identified differences in decision policies across loan officers. This implies that loan officers cannot be seen as a homogeneous group of individuals who reach similar conclusions about a specific loan or borrower. In connection with the influence of the borrowers' characteristics, Bruns et al. (2008) demonstrated that the similarity between the loan officers' and the applicants' specific human capital is a significant indicator of loan approval. However, this did not hold true for similarities in general human capital.

As mentioned, characteristics of the borrower form a third category of influence. In this regards and based on the work of Shiller (1984), McNamara & Bromiley (1997) argued that bankers are susceptible to the excitement of the borrowers industry. Specifically, they showed that the more exciting an industry was perceived by a loan officer, the more likely it was that the risk of the borrower would be underrated. To further highlight the importance of the borrowers' characteristics in lending behavior, the reader is referred to studies by Carter et al. (2007b), Buttner & Rosen (1989) and Fay & Williams (1993) who present evidence how the borrowers' gender influences lending decisions, usually in favor of men. It has to be pointed out that even though no explicit evidence could be found to justify arguments that women are worse than men in terms of borrower quality (see e.g. DeCarlo & Lyons, 1979), bank loan officers still seem to treat them differently, which indicates that different beliefs or perceptions have to be in place so that behavioral research is important to understand underlying mechanisms. Ravina (2012) expanded on this by illustrating how borrowers' beauty affects loan availability and contract terms. They basically state that the better a borrower looks, the more likely they are to receive a loan and get better conditions. In a similar fashion, Herzenstein et al. (2011) examine how stories about the borrower influence lending decisions (in regards to unsecured personal loans). They e.g. found that identity claims which focused on being trustworthy or successful were associated with increased loan funding but at the same time did not predict loan performance accurately.

In addition, McNamara & Bromiley (1997) argue that bank loan officers' are also influenced by organizational doctrines. In this context, they found that loan officers working for banks promoting a profit orientated philosophy make systematic errors when evaluating a borrower's risk. In such an environment, they e.g. tend to underrate the risk of large loans in comparison to smaller ones owing the fact that large loans are associated with higher absolute profits, which according to neoclassical theories might influence the final loan availability or loan contract term decisions but should not influence the risk rating. Those findings demonstrate the individual loan officers' susceptibility to organizational characteristics.

Schneider & Church (2008) presented further evidence on the susceptibility of loan officers to behavioral factors by showing that an adverse auditors' internal control opinion negatively affects the assessment of risk. Conversely, Wright & Davidson (2000) found no effect between auditor attestation and risk assessment.

Finally, Lipshitz & Shulimovitz (2007) conducted in-depth interviews with 14 loan officers in Israel and concluded that positive and negative emotions affect bankers' judgment and decision making. Similarly, Kida et al. (2001) suggested that managers tend to avoid superior alternatives that elicit negative feeling in comparison to inferior alternatives which are not associated with such feelings. Those findings are in line with models of emotions within behavioral research (see e.g. Schwarz, 2000; Mellers et al., 1997 and Damásio, 1995).

In addition to those research efforts, a number of studies presented evidence on the relative importance of specific cues in lending behavior. Jankowicz & Hisrich (1987) argue that experience and track record of the applicant are the most important cues in evaluating a borrower. Similarly, Rosman & O'Neill (1993) found that commercial lenders tend to minimize the use of financial forecasts. In contrast, Fletcher (1995) and Mason & Stark (2004) report results that indicate an emphasis on financial information and a capital-based approach in the context of bankers' risk assessment. Those outcomes are in line with the findings that were previously discussed in regards to variations in lending strategies across loan officers.

The presented empirical results point to the conclusion that behavioral factors significantly influence lending decisions, which cannot be explained in terms of neoclassical theories.

Thus, the concepts and findings of behavioral economics should be an essential part of research aimed at understanding lending behavior.
Besides another theoretical basis, scholars using the behavioral research framework typically use different empirical tools. This stream of research especially favors experimental approaches in a naturalistic decision making context, which are not without controversy, but offer the possibility of isolating, manipulating and therefore testing particular influence factors precisely. In addition to experiments, some of the above presented studies used surveys to find out about cues and underlying processes that are important to the lender.

2.2 Research Regarding Lending Behavior toward Family Firms

2.2.1 Method

The review is driven by theoretical pre-considerations and follows a clear process. This section will illustrate the chosen method for identifying relevant articles in regards to the question whether lenders deal differently with family firms. In addition, it will describe the framework that was used for analyzing the articles.
In order to not be influenced by a researcher bias (Mulrow, 1994; Tranfield et al., 2003), the method for conducting the review is generally based on the systematic approach proposed by Fink (2010). However, the proposed selection process was modified a bit as the present review used a three-stage approach. The first step consisted of a title and abstract search in various databases using pre-defined keywords. The search was conducted in four different databases, namely (1) Scopus, (2) Web of Science, (3) EBSCO Business Source Elite and (4) EconLit because those are the most likely to include studies about the topic in focus. The review should only include studies that are concerned with family businesses. A number of studies focus on seemingly related subjects like e.g. small businesses or owner-managed companies (Shuto & Kitagawa, 2011 or Ortiz-Molina & Penas, 2008). Research has shown that e.g. small business family firms differ significantly from small non-family firm (Kimhi, 1997), so that it would not be appropriate to include those studies when reviewing literature about differences in lending behavior toward family firms. Therefore, this particular review excluded studies that do not have a reference to family firms in their title or abstract (using this approach, it were possible to include studies that might not have focused on family businesses but use it as a variable in their empirical tests and found a significant influence like e.g. Voordeckers & Steijvers, 2006). In this context the following keywords were used: FAMILY FIRM*, FAMILY BUSINESS*, FAMILY CO*, FAMILY INVOLVEMENT and FAMILY OWN*. Using asterisks allowed the inclusion of variations in the ending of the keywords, so that FAMILY CO* would include terms like "family company" and "family controlled". As a second criterion, the review only included studies that concentrated primarily on lending behavior and especially regarding access to credit and loan contract terms. So in order to be included, articles had to contain one of the following keywords: LOAN*, DEBT*, LEND*, CREDIT* and BORROW*. In addition, the present literature review included all studies that

have been conducted prior 2012. As a consequence of the emerging nature of this field of study the review was intended to be based on a broad basis so that no further criteria for inclusion respectively exclusion was required. The first step of this review's selection process resulted in 286 articles using Scopus, 140 articles using Web of Science, 130 articles using EBSCO Business Source Elite and 87 articles using EconLit. After eliminating duplicates, 433 articles could be identified using the presented selection criteria.

In a second step, all of the 433 abstracts were read in order to apply a finer filter after a rather basic selection in the first step where a wide range of articles were included. In particular, the second criterion of this method's first step (research focus had to be lending behavior) was reapplied more rigorously. Thereby, all articles were eliminated that e.g. dealt with capital structure decision respectively capital structure preferences or articles that discussed the effect of debt on performance. The articles had to discuss differences in lending behavior toward family firms. If an articles' abstract did not provide a reason for exclusion without any doubt, it was retained and reassessed in the third part of the selection process. This was the only criterion that was used in this step as the goal was to conduct a broad scoping review of the research question in focus. The second step resulted in 19 articles.

In the final step, the full texts of all twelve articles were read in order to find articles that do not fit in this review but could not be extracted within the first two components of the selection process. In this case, 10 further articles could be dismissed that related to different topics, leaving 9 relevant articles for the review. Additionally, the article of Ellul et al. (2007) was added, which was not included in the searched databases, but discusses the topic in focus and might thus provide valuable insights. Table 1 gives an overview of the reviewed studies.

Because this literature review is a scoping review, a broad concept was used for systemizing the current literature. In this context, it was decided to structure the review on a macro level according to the triad of evidence which should be the underlying basis of every piece of academic research (Laudan, 1984). Therefore, the relevant literature will be discussed in terms of (1) research aims and topics, (2) theoretical frameworks and (3) empirical approaches and methods used. From a micro structure perspective, the author chose to use both the identified major research streams within the extant literature i.e. neoclassical models, agency theory and behavioral economics as well as the two major decisions of lending behavior i.e. the loan availability and loan contract term decisions. In a final section, the currently available literature on differences in lending behavior toward family firms will be critically discussed. Within those sections, the review will apply a concept-centric approach in order to synthesize the literature adequately and avoid a pure listing of citations (Webster & Watson, 2002).

Study	Main Research Question	Type of Study	Type of Debt
Anderson et al. (2003)	What is the effect of equity ownership structure on the cost of debt?	Empirical	Public debt
Bagnoli et al. (2011)	Does family involvement influence the use of covenants in private bank debt contracts?	Empirical	Private debt
Bopaiah (1998)	Does family ownership influence credit availability and credit terms?	Empirical	Private debt
Boubakri and Ghouma (2010)	Do ultimate ownership and family control have an effect on bond costs and ratings und different credit protection environments?	Empirical	Public debt
Chua et al. (2011)	Does family involvement influence a new ventures access to debt financing by borrowing family social capital?	Empirical	Private debt
Ellul et al. (2007)	Does a founding family exacerbate or mitigate the agency cost of debt and does this behavior change in the presence of different investor protection regimes?	Empirical	Public debt
Niskanen et al. (2010)	What is the impact of family ownership on loan availability and credit terms?	Empirical	Private debt
Steijvers and Voordeckers (2009)	Does family ownership influence the explicit (interest rate) or implicit (collateral) loan price?	Empirical	Private debt
Steijvers et al. (2010)	Do relationship characteristics (between lender and borrower) and family ownership influence the use of collateral in SME lending?	Empirical	Private debt
Voordeckers and Steijvers (2006)	What are the determinants of business and personal collateral in SME lending and what is the effect of family involvement in this context?	Empirical	Private debt

Table 1: Overview of the Reviewed Studies

2.2.2 Theoretical Arguments

As previously seen, it is assumed that differences in lending behavior between borrowers in general can be studied differently depending on the theoretical perspective someone takes. Within the extant literature scholars typically use neoclassical models, agency theory or behavioral economics – all revealing different facets of the underlying mechanisms. In the following, those three perspectives will be used to examine what kind of theoretical arguments scholars used when investigating the question of whether and how lenders deal differently with family firms and thus seeing what facets have been explored.

Starting with the neoclassical perspective, it was found that no study explicitly argues with those kinds of models in their theoretical section. None of the reviewed studies includes resource-based arguments stating that family firms might develop or hold unique resources leading to a competitive advantage in comparison to non-family firms. It is only that scholars include some of the resulting variables in their empirical models as control terms like e.g. profitability, leverage, industry or firm size.

Moving to the next theoretical perspective, is was discovered that all of the reviewed studies are mainly arguing from an agency theoretical perspective. Within this framework scholars propose that family firms represent a whole set of opposing forces that alleviate or intensify agency conflicts so that family firms either benefit or suffer regarding credit availability and/or contract terms (implicit and explicit). In the following, the commonly used arguments will be presented of why family firms have a positive respectively negative effect on inherent agency costs. All reviewed articles recognize the janiform nature of family firms with respect to debtholder-shareholder agency conflicts.

In a first step, the arguments proposing a positive effect of family firms will be presented. In comparison to non-family firms, family firms are generally characterized by concentrated ownership, where family members are poorly diversified (Anderson et al., 2003). As a consequence family businesses have different incentive structures. So, firm survival becomes an essential goal as family shareholders have a substantial part of their wealth invested in the business and hence at risk. This in mind, scholars argue that family firms have longer investment horizons and act more risk-averse, which ultimately lowers the risk of moral hazard problems (Kang, 2000; McConaugby et al., 2001; Le Breton-Miller & Miller, 2006; Naldi et al., 2007). Similarly, the goal of dynastic stability, i.e. the intention to pass the company from generation to generation is an essential characteristic of family businesses which also leads to less exposure of risk and thus to lower agency conflicts (Arregle et al., 2007; Chua et al., 1999; Litz, 1995). As a consequence of such a long-term orientation, scholars argue that family firms can build longer and more intense relationships with lenders. This, in accordance with agency theory, results in lower informational asymmetries as a more personal and better informed relation between the principal and the agent exists. Longer time horizons also influence the behavior toward other stakeholders. Scholars argue that family firms pursue non-economic goals like reputation (Zellweger et al., 2011) which yields to lower moral hazard issues. In addition, prevalent kinship and altruism are supposed to lower self-interest of family agents which would also lower agency costs (see Chami, 1997 and Karra et al., 2006). According to Fama & Jensen (1983) family owned and managed firms have advantages in monitoring and disciplining decision agents (long term orientation, cohesive management structure and many levels of interaction among themselves) and thus a lower risk of moral hazard. In addition to those basic and pure agency related arguments, Chua et al. (2011) use social capital theory to suggest how new ventures can borrow family social capital and therefore reduce agency costs of debt in order to get better access to debt financing.

In contrast to those arguments, scholars theoretically claim that family firms also have negative effects on agency costs of debt. Besides its positive effects, parental altruism also has a dark side from a debtholders' perspective as it might exacerbate agency conflicts. Family members get the opportunity to free ride without being monitored or disciplined by the parents which represent an increase of moral hazard risks (Schulze et al., 2003). Similarly, concentrated ownership increases the risks associated with moral hazard, because blockholders gain the power to expropriate wealth from stakeholders (Mueller & Inderst, 1999; Claessens et al., 2002). In addition, Lubatkin et al. (2005) and Schulze et al. (2001) hypothesize that family firms are more susceptible to self-control issues (partly because of parental altruism) which intensifies agency conflicts. Likewise scholars point to the higher risks of moral hazard due to entrenchment within family firms (Gomez-Mejia et al., 2001). Anderson et al. (2003) state that family firms are more likely to pay special dividends and offer excessive compensation to family members in comparison to non-family firms. Besides linking family involvement to moral hazard conflicts, literature claims that lenders face more informational problems when working with family firms. Family firms are said to have a "keep it in the family" tradition (Poutziouris, 2001) which leads to higher informational asymmetries and thus increased agency cost of debt. Moreover, informal management styles and rather low levels of formal documentation aggravate this effect (Ali et al., 2007; Chen et al., 2008; Daily & Dollinger, 1991).

Ellul et al. (2007) include the investor protection environment (IPE) which is the way how market participants are disciplined as a moderator variable in their theoretical model and argue that the total effect of family involvement on lending behavior depends on the IPE. In case of a well-functioning market i.e. a high IPE, negative agency aspects of family firms become less relevant as the market limits the possibility of wealth expropriation so that family firms benefit from their positive facets. In case of a low IPE, the authors suggest that family firms suffer from higher agency costs as the environment will not be able to repress their dark side, thus making it possible for them to take advantage of their powerful position and expropriate debtholders' wealth.

On this basis, three agency theoretical hypotheses from the reviewed studies could be extracted which were subject to empirical tests: (1) Family firms have a better (worse) access to debt financing due to lower (higher) agency costs of debt, (2) Family firms get better (worse) conditions when obtaining debt because of lower (higher) agency costs of debt and (3) New ventures enjoy better access to debt financing by borrowing social capital from the family and thus reducing agency costs of debt.

Finally, it was found that none of the reviewed studies uses concepts from behavioral research to investigate differences in lending behavior toward family and non-family firms.

2.2.3 Empirical Approaches and Results

Without exception, scholars relied on historical data with different levels of quantity and quality. In addition, nine out of ten reviewed studies used regression models to test the influence of family firms on lending behavior. Only Steijvers et al. (2010) applied an alternative approach using decision tree analysis. Researchers included different combinations of variables in their tests. Typically, they tested the direct effect of family firm variables on credit availability or on specific loan contract terms while controlling for a number of other independent variables (see Table 2 for a synoptic illustration of the used variables). Only Chua et al. (2011) and Boubakri & Ghouma (2010) investigated potential indirect effects.

Reviewing the studies in focus, it was found that the gathered empirical evidence in regards to the influence of family firms on lending behavior proves to be as ambiguous as the results of the studies regarding agency conflicts within a general lending context. While some authors claim that family firms have lower agency costs and thus benefit in terms of credit availability and/or loan contract term, others present contrary empirical results. Nevertheless, some similarities in regards to the influence of family firms on specific contract terms could be found. Investigating the impact on credit availability, Bopaiah (1998) found that family ownership has a direct and positive effect. Even though Chua et al. (2011) showed that family governance and management has a positive impact on the approved loan amount, they could not verify a direct effect of family ownership. However, they detected an indirect effect of family ownership mitigated by the relationship with lenders. Contrary to those findings, Niskanen et al. (2010) showed that loan availability decreases with family ownership. Additionally, Chua et al. (2011) indicate another indirect relationship between family involvement and loan amount. They find that family governance and the intention for transgenerational succession are positively correlated with obtaining third-party guarantees which then influences the granted loan amount. No other study investigated further direct and indirect effects on credit availability of family firms. The other studies examined the impact on rating results (one study) and specific loan contract terms, namely covenants (one study), collateral (four studies) and interest rates in the form of yield spreads (six studies). Boubakri & Ghouma (2010) and Bagnoli et al. (2011) found that family firms have to cope with higher agency costs of debt as they are associated with lower credit ratings (Boubakri & Ghouma, 2010) and their debt contracts are more likely to include restrictive covenants, especially covenants that minimize risks of moral hazard in the form of restricting the firm's ability to expropriate wealth from bondholders with liquidity and net worth covenants (Bagnoli et al., 2011). Evidence about the impact on interest rates is again ambiguous. Using a sample of U.S. public debt, Anderson et al. (2003) identified a beneficial effect of family ownership on interest rates. Ellul et al. (2007) confirmed those findings. But, they also found that the quality of the IPE acted a moderator variable in their sample resulting in a negative impact of family firms in a low creditor protection environment and a positive impact in a high creditor protection environment. In contrast, Bopaiah (1998) and Niskanen et al. (2010) could not find a significant direct relationship between family ownership and explicit loan price. Moreover, Boubakri & Ghouma (2010) concluded that family firms are associated with higher costs of debt even when controlling for different IPEs. Similarly, Steijvers & Voordeckers (2009b) determined a negative effect. They found that family firms have a higher likelihood of pledging personal collateral which prompts banks to charge higher interest rates.

	Anderson et al. (2003)	Bagnoli et al. (2011)	Bopaiah (1998)	Boubakri and Ghouma (2010)	Chua et al. (2011)	Ellul et al. (2007)	Niskanen et al. (2010)	Steijvers and Voordeckers (2009)	Steijvers et al. (2010)	Voordeckers and Steijvers (2006)
Dependent variables										
Availability of credit / Amount of loan			X		X		X			
Yield spread / Interest rate	X		X	X		X	X	X		
Use of covenants		X								
Use of collateral							X	X	X	X
Type of collateral used								X	X	X
Rating				X						
Independent variables										
Family characteristics										
CEO-type	X	X								
Dual-class stock system		X		X		X				
Family firm (dummy)	X	X	X	X		X	X	X	X	X
Family governance	X				X					
Family management / Owner management			X	X	X	X				
Family ownership	X	X	X		X					
Intention for dynastic stability					X					
Non-family blockholders / Outside blockholders	X					X				
Non-family managers					X					
Other types of controlling shareholders				X						
Outside board members (# of outside board members)					X					
Size of family ownership	X					X	X	X*		
Relationship characteristics										
Length of of borrower-lender relationship			X					X	X	X
Market power of banks			X				X	X*		
Number of bank relationships			X						X	X
Relationship intensity			X		X		X	(X)	(X)	(X)
Loan characteristics										
Age of debt	X									
Bank judging time										X
Debt liquidity	X									
Debt maturity / duration	XD	X	X	X		X		X		X
Debt amount (Loan amount, Issue size)		X	X	X		X			X	X
Reference value for interest rate		X	X			X				
Third party guarantees					X					
Type of collateral			(X)					X		
Type of interest rate			X							
Use of collateral			X				X	X		
Yield spread / Interest rate		X						X		
Firm characteristics										
Country										
Equity					X					
Firm age			X		X		X	X*		X
Firm growth		X								
Firm location				X	X		X			
Firm risk	X	X		X						
Firm size	X	X	X	X	X		X	X	X	X
Firms delinquency								X*		
Industry	X	(X)		X	X	X		X		
Legal form			X					X		
Level of trade credit use										X
Leverage	X	X	X	X		X	X	X		
Liquidity			X							
Mother or affiliate company										X
Performance / Profitability	X		X	X		X	X	X*		
Rating	X	X				X				
Characteristics of the macro-environment										
Country-level condition				X		X				
Investor Protection Environment Characteristics				X		X				
Size of debt market										
Other characteristics										
Assistance with disclosure					X					
CEO/owner characteristics								X*		
Time	X			X		X				X

Table 2: Used Variables within the Reviewed Studies

Empirical results are mainly in line in regards to the influence of family involvement on the use of collateral though it has to be remarked that such a result is not surprising when considering that almost all studies in this context have been conducted by the same authors partly

even using the same data set. So, Niskanen et al. (2010), Voordeckers & Steijvers (2006), Steijvers et al. (2010) and Steijvers & Voordeckers (2009b) found that family firms generally have a higher likelihood of pledging collateral. However, when controlling for collateral type, Steijvers & Voordeckers (2009b) provide evidence that family firms are only associated with higher requirements in regards to personal collateral. They do not find any significant relationship with business collateral. While as well controlling for collateral type Voordeckers & Steijvers (2006) assess that family firms have an influence on any kind of collateral.
In addition to examining direct and indirect effects on credit availability and contract terms, Steijvers & Voordeckers (2009b) found additional evidence for a substitution effect between explicit interest rates and business collateral requirements. Using a simultaneous system of equations model including interest rate premium, business collateral and personal collateral as dependent variables, they suggest that both family and non-family businesses can choose to either pay a higher interest rate with lower levels of business collateral or vice versa. This relationship does not hold true for personal collateral in their sample indicating that personal collateral is used as a particular agency mitigating mechanism for family firms as family members will suffer personally in case of default and thus have less incentives to expropriate debtholders wealth.
Trying to conclude, it has to be stated that the currently available literature and the related empirical evidence do not justify any inference about the existence and reasons of differences in lending behavior toward family and non-family businesses. It's either that currently available studies contain crucial methodological flaws or that the underlying theoretical models are not adequate and/or insufficient. The thesis will critically elaborate on those issues in the next section.

2.2.4 Critique

In this section, the available studies will be critically assessed from (1) a theoretical and (2) an empirical perspective.
As seen previously, research on lending behavior uses three main theoretical frameworks – neoclassical models, agency theory and behavioral economics. All those concepts can be used to explain differences in lending behavior toward family and non-family firms. So, family firms can differ significantly and objectively from non-family businesses leading to variations in access to debt and contract terms. In addition, family firms might face higher or lower agency costs which cause potential differences. Lastly, lenders might deal differently with family firms as a result of behavioral factors without objective differences between family and non-family firms. Unfortunately, currently available literature focuses almost solely on agency theoretical aspects, mentioning neoclassical arguments only incidentally and ignoring behavioral concepts completely. Consequently, current research does not cover important facets of the topic and thus appears to be incomplete. In addition and as already discusses above, the agency theoretical perspective holds the potential of not explaining lending behavior ade-

quately as it only represents a partial view on the topic. It is only useful to explain problems that arise from informational asymmetries and goal divergences. Classical agency theory does not care about actual differences between two companies if they do not lead to agency conflicts (contrariwise, neoclassical theories do care about agency conflicts). In addition, the underlying assumption of agency theory is that people act rational under the constraint of informational asymmetries. As demonstrated by behavioral research, this assumption does not hold in reality so that the agency theoretical perspective becomes useless to describe and explain real world behavior. Hence, it is an inappropriate and unjustifiable assumption when studying human behavior.

Furthermore, the underlying theoretical understanding of family firms within currently available studies which also influences empirically used definition of this particular type of business is deficient. All of the reviewed articles regard family firms as a more or less homogeneous group even though research indicates a significant variability between them (Chrisman et al., 2007; Sharma, 2003; Chua et al., 2012; Chrisman & Patel, 2012; Bennedsen et al., 2010). Only some researchers partly distinguish between different types of family management and family governance. Furthermore and partly as a result of the slack theoretical handling, the empirical models use rather fuzzy definitions of family businesses. Most of the empirical studies define family firms with respect to family ownership (typically if family ownership is greater than 50% than the company is seen as a family firm). Numerous authors have discussed the inappropriateness of such definitions and stated that family firms cannot be described solely in terms of the ownership structure (Astrachan et al., 2002). Only Chua et al. (2011) include aspects like intention for transgenerational succession. Such fuzzy definitions can have caused further ambiguity of empirical results. So, some scholars defined companies like Oracle and Yahoo as family firms, which leaves serious doubt in regards to the gathered empirical evidence.

From a methodological perspective, endogeneity is generally one of the major threats to the viability of empirical results. Caused by omitted variables, simultaneity and/or measurement errors it leads to biased and inconsistent estimates making any reliable inference impossible (Shaver, 1998; Antonakis et al., 2010). This in mind, studies in the context of lending behavior are expected to be particularly affected by those threats as important variables like e.g. loan availability or various loan contract terms are characterized by strong interrelations. Taking additionally into account that none of the reviewed studies includes all variables (see table 2), endogeneity becomes a crucial aspect of the empirical tests. Two of the ten reviewed papers ignore this problem completely (Bopaiah, 1998 and Niskanen et al., 2010), leaving the reader with serious concerns with respect to their gathered empirical evidence. So, e.g. Niskanen et al. (2010) did not include variables like debt maturity or debt amount which might correlate with other independent variables they included in their study like the use of collateral or family involvement (see Steijvers & Voordeckers, 2009b who discuss the interrelation). Fortunately, all of the other eight studies address endogeneity issues, which is respectable considering the findings of Antonakis et al. (2010) who estimate that only between 10% and 44% of all studies within social sciences address such problems. However, the whole field suffers from the fact that scholars do not have access to the data they would need to completely get endogeneity problems under control. In general, one way to deal with this kind of problem is to use instrumental variables and to estimate the parameters indirectly (the most common estimation approach is the two-stage least squares method - 2SLS; see Roberts & Whited, 2012 for further details on the method and alternative ways). In this context, one necessary condition is that instrumental variables do correlate with the included independent variable but not with the omitted variable. So, e.g. Steijvers & Voordeckers (2009b) do not include the variables debt amount and firm risk in their empirical model which potentially correlate with the included variable interest rates and thus lead to potential endogeneity problems. As a consequence, they use firm age and market power of banks as instrumental variables in order to correctly estimate the effect of interest rates. But debt amount and firm risk might also correlate with firm age which would again cause endogeneity. Unfortunately, the usually available data sets in the context of lending behavior are a limiting factor, making it hard to fully control for problems of endogeneity.

2.2.5 Recommendation for Future Research

Based on the above critique of the currently available literature, which revealed both theoretical and empirical shortcomings in explaining differences in lending behavior toward family and non-family businesses, five specific recommendations for future research will be outlined in this section. The first three are concerned with a theoretical perspective whereas the others address empirical issues.

Theoretical diversity: Scholars should apply multiple theories in order to answer the question whether lenders deal differently with family and non-family firms. More specifically, two theoretical frameworks are suggested, namely (1) RBV and (2) behavioral economics.

Based on a RBV, researchers could answer the question whether family firms as lenders are different from non-family firms without tenaciously focusing solely on agency conflicts. So, questions like "Do family firms have lower operational risks?", "Do family firms perform better and thus are better lenders?" or more generally "Do family firms have competitive advantages in comparison to non-family firms, therefore get better credit ratings which then leads to better access to debt and/or more favorable loan contract terms?". All those questions have not yet been addressed adequately within the research context of lending. Nevertheless, a large part in family business research is concerned with finding general differences between family and non-family firms based on internal aspects and arguments. Scholars exploiting the research question in focus on the basis of this theoretical foundation could therefore also contribute to the available extant literature in family business research. However, it has to be mentioned that research using the RBV also produced highly ambiguous results.

Furthermore, behavioral economics is an interesting and promising theoretical framework for future research regarding the question whether lenders deal differently with family and non-family firms. Unlike standard economic theories, behavioral models do not use simplistic assumptions about human nature and are thus better suited for analyzing behavior. As seen above, lenders are susceptible to a variety of behavioral factors which was previously assigned to one of the following categories in the context of lending: task characteristics, characteristics of the loan officer, borrower characteristics, characteristics of the lending organization, external information and opinions and emotions. In the following, some suggestions are presented of how behavioral concepts might explain potential differences in lending behavior toward family and non-family firms, but need further research.

Starting with the loan officers' characteristics, it is argue that those might affect lending behavior causing differences between family and non-family firms. As seen above, Bruns et al. (2008) found that the similarity between a lenders' and a borrowers' specific human capital is a significant indicator of loan approval. Taking additionally into account that family firms personify a particular set of values as a consequence of the inevitable entanglement between the family and the business (Aronoff & Ward, 1995; Carrigan & Buckley, 2008; Tagiuri & Davis, 1996), it is assumed that bank loan officers having a strong family background or striving for such values might favor family over non-family firms even if this might not be the rational choice in a neoclassical sense so that family firms might benefit in terms of credit availability and/or loan contract terms in such a situation.

Additionally, it is assumed behavioral aspects associated with the borrowers' characteristics or more specifically with the communication of these to influence lending decisions. Inspired by the work of Micelotta & Raynard (2011) who found that family firms use different strategies to communicate family involvement and based on the widely confirmed susceptibility of decision makers in regards to the presentation of a decision task, it is proposed that lending behavior is influenced by the form of communicating family involvement. So, firms communicating on the basis of a family preservation strategy (intimate connection between the family and the company is highlighted) will probably differ more extremely from non-family firms in the context of lending behavior than family firms using a family subordination strategy (familial component of the business is downplayed).

Besides those factors and as previously seen, McNamara & Bromiley (1997) argue that differences in lending behavior can also be explained on an organization level based on the characteristics of the lending organization. In this context, it is supposed that e.g. private family-owned banks with a long tradition might be more susceptible to emotional factors, potentially even favor an inferior family firm over a superior non-family firm, feeling obliged to support those kinds of companies. On the other hand, it is presumed that large private banks to rather rely on hard financial data than on soft information like family characteristics when making decisions regarding credit availability and loan contract terms.

Furthermore, external information and opinions generally influence loan officers in their judgment and decision making. Trotman & Trotman (2010) argue that auditors are affected by family firms in their decisions, so that external information from auditors of family and non-family firm will be different. It is proposed that loan officers either use this information equally in both cases or anticipate such differences and discount external information regarding family firms.

Finally, emotional aspects might cause differences in lending behavior toward family and non-family firms. According to Rottenstreich & Shu (2007), decision-tasks that are associated with a high degree of affect facilitate automatic decision processing resulting in the use of heuristics whereas affect-poor decision-tasks facilitate deliberate valuation by calculation relying rather on hard facts. So, if lending decisions involving family firms provoke affect rich reactions, it is likely that the loan officer's behavior will be based on automatic processing and thus potentially deviate from neoclassical models. In addition, Kida et al. (2001) report that managers tend to avoid superior alternatives that elicit negative feelings in comparison to inferior alternatives that are not associated with such feelings. In regards to this dissertation's specific research question it means that a loan officer will decide in favor of a potentially inferior family firm if the alternative i.e. deciding in favor of the superior non-family firm or to put it differently deciding in disfavor of the inferior family firm is associated with negative feelings and vice versa. On the other hand, Isen et al. (1988) argue that positive affect results in a risk-averse behavior when people consider potential losses. So, if loan officers focus on the risk of default when evaluating a credit (thus considering the potential losses) and assuming that family firms evoke positive feelings within bank loan officers (as a result of past experiences or generally existing images of family firms within society or within a particular lending organization), it can be supposed that lenders behave rather cautiously when dealing with family firms potentially resulting in unfavorable reactions.

Those are just some suggestions on how behavioral findings might explain potential differences in lending behavior toward family firms by providing an altered perspective on the underlying research question. But we clearly need more research in this direction as it might reveal new interesting insights and thus contribute to a better understanding of family firms in the context of lending.

Definitional clarity and heterogeneity of family firms: Scholars are called to use more precise definitions of family firms. In addition, they should distinguish between family firms and other types of companies like owner-managed firms. Accepting the different nature of the two will contribute to unambiguous arguments and thus a better understanding of the phenomena.

As seen in the extant literature, family firms are not all the same. They do differ in various aspects (Chrisman et al., 2007; Chua et al., 2012; Chrisman & Patel, 2012). Therefore, scholars should accept this heterogeneity. This is especially true when scholar use a rather objective orientated theoretical framework assuming that lending differences are caused by real differences between companies. Not differentiating between different types of family firms theoretically will also bias empirical findings and might also cause ambiguous results depending on the composition of the sample. Unlike currently available literature, future research should embrace the divergence of family firms and analyze differences between the various types of family firms. Maybe it is not the question whether family firms differ from non-family firms, but whether family firms differ from each other and how particular family firms differ from non-family ones. As a welcomed side-effect, this type of research can make valuable contributions to the general literature on family businesses by either verifying existing or identifying new types of family firm categories and describing their effects on lending behavior toward them.

Context-dependent behavior: As shown previously, empirical studies reveal an inconsistent pattern of the influence of family firms on lending behavior. This thesis argues that this might be partially caused by an insufficient recognition of the conditional influence of family involvement on lending behavior causing lenders to not always favor either family or non-family firms but to rather adopt their behavior in accordance to a specific context. Currently, only Ellul et al. (2007) explicitly discuss the impact of contextual variations demonstrating that differences in lending behavior toward family and non-family firms are not homogeneous but vary depending on the IPE. In a similar fashion, Gedajlovic et al. (2012) argue that the form of influence of family firms largely depends on specific contextual institutional factors. More specifically, they state that the influence of family firms is different in emerging and advanced economies. As a consequence, researchers are called to explicitly investigate further contextual aspects with respect to the conditional influence of family involvement on lending behavior. It might help to obtain a more differentiated view on the topic by explaining how, why and under what circumstances lenders treat family and non-family firms or distinct types of family firms differently. Having said this, this thesis suggests future research in this field to particularly test the influence of family firms on lending behavior depending on the economic situation of the company. So, it is proposed that, all else equal, lenders will favor a family over a non-family firm as long as both companies face good economic conditions, but disfavor the family business if both companies are in crisis revealing a reversal of preferences. Arguing from a behavioral perspective, lenders might have developed conditional stereotypes assuming that family firms in critical situations face more problems like emotional intra-family conflicts that make it hard to recover from the economic situation and thus favor non-family firms or family firms with low levels of family involvement. On the other hand, lenders might be able to recall more positive characteristics of family firms in case of a flourishing economic situation when compared to non-family firms leading to a preference for family firms (see the work of Tversky & Kahneman, 1974 in regards to the availability heuristic). This might explain a potential reversal of behavior in both situations.

Ultimately, it has to be stated that context-depend behavior has been mostly neglected within currently available studies, though it offers interesting insights to the research question. Thus, it is highly recommended that scholars pay more attention to those aspects.

Methodological rigor and plurality: Currently available studies on the question whether lenders deal differently with family firms suffer from imperfect data sets making it difficult to fully control for endogeneity. Therefore, scholars are encouraged to generate more studies on this topic using "better" and different data sets and pay more attention to the consequences of endogeneity as it represents a major threat not only in this context but also in other areas within social sciences. In addition, empirical models should be tested on different data sets in order to avoid generating solely sample based knowledge and further test empirical results. As said before, endogeneity is one major threat within current research on the question in focus. One way to avoid those problems and be able to make valid causal claims is to use randomized experiments. In this context, Antonakis et al. (2010) regard experiments as the "gold standard" (p. 1086) or the "failsafe way to generate causal evidence" (p. 1086). This thesis therefore recommends supplementing currently available literature with different empirical approaches, especially with experiments. Even though experiments do have disadvantages as well (see e.g. Bryman & Bell, 2007 or for a critical examination of experiments), they offer the possibility to micro-test causal relationships. In addition, scholars are almost obliged to make use of experiments when following this dissertation's recommendations for future research. As this review called scholars to expand their theoretical horizon when answering the research question in focus and in particular research based on concepts from behavioral economics, it implicitly proposed experiments as a methodological approach due to the fact that this kind of research literally screams for such methods.

Longitude studies: Reviewing available empirical evidence, it was previously shown that scholars using the same data set from different periods of time reported different results on whether family businesses face higher or lower agency costs of debt (Bopaiah, 1998 and Steijvers et al., 2010). One reason for this equivocality might lie in methodological flaws of one or both studies. Drawing on another explanation, this divergence in results might also be caused by changes of lending behavior over time. So, scholars could investigate the changes of differences in lending behavior toward family firms in dependence of time as either family firms might have changed and thus be better or worse borrowers or bankers changed their behavior without family firms having changed necessarily. In this context, longitude studies might be an interesting path for research. Scholars could use the data set from the National Survey of Small Business Finance (NSSBF) as they collected data from 1987 till 2003. This could help to achieve a broader look at the topic if they handle potential problems related to endogeneity.

2.2.6 Limitations of the Literature Review

At this point potential limitations of the conducted review are to be discussed. As a consequence of primarily using scientific databases for identifying relevant studies, this review might face a publication bias. However, the reference lists of the reviewed studies were also scanned but did not reveal any further sources of interest. In addition, the results of the reviewed studies are extremely diverse. Therefore, we can be confident that the effects of publication bias are relatively small.

Another potential limitation might be caused by the selection process itself and the criteria used. Defining criteria for inclusion or exclusion too narrowly might lead to overlooking relevant studies and thus drawing false conclusions. One might assume that this might be the case within this review when considering that it identified only ten relevant studies to review. In order to not suffering from this bias this study defined the criteria within this review very loosely in order to include as many studies as possible. Furthermore, it used a time consuming process for fine selection. However, this chosen approach ignores studies that might discuss the research question without including the used keywords in their title or abstract. Nevertheless, the risk of this limitation is very low for the present review.

2.3 Other Important Theories within Family Business Research with Relevance to Lending Behavior

According to Siebels & Knyphausen-Aufseß (2012) who recently did an exhaustive review on theory in family business research, three theories are predominant within family business research, namely agency theory, stewardship theory and the RBV. In addition, Chrisman et al.'s (2010) paper titled "Intellectual Foundations of Current Research in Family Business" found that the most influential papers within family business research use either agency theory or the RBV as a theoretical foundation. Hence, it can be assumed that those theories - especially agency theory and the RBV - are the essential theories to describe the unique character of family firms. In addition, the theoretical concept of SEW started to gain a lot of attention in recent years (Berrone et al., 2012; Gomez-Mejia et al., 2007; Stockmans et al., 2010; Cruz et al., 2011). Berrone et al. (2012) even claim that the SEW approach might evolve to be the dominant paradigm in family business research as SEW is the most important differentiator of family firms. Therefore, it might also be considered an important theoretical framework within family business research that might help answer the leading research question in focus.

However, except for the agency theoretical perspective, current research that investigated lending behavior toward family firms has largely ignored all of the other theories which are predominant in family business research and might have provided additional insights and revealed interesting relationships. As a consequence, these additional important theoretical frameworks will be included in the review and used to develop the dissertation's theoretical model. Hence, this study employs the agency theoretical perspective, the SEW approach and the RBV. Please note that the agency theoretical perspective in this thesis encompasses both agency and stewardship theory. And because this perspective has already been discussed earlier, this section will not elaborate upon this approach again (see sections 2.1.2 and 2.2.2).

In the following, an abridgment of the SEW approach and the RBV will be presented – both from a theoretical and empirical perspective. However it has to be noted that those two theoretical concepts will be described in general terms within this section. The relevance with respect to lending behavior and to this study will be discussed in the third chapter.

2.3.1 Socioemotional Wealth

The SEW perspective was originally developed by Gomez-Mejia et al. (2007) in order to explain unique behavioral characteristics of family firms which could not be described adequately with just one of the other dominant theories within family business research, i.e. agency theory, stewardship theory or the RBV (Berrone et al., 2012; Cennamo et al., 2012; Gomez-Mejia et al., 2011). It basically builds upon behavioral agency theory and applies the principles of this theoretical approach to the family firm context. In general, behavioral agency theory represents a combination of agency and prospect theory and assumes that an agent's behavior will depend upon his/her personal reference point. When finding themselves below the reference point, i.e. in a loss mode regarding their personal wealth, agents tend to behave risk seeking. In contrast, when being above the reference point with respect to their personal wealth, i.e. in a gain mode, the very same agents tend to behave risk-averse (Wiseman & Gomez-Mejia, 1998; Gomez-Mejia et al., 2007). By including a prospect theoretical perspective into agency theory, the authors were able to describe an agent's behavior in a more nuanced way. As mentioned, Gomez-Mejia et al. (2007) took advantage of this theoretical concept and applied it to the family business domain arguing that SEW is the most critical factor for the formation of reference points within family firms which on their part affect the companies behavior. Putting it differently, the SEW model assumes that family firms will assess all actions in terms of how those will affect their SEW. In this regard, the term SEW captures all of the affective endowment that an owning family has with respect to the business which might include aspects like e.g. the family's desire to exercise control, the satisfaction of needs for belonging and family identity, the preservation of generational stability and the development and maintenance of social status (Gomez-Mejia et al., 2007; Berrone et al., 2012). Berrone et al. (2010) noted that though non-family agents and managers in non-family firms might also experience some of those SEW-related aspects, "the value of socioemotional wealth to the family is more intrinsic, its preservation becomes an end in itself, and it is anchored at a deep psychological level among family owners whose identity is inextricably tied to the organization" (p. 87). When the family's SEW is at risk, the family will find themselves below the reference point, i.e. agents will be in a loss mode and thus try to undertake all possible actions to avoid any potential losses with respect to their SEW, even if that jeopardizes the firm's performance or comes at the expense of external stakeholders in the form of expropriating their wealth (Gomez-Mejia et al., 2007; Gomez-Mejia et al., 2011; Berrone et al., 2012). Within their original paper, Gomez-Mejia et al. (2007) used data from Spanish olive oil mills to make their case and demonstrate the concept of the SEW approach. They showed that family firms were willing to accept a greater probability of organizational failure and a below-target performance in order to preserve their SEW. So, according to the SEW concept, family firms tend to prioritize risk-averse behavior toward issues that are related to their SEW in comparison to risk-aversion with respect to financial losses. When presented with two alternative strategies - one that might diminish the family's SEW but does not risk the financial position of the firm and the other preserving the family's SEW but risks the financial situation of the firm - a family firm will choose the later alternative. Thus, the SEW construct postulates that family firms' decision making is not driven by pure economic logic, but rather by considerations regarding the preservation of their SEW - especially in situations when their SEW is at risk.

As mentioned before, SEW is a multidimensional concept that captures all of the affective endowment that an owning family has with regards to the business which might include aspects like e.g. the family's desire to exercise control, the satisfaction of needs for belonging and family identity, the preservation of generational stability and the development and maintenance of social status (Gomez-Mejia et al., 2007; Berrone et al., 2012). In order to make the concept more concrete and applicable, Berrone et al. (2012) broke down this concept into five dimensions that they labeled as FIBER. In particular, they consist of the dimensions (1) family control and influence, (2) family members' identification with the firm, (3) binding social ties, (4) emotional attachment and (5) renewal of family bond to the firm through dynastic succession. In the following, those dimensions will be discussed shortly as those on the one hand will enhance the readers understanding of the SEW concept and on the other hand will be an essential part of this study's theoretical and empirical model. The first dimension - family control and influence - addresses the family's need for control and influence that it can exert over the company and its decisions by e.g. holding a majority in the business, appointing the CEO and other members of the top management team or filling the board with family members who then are able to influence the business. In addition, numerous authors have documented the importance of control and influence for family firms (Zellweger et al., 2011; Gomez-Mejia et al., 2007; Croci et al., 2011). Hence, family control and influence is an integral part of SEW. The second dimension titled "family members' identification with the firm" refers to the close relationship between the family and the business and the desire that family members strongly identify with the firm and are proud to be members of the family business. Berrone et al. (2012) noted that the identity of the family is inextricably tied to the organization and influences both employees and external stakeholders (like e.g. customers or suppliers) by projecting the family's image to the company. Hence, family firms who aim to preserve their SEW will try to ensure a high level of family members' identification with the firm which makes the family members' identification with the firm an important dimension within the SEW model. The third FIBER dimension is called "binding social ties" and relates to the family firms' social relationships. According to this dimension of the SEW construct, family firms strive for a positive reputation of their family and their company within society, strong relationships with their stakeholders and an essential role in their community (Berrone et al., 2012; Zellweger & Astrachan, 2008). Cennamo et al. (2012) argues that this desire is based on normative rather than instrumental motives, i.e. family firms do not strive for those aspects because they expect a financial return but instead are intrinsically motivated and hope for non-economic benefits, like e.g. relational trust, feelings of closeness and belonging as well as solidarity (see also Dyer & Whetten, 2006; Chrisman et al., 2007). Similarly, numerous scholars argue that family firms are deeply embedded in their community and tend to sponsor local activities and organizations like e.g. local charities, local events and local sports clubs (Berrone et al., 2010; Uhlaner et al., 2004). Further, Berrone et al. (2012) defined "emotional attachment" as a fourth dimension of SEW. This category describes the role of affective considerations or emotions within the family business context. Although emotions are an important part in every organization (Ashforth & Humphrey, 1995), the inextricable connection between the family and the business system in case of family firms leads to a particular relevance and embeddedness of emotions within this type of organization (Eddleston & Kellermanns, 2007; Tagiuri & Davis, 1996). So, Schlippe et al. (2008) note that the business system typically follows an economic logic whereas the family system pursues an emotional logic, which causes the family firm to be particularly susceptible to emotional issues (see also Berrone et al., 2010; Baron, 2008). Besides their omnipresence in family firms, emotions also hold a value for family members. So, a strong emotional attachment helps the family to maintain a positive self-image. Thus, a loss of the firm would be related to a loss of one's identity (Berrone et al., 2012). Similarly, Kleine et al. (1995) note that a family's emotional attachment might "facilitate self-continuity by connecting a person with a desirable past self (e.g., memories), a present self (me now), or a future self (who I am becoming)" (p. 328). Hence, emotions within the family firm might support the satisfaction of the family members' desire for belonging, affect and intimacy and thus play an integral part in the SEW model (Berrone et al., 2012). Moreover, Zellweger et al. (2011) noticed that the companies perceived value from the owner's perspective increases with the level of emotional attachment which additionally indicates and emphasizes the importance of emotions. Finally, the FIBER dimensions include "renewal of family bonds through dynastic succession" as the fifth category. This dimension refers to the owners' intention to past the business to future generations in order to secure family tradition and legacy (Berrone et al., 2012; Zellweger & Astrachan, 2008; Astrachan et al., 2002). Zellweger et al. (2011) even suggest that the intention for generational stability is the central dimension of the SEW approach. Similarly, Chua et al. (2003) found that succession is one of the most important concerns of family firm owners. Numerous scholars support this view by stating that transgenerational sustainability is one of the main goals and key differentiators of family firms (Kets de Vries, 1993; Zellweger et al., 2011). In addition, it has to be mentioned that the focus on this goal has important implications for the behavior of family firms as it leads to a long-term orientation in their decision making. So, investment decisions, for instance, will be calculated on longer time horizons with the ambition to maintain the company for future generations. All of those five dimensions describe the term SEW within the SEW construct. Originally, the SEW model was developed to explain differences between family and non-family members. However, Berrone et al. (2012) argue that the SEW concept might also be used to explain differences across family firms. Numerous scholars state that family firms are not a homogeneous group of companies as assumed by most of the current research attempts, but do significantly differ from each other (Zahra et al., 2004). Chua et al. (2012) as well as Chrisman & Patel (2012) even claim that differences between different kinds of family firms are probably the more appropriate research topic than differences between family and non-family firms as some family firms might e.g. behave more like purely economically driven non-family firms whereas others might behave conversely. On this basis, Berrone et al. (2012) argue that family firms might differ with respect to the importance they attach to issues that are related to their SEW and thus to the different FIBER dimensions. Gomez-Mejia et al. (2007) demonstrated that family firms display a higher preference for SEW preservation when the level of family involvement is high. Thus and drawing upon the SEW model, it is assumed that firms with a low level of family involvement will probably behave differently in comparison to family firms with a high level of family involvement as they will have a different reference point for their decisions and thereby their behavior. As a consequence, the SEW approach promises to be a useful theoretical framework for the current research project.

Besides the presented theoretical foundations of the SEW approach, numerous scholars have applied it to a wide range of areas including e.g. executive pay (Gomez-Mejia et al., 2003), firms risk-taking behavior (Gomez-Mejia et al., 2007), governance arrangements (Jones et al., 2008); diversification decisions (Gomez-Mejia et al., 2010b), family firms innovation strategies (Gomez-Mejia et al., 2010a) and human resource management practices (Cruz et al., 2010; Cruz et al., 2011) in order to test the model empirically. Overall, those studies have produced ample evidence that mainly support the assumptions and arguments of the SEW concept. In the following, a sample of empirical papers will be presented that examines family business related topics while relying on the SEW model. As mentioned, Gomez-Mejia et al. (2007) were the first to gather empirical evidence in favor of the SEW approach. In addition, Jones et al. (2008) demonstrated that family-owned firms tend to prefer affiliate directors in their boards even if this causes a diminished ability to monitor the management's activities. They argue that affiliate directors can execute an advising function without reducing the family's control over the business and thereby not threatening their SEW. In a similar fashion, Cruz et al. (2010) found that family firms which top management team majorly consists of family members tend to design agency contracts in a way that the top management teams welfare will be protected even if this might be counterintuitive from a purely agency theoretical perspective. However, the authors argue that this behavior finally protects harmony within the family and thus preserves their SEW.

Using data from a sample of 360 firms (of which 160 were family controlled), Gomez-Mejia et al. (2010b) investigated differences in firms' decisions to diversify and found that family firms are less likely to engage in corporate diversification even though it increases their economic risk that is related with the business as diversification might reduce volatility in earnings and improve the likelihood of firm survival. They basically argued that diversification is associated with potential losses in SEW. Because diversification typically requires external funding which comes along with several rights to influence the company (e.g. covenants, position of lenders in the board) the family's ability to exercise unconstrained authority and control will be limited, so that their SEW will be diminished. In addition, they suggested that diversification requires outside management talent which is not available within the family and thus further risks the family firms SEW (see also Chrisman & Patel, 2012 for a further examination of the topic of diversification in family firms on the basis of the SEW concept and prospect theory).

Applying the SEW model to a different topic, Berrone et al. (2010) found evidence that family firms tend to care more about their environmental impact in comparison to non-family firms (i.e. pollute less and/or invest more in environmental projects) in order to enhance the family's image within the local community and thus preserve or increase their SEW. They found that this relationship is particularly strong on a local level, i.e. when the company operations and their production sites are mainly concentrated in a local area.

Using a sample of 392 small and micro firms, Cruz et al. (2012) present empirical results that demonstrate how small and micro family controlled firms tend to accept cuts in performance in order to employ family members. They assert that employing family members holds socio-emotional rewards for the family like e.g. kinship ties, collective social capital, relational trust and/or interpersonal solidarity.

Drawing upon the SEW model, Stockmans et al. (2010) gathered empirical evidence that suggests that family firms tend to engage in upward earnings management when the firms' actual performance is poor in order to preserve their SEW. They argued that when actual performance is poor, external stakeholders like e.g. lenders will try to protect their wealth by pressing the family firm to add independent directors, change the firm's strategy or gain a seat on the board of directors themselves. As this would cause of loss in control from the perspective of the family firms and thus diminish their SEW, family firms will try to avoid those consequences by managing their earnings upward.

Using regression analysis on two data samples from two different countries (Switzerland and Germany), Zellweger et al. (2012) examined the relevance of SEW for family firms. They found that a family's intention for transgenerational control (which is part of SEW) had a significant positive effect on the owners asking price, i.e. the selling price at which they would accept to sell the company. In addition, they showed that the duration of family control had a mixed impact on the perceived asking price, which contradicts with the findings of Gomez-Mejia et al. (2007). However, Zellweger et al. (2012) argue that those differences can be explained by differences in sampling, measures and the examined decisions (decision whether to join a co-op vs. decision whether to sell the total company). Hence, it can be assumed that the findings of Zellweger et al. (2012) are basically in line with the SEW concept and other empirical findings regarding this topic. Moreover, it has to be noted that Zellweger and colleagues have already examined this effect before the term SEW came up. However, they termed the value that family owners assign to the socioemotional endowments as the "emotional value" of the firm (see Zellweger & Astrachan, 2008; Zellweger, 2006).

In 2010, Gomez-Mejia et al. (2010a) analyzed a sample of 610 publicly traded high technology firms and found empirical support for the propositions made by the SEW model. In particular, they demonstrated that family-controlled firms within high technology industries tend to invest less in R&D in order to protect their SEW despite the fact that lower investments in innovation increase business risks in those industries. The authors argue that increased R&D efforts require outside managerial talent (as it is typically not available within the firm) and thus causes a loss in control which will be perceived as a loss in the families' SEW. In addition, Gomez-Mejia et al. (2010a) state that most R&D projects of publicly traded high technology firms are financed by issuing new stock to outside investors. However, as this would also cause a loss in control, family firms will perceive such actions as a threat to their SEW. Hence, family firms will tend to avoid above-average investments in R&D.

Reviewing the empirical literature and as already stated previously (see section 2.2), it was found no empirical paper that examined lending behavior toward family firms using a SEW perspective.

Overall, the gathered empirical evidence mainly supports the notions of the SEW model. Nevertheless, the number of currently available studies that explicitly use the SEW model as their primary framework and derive testable hypotheses on this basis are limited (see e.g. review of Berrone et al., 2012). Therefore, Gomez-Mejia et al. (2011) applied the empirical results of various studies within the field of family business research that do not use the SEW model as their primary theoretical framework to the SEW approach and found that most empirically observed phenomena could be explained when using the SEW model which further suggests the fit and utility of the SEW approach within family business research. According to pecking order theory, for instance, firms will prioritize internal funds over debt and debt over new external equity. Within the field of family business research, empirical data suggest that this relationship proves to be especially true for family firms, which try to avoid issuing new equity to external investors even though this might increase the firms' financial risk and decelerates growth (Coleman & Carsky, 1999; Croci et al., 2011; Erikson et al., 2003; Morck & Yeung, 2003; Poutziouris, 2001; Romano et al., 2001). Most scholars rely on pecking order theory to explain this phenomenon. However, the SEW approach could be used to supplement the argument and enable researchers to explain differences more precisely. As a consequence, the current study will build upon the SEW construct to develop its theoretical model to explain differences in lending behavior toward different types of family firms.

2.3.2 Resource-Based View

The RBV has become one of the most widely accepted theoretical concepts within the field of strategic management (Powell, 2001; Priem & Butler, 2001; Newbert, 2007) and a central theoretical framework within family business research (Chrisman et al., 2005; Chrisman et al., 2010; Siebels & Knyphausen-Aufseß, 2012). Due to its relevance for the current study, the concept will first be presented on a general level and then described against the background of family business research. In both cases, the author will outline (1) the basic theoretical arguments as well as (2) the generated empirical evidence in the respective domain.

In general, the RBV provides a theoretical basis for analyzing firms from an internal, resource-based perspective rather than an external, market-orientated view. Wernerfelt (1984) was one of the first to coin the term "Resource-Based View" and to start formalizing the concept (see Fahy & Smithee, 1999). However, he was not the first to discover the concept. Its origins can be traced back to earlier research, in which authors have emphasized the importance of a firm's resources and its impact on the company's performance (see Penrose, 1959; Pfeffer & Salancik, 1978; Selznick, 1957; Rubin, 1973). In addition, it was not until the publication of the work of Prahalad & Hamel (1990) and Barney (1991) that the RBV received wide attention and attracted new research in this field. Before those two papers, the majority of scholars relied on the external view of the firm which put the determinants of a firm's success outside the firm (see Bain, 1968; Porter, 1979; Porter, 1985). The RBV was initially developed as a counter position to this market orientated view. Nevertheless, it does not replace theories that focus on externalities, but rather complements them. In this context Barney (1991) states that firms "obtain sustained competitive advantages by implementing strategies that exploit their internal strengths, through responding to environmental opportunities, while neutralizing external threats and avoiding internal weaknesses" (p. 99). Having this in mind, the RBV provides a theoretical framework for identifying and explaining the sources of the internal strength and weaknesses (Wernerfelt, 1984; Barney, 1991; Prahalad & Hamel, 1990).

In essence, the RBV conceptualizes firms as a bundle of resources and assumes that those resources are heterogeneously distributed among firms while at the same time being imperfectly mobile so that firms might differ in terms of their resource endowments. In addition, these assumptions imply that those differences can persist over time. On this basis, the RBV argues that firms will outperform competitors if they are able to acquire, manage and leverage valuable and rare resources that lead to competitive advantages which on their part allow individual firms to earn economic rents and thereby achieve above-average returns (Peteraf, 1993; Henderson & Cockburn, 1994; Barney, 1991; Prahalad & Hamel, 1990). Moreover, Barney (1991) claims that if those resources are not only valuable and rare, but also inimitable and non-substitutable (VRIN), firms will be able to develop sustained competitive advantages (SCA), i.e. advantages that cannot be easily duplicated by competitors. At this point, it has to be emphasized that the RBV does not suggest that a company can or let alone will outperform competitors by simply possessing VRIN resources. The company has to use those resources efficiently and exploit their full potential in order to achieve above-average returns (Mahoney & Pandian, 1992; Barney, 1997; Peteraf, 1993; Lado et al., 1992). Therefore, the RBV represents a dynamic rather than static theoretical framework which allows researchers to include all potentially idiosyncratic firm-level characteristics in their analysis (Newbert, 2007).

A further issue that needs to be addressed is the definition of the term "resource" in the context of the RBV. Reviewing the literature, it was found that scholars use numerous and partly opposing definitions when speaking about resources. So, Grant (1991), for instance, uses the term "resources" to refer to inputs into the production process. In contrast, Wernerfelt (1984) defines resources as all assets that are semipermanently tied to the firm without necessarily used within the production process. Other scholars use terms like e.g. competencies (Prahalad & Hamel, 1990), skills (Grant, 1991), strategic assets (Amit & Schoemaker, 1993) or assets (Ross et al., 1996) to describe the term resources. In addition, some scholars use the terms "resources" and "capabilities" interchangeably while others strictly distinguish between these two (see e.g. Wernerfelt, 1984; Barney, 2005; Ray et al., 2004; Grant, 1991). So, Cabrera-Suárez et al. (2001) define resources as all tangible and intangible assets of a firm and refer to capabilities when speaking about a firm's capacity to deploy these resources. Within this study, the term "resources" will be used in a broad sense to refer to all assets (tangible and intangible) and capabilities that a firm can utilize to generate economic rents.

From an empirical perspective, scholars have produced an enormous amount of empirical evidence. Reviewing and assessing 166 empirical studies, Barney & Arikan (2001) concluded that only two percent of the reviewed studies were partially or fully inconsistent with the RBV. Thus, on the basis of this review, it can be concluded that the RBV has been majorly confirmed by empirical studies. However, Newbert (2007) questions the validity of those findings. They argue that Barney & Arikan (2001) use an inadequate method for examining the actual level of support for the RBV as Barney and Arikan assume that a reviewed article is in line with the RBV as long as the findings do not show significant inconsistencies, so that e.g. insignificant regression coefficients are not interpreted as inconsistencies. In addition, he notes that Barney and Arikan's choice of method might be subject to a strong selection bias as they did not use a systematic approach (Newbert, 2007). As a response to that criticism, Newbert (2007) conducted a systematic and meta-analytical review (sample of 55 studies) and found that only about 53 percent of tests were empirically supported. Additionally, he concluded that capabilities, i.e. the firm's capacity to deploy resources, contribute more significantly to a firm's performance that their assets, which emphasizes the importance of a firm's ability to make efficient use of their available resources and that the possession of resources does not automatically lead to competitive advantages. All in all, the empirical evidence regarding the RBV is comparable to the empirical results of other theories like e.g. transaction cost economics (Newbert, 2007) and thus can be seen as an adequate theoretical concept.

After having discussed the RBV in rather general terms, this part of the thesis will present how scholars adapted the RBV as a theoretical framework within the context of family business research in order to explain the unique character of family firms. As having said before, family firms are subject to the inextricable entanglement between the family and the firm. Scholars that applied the RBV to the domain of family business research basically argue that this entanglement and the resulting involvement of the family represent an additional resource for the firm that can be exploited (Cabrera-Suárez et al., 2001; Habbershon & Williams, 1999; Dyer, 2006). Habbershon & Williams (1999) who were among the first to introduce the RBV to family business research state that family firms are characterized by "the unique bundle of resources a particular firm has because of the systems interaction between the family, its individual members and the business" (p. 129). They label the resulting resources that are idiosyncratic to a particular family firm as their "familiness". Put differently, a family firm's familiness represents the additional resources (assets and capabilities) that are at the firm's disposal as a consequence of the close connection between the family and the firm and might be used to develop competitive advantages. Those family specific resources might consist of e.g. deeply embedded informal decision-making processes, relational mentoring practices between parents and children or stakeholder relationships that the family has with suppliers, lenders or customers (Habbershon & Williams, 1999). Thus, familiness mostly consists of intangible resources. Additionally, Eddleston et al. (2008) propose that family firms tend to evaluate, build and deploy resources differently in comparison to non-family firms as a result of the tradeoffs they make between economic and non-economic goals. Hence, according to the RBV, family firms differ in terms of their resources and the way they exploit the potential of the resources at hand. Habbershon & Williams (1999) term the components of familiness that provide the family firm with advantages as "distinctive familiness". However, they note that not all family-related resources will positively influence the firms' performance. Thus, it is argued that if a firm's familiness is not managed and monitored, family involvement might quickly become a familial encumbrance. Habbershon & Williams (1999) refer to all of the negative aspects of familiness as a family firm's "constrictive familiness". This type of familiness might be manifested in negative consequences regarding the cost of capital (Steijvers et al., 2010), unfavorable HR policies with respect to incompetent family members (Lubatkin et al., 2005) or other areas of a firm's decision making that can be negatively influenced by the family system (Habbershon et al., 2003). Additionally, Habbershon et al. (2003) note that the direction of how family involvement affects an individual business, i.e. positively in the form of distinctive familiness or negatively in the form of constrictive familiness depends upon the characteristics of a particular family firm and the specific context in which the interaction between the family and the firm occurs (Habbershon et al., 2003). In an attempt to concretize the construct of familiness, Sirmon & Hitt (2003) defined five categories where family involvement might result in family-related idiosyncratic resources, namely (1) human capital which refers to the knowledge, skills, and capabilities of family members and employees and includes aspects like e.g extraordinary commitment or warm, friendly, and intimate relationships, (2) social capital which relates to the firm's relationships with stakeholders as a consequence of the family's own social capital or their style of creating and maintaining those relationships, (3) survivability capital which encompasses all of the pooled personal resources that family members are willing to contribute to the business, (4) patient capital that refers to the longer time horizons of family firms and (5) governance structure as a result of the peculiar principal-agent situation. However, this categorization can be criticized, especially in regards to its applicability as the individual categories are not mutually exclusive which makes it hard to assign individual items to one group (see e.g. the categories human capital vs. survivability capital). Despite the critique of this particular approach to concretize the construct of familiness, scholars remark that the concept of familiness itself is a rather fuzzy one and requires further specification in order to be applied adequately. In addition, this factor also contributes to the widely spread notion that the RBV is a valuable theoretical concept within the field of family business research, but, due to the ambiguity of the familiness construct, currently remains an umbrella theory that includes a variety of family-related aspects without being able specifying them rigorously (Lambrechts et al., 2009; Sharma, 2008; Moores, 2009). Similarly, Chrisman et al. (2005) argue that "we do not yet fully understand sources or types of familiness" (p. 238), which causes the familiness construct to resemble a black box. As a consequence and from a theoretical point of view, it can be concluded that the RBV represents a useful theoretical basis for the study of family firms but also holds some challenges that need to be addressed.

Reviewing the empirical literature on the RBV in the context of family business research, Huybrechts et al. (2011) found that the majority of studies mainly support the core propositions of the RBV regarding the effect of familiness. However, they note that only few studies exist that explicitly examine the relationship between familiness and the firm's performance. In addition, they report that most of the reviewed studies have focused on the human resource component of the familiness construct since data on this aspect might be easier to obtain in comparison to the other dimension like e.g. social capital or organizational culture. At this point, it needs to be stated that the review and the conclusions of Huybrechts et al. (2011) should be used with caution as the authors waive to explain their method for identifying relevant studies so that the risk of a selection bias remains.

Using a qualitative research approach, Tokarczyk et al. (2007) found that familiness is positively related to the long-term success of the business and a market-orientated culture which again positively affects the firm's viability. Likewise, Eddleston et al. (2008) demonstrate that reciprocal altruism, a family-related characteristic which influences the way resources are deployed, is positively correlated to family firm performance. Moreover, Naldi et al. (2008) present empirical evidence that family related knowledge and reputational assets positively affect the company's performance. In contrast, Levie & Lerner (2009) demonstrated that family firm owners/managers are characterized by lower levels of human capital, are more likely to show opportunism, are more likely to operate in relatively unattractive niches and are less likely to take in external equity than external debt in contrast to non-family business owners/managers, which demonstrates the constrictive aspects of family-related resources. However, Levie & Lerner (2009) also found that firm performance did not differ between family and non-family firms. They argued that the negative effects of familiness might be offset by the positive impact of familiness in the form of reputational capital. These findings additionally underline the janiform nature of family firms, stating that family involvement might have both positive and negative effects on a company's performance.

Finally, when reviewing the literature, it was found that no paper explicitly relied on the RBV to investigate lending behavior toward family firms. Nevertheless, the RBV framework might provide researchers with additional theoretical arguments regarding the effect of family involvement on the loan officers' decision making process as it explains why and how family involvement might influence the firm's behavior and thereby its performance. Therefore, this approach will be used to form the theoretical model of this particular study (see next chapter).

2.4 Interim Conclusion

At the beginning of this literature review, four goals were formulated, namely to (1) give an overview of what is already known with regards to the leading research question in focus, (2) identify considerable research gaps which also provide additional arguments for the relevance of this study, (3) make propositions for future research of which some are aimed to be pursued by this study and (4) establish a theoretical basis to develop the theoretical model of this research project. This section will reflect upon these goals, sum up the generated insights and prepare the ground for the upcoming chapters.

Previously, it was found that scholars typically use neoclassical approaches, agency theory and behavioral economics to explain lending behavior in general. However, within the field of family business research, scholars that examine lending behavior toward family firms majorly rely only upon the agency theoretical perspective and ignore other potentially relevant theoretical frameworks. In addition, current research focuses mainly on differences in lending behavior toward family and non-family firms while completely neglecting the frequently mentioned heterogeneity within the group of family firms which is said to be of even greater importance (Chua et al., 2012; Chrisman & Patel, 2012; Bennedsen et al., 2010; Sharma, 2003). On top of those issues, it was found that the generated empirical data of the existing studies have produced highly ambiguous results and are not sufficient to answer the main research question in focus adequately, i.e. whether lenders deal differently with family firms or more specifically with different kinds of family firms. When starting to tackle the underlying research questions from the perspective of family business research rather than research on lending behavior, it was shown that scholars in this field typically rely on the agency perspective, the RBV and most recently the SEW approach to explain the unique characteristics of family firms. And again, when considering that scholars who examined lending behavior toward family firms mostly relied only on agency theoretical arguments while neglecting other potentially relevant theoretical perspectives (the RBV and the SEW concept), gaps within the currently available literature start to unveil. All of these aspects underline the relevance of examining the leading research question with additional studies.

Besides identifying relevant gaps within currently available research, this review made propositions for future research of how to address these issues and thereby contribute to a better understanding of lending behavior toward family firms. In particular, it was suggested that future research might benefit from (1) adapting new theoretical frameworks to the study of the research question in focus, namely the behavioral economics, the RBV and the SEW model, (2) examining differences in lending behavior toward different types of family firms as those differences might be the more relevant research topic and explain much of the found ambiguity within currently available studies, (3) recognizing the conditional influence of family involvement on lending behavior which might cause lenders to not continuously favor either family or non-family firms or different types of family firms but to rather adopt their behavior in accordance to a specific context, (4) paying more attention to methodological rigor and plurality in order to avoid potentially existing biases within the currently available studies by e.g. using different methods like experiments which are said to be the "gold standard" to generate causal evidence (Antonakis et al., 2010) and thereby supplementing currently available literature and finally (5) conducting longitude studies regarding lending behavior toward family firms as the ambiguity of the currently available literature might be partly caused by changes over time. As mentioned in the introduction of the literature review, some of those propositions will be addressed within this dissertation. More specifically, the current study aims to (1) apply new theoretical perspectives to the research question, (2) start examining the differences in lending behavior toward varying types of family firms and thereby addressing the issue of heterogeneity of family firms, (3) analyze the impact of an alternative contextual factor and (4) employ an experimental approach to generate empirical data in order to supplement the generated and currently available data sets.

The fourth goal of this literature review was to establish a theoretical basis for the development of the theoretical model of this research project. This was achieved by providing on overview of the research with respect to lending behavior (sections 2.1 and 2.2), the agency theoretical perspective (sections 2.1.2 and 2.2.2), behavioral economics (section 2.1.3), the SEW concept (section 2.3.1) and the RBV (section 2.3.2). The underlying theoretical research model of the study at hand will be mainly developed on the basis of those concepts, which brings us to the next chapter.

3 Theoretical Model and Hypotheses Development

The focus of this chapter is to develop a testable theoretical model on the basis of the previously reviewed literature in order to examine the influence of family involvement on loan officers' lending decisions. Therefore, this part of the thesis will start by giving an overview of the overall theoretical model in section 3.1. Thereafter, the individual effects and the corresponding hypotheses are developed. Finally, this chapter will be closed by recapitulating its content and summing up all of the developed hypotheses.

3.1 Theoretical Model

Based on the literature on lending behavior in general, lending behavior toward family firms and family business research in general, the theoretical research model of this study was developed. It is illustrated in Figure 3.

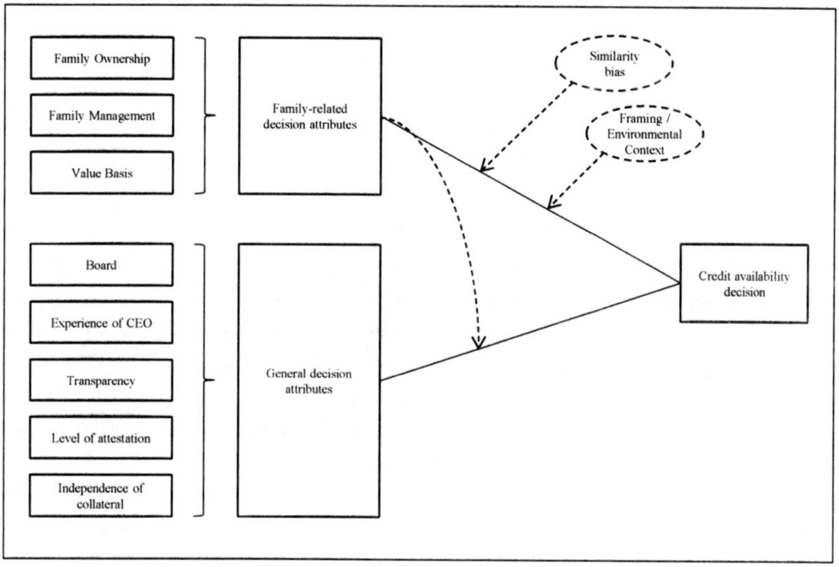

Figure 3: Overview of the Theoretical Model

The presented theoretical model was constructed according to the main goal of this study which is to investigate different facets of the influence of varying levels of family involvement on loan officers' judgment and decision making. Therefore, a main-effects model was derived, which incorporates variables that directly influence the bank loan officers' credit availability decisions. Afterwards, moderating effects have been included on the basis of the available literature. More specifically, the impact of the similarity bias and the framing effect are examined. Finally, interaction effects are hypothesized. In the following, the individual hypotheses regarding those categories are developed and discussed.

3.2 Main Effects

This study focuses on the loan officers' credit availability decision. According to literature and as described previously, bank loan officers typically use multidimensional frameworks to assess loan applications and to make their decisions. One of the most well-known concepts in this regard are the five Cs of lending, which consist of (1) character i.e. the integrity, credibility and overall willingness of the applicant to repay the loan, (2) capacity i.e. the ability of a firm to service their liabilities in terms of cash-flow and management experience, (3) capital i.e. the capitalization of the company or the amount of equity available to operate the business, (4) collateral i.e. the firms and owners available collateral (5) conditions i.e. the firms environmental conditions that might influence their debt repayment like e.g. macroeconomic conditions or competitive environment (see e.g. Beaulieu, 1994 or Jankowicz & Hisrich, 1987). This study's theoretical model or more specifically this study's main effects are basically constructed on the basis of the five C's of lending with a focus on character. So, the level of family involvement, the board function, the borrower's transparency and the level of attestation refer to issues relating to the category of character. The experience of the CEO refers to the category capacity. Finally, the independence of collateral is based on the factor collateral. Though factors from the category "conditions" are not included in the main effects model, they are included in the overall theoretical model as a moderating effect (see section 3.3.2).

However, not all aspects were included in the model. It focuses only on those factors that are the most relevant for this study and its leading research question. All aspect that were unlikely to add significant value to this study or which were likely to bias the model were suspended from the model. It, for instance, explicitly excluded hard financial variables like e.g. profitability, liquidity or the prospective borrowers' capitalization in this study's model. Those factors have already been shown to significantly influence lending decisions (see e.g. Ulrich & Arlow, 1981 or Fletcher, 1995). Nevertheless, they would create significant problems which could compromise this study's objectives. According to Beaulieu (1994), lenders use soft information only when financial information is positive. Negative financial information functions as a deal breaker. Including those types of factors would make it impossible to investigate the influence family-related factors have on the loan availability decision. Therefore, such aspects have been excluded from the theoretical model by assuming that those aspects are given and equal across all borrowers.

In the following, the model's main effects will be described and testable hypotheses are developed on the basis of the currently available literature.

3.2.1 Family-Related Decision Attributes

Family business research claims that family involvement influences bank loan officers' judgment and decision making (see e.g. Anderson et al., 2003; Chua et al., 2011; Steijvers & Voordeckers, 2009b). Unfortunately, scholars have produced mixed empirical results regarding the direction of this effect, which is due to a variety of reasons (see previous chapter). Within this paragraph, the author will use (1) agency theory, (2) the SEW approach and (3) the RBV to develop testable hypotheses regarding the influence of family involvement on bank loan officers' judgment and decision making.

Using agency theory, it can be argued that a higher level of family involvement in terms of the share of ownership leads to a lower risk of moral hazard (Anderson et al., 2003). A higher stake in the company usually comes along with financially less diversified family members as those have a substantial part of their wealth invested in the business. Consequently, family members will have stronger incentives to assure the firm's survival which causes longer investment horizons and risk-averse behavior so that the risk of moral hazard might be perceived lower in firms with a high degree of family involvement (Kang, 2000; McConaugby et al., 2001; Le Breton-Miller & Miller, 2006). This effect might even be higher if the majority of the family is employed by the firm as the family does not have an alternative source of income in case of a negative situation on the corporate level like e.g. bankruptcy. In addition and as presented in the last chapter, long-term orientation opens up the chance to develop longer and more intense relationships with lenders, which according to agency theory would lower informational asymmetries and thus lead to a beneficial treatment of those firms by the loan officers in terms of credit availability. Considering that a high degree of family involvement is typically affiliated with a high stake in the business, both financially and emotionally (Anderson et al., 2003; Steijvers & Voordeckers, 2009b), it is proposed that loan officers will perceive firms with a high level of family involvement to represent a higher level of long-term orientation in comparison to firms with a lower level of family involvement, so that family involvement would be positively related to loan availability. Besides this effect, a higher degree of long-term orientation is associated with a more intense pursue of non-economic goals like e.g. the creation of reputation and trust (Zellweger et al., 2011). This would also lower the risk of moral hazard and thus increase the availability of credit. A further argument for the positive effect of family involvement is caused by the degree of kinship and altruism found in a family firm. According to Chami (1997) and Karra et al. (2006), the higher family involvement (especially the higher the overlap between the company's and the family's value basis), the higher the influence of kinship and altruism, causing family agents to have a lower self-interest which leads to lower agency costs as the risk of moral hazard is lower. Hence, the availability of credit should increase with the degree of family involvement.

Besides providing arguments for the positive effects of family involvement, agency theory can be used to explain, why a high level of family involvement might also be perceived negatively by bank loan officers. A higher degree of family involvement, especially in terms of ownership share and management control, makes it easier for family members to pursue policies that are unfavorable for lenders like e.g. the consumption of perks or the entrenchment of ineffective family members. Thus, the concentrated power that comes along with the high level of family involvement might be perceived as a threat to bank loan officers because it increases the risk of moral hazard and makes it necessary to implement costly agency mitigating mechanisms (Chua et al., 2011; Gomez-Mejia et al., 2001; Mueller & Inderst, 1999). Hence, family influence might be negatively correlated with credit availability. In addition, parental altruism might also be perceived negatively as it gives family members the opportunity to free ride without being monitored or disciplined (Schulze et al., 2003). Thus, loan officers might perceive a higher risk of moral hazard with an increased level of family involvement and thus ration credit. Similarly, higher family involvement might be associated with a higher likelihood of special dividends and/or excessive compensation to family members which would increase the risk of wealth expropriation from debtholders and thus the risk of moral hazard (Anderson et al., 2003). Besides the potential risk of moral hazard issues related with the level of family involvement, loan officers might also perceive more informational problems with firms that are highly interconnected with a family. Poutziouris (2001) noted that family firms tend to have a "keep it in the family" tradition, which leads to higher informational asymmetries and thus increased agency costs of debt. This effect might be even stronger, when family involvement with respect to ownership and management is high as there is no need for any additional communication with "outsiders". Similarly, when the overlap between the company's and the family's value basis is high, the role of the "keep it in the family" tradition increases. Thus, a family firm with a typical corporate value basis should not be prone to such an isolated and closed communication culture. In addition, some authors found that family involvement is positively correlated with an informal management style and low levels of formal documentation which might aggravate the effect associated with increased informational asymmetries (Ali et al., 2007; Chen et al., 2008; Daily & Dollinger, 1991). So, based on those agency theoretical arguments, it can be concluded that loan officers have good reasons to perceive an increased influence of the family on the business as either positive or negative and thus make their credit availability decisions accordingly.

Drawing upon the SEW concept, it is possible to develop further arguments for the opposing effects of the impact of family involvement. According to Cennamo et al. (2012), an increased importance of SEW causes firms to invest in proactive stakeholder engagement (PSE) activities as those hold a socioemotional, i.e. non-economic reward for the family. PSE, in this context, is the term that describes a firm's tendency to not just simply respond to stakeholder issues, but to take a more active role and to anticipate the stakeholders' needs in order to develop suitable solutions for those. Cennamo et al. (2012) argue that this PSE orientation of family firms is driven by a combination of both instrumental and normative motives. From an instrumental point of view, family firms with a strong focus on SEW invest in PSE activities as they expect non-economic returns in the form of social legitimacy or reputation which might help to secure a transgenerational survival of the firm and thereby secure the family's SEW. Complementary to this perspective, the normative view asserts that family firms with a strong emphasis on SEW will invest in PSE activities, like e.g. considering others' interests when making decisions or donating to charity, in order to meet the family's and the firm's moral duties within society. Thus, the normative view differs from the instrumental perspective in that it does not define stakeholders as means to an end but rather sees them as ends in themselves. In both cases, the resulting behavior would serve as a positive signal for lenders as the risk and hassle of working with such clients would be lower. Hence, firms with PSE should be favored in terms of credit availability. Additionally, Gomez-Mejia et al. (2007) found that the importance of SEW comes along with the level of family involvement. They state that the stronger the role of the family within the business, the more likely the firm is to strive to protect its SEW. Consequently, it can be hypothesized that the level of family involvement should be positively correlated with the loan officers' credit availability decision. This relationship should be even stronger, when the connection between the family's and the company's value basis is intense, as family principals are more likely to attend to an enlarged set of internal and external stakeholders in this situation (Cennamo et al., 2012).

On the other hand, family involvement might also signal an opposing message to bank loan officers according to the SEW approach. As seen previously, Gomez-Mejia et al. (2007) argue that the primary reference point for private family firms is the loss of their socio-emotional wealth. In order to avoid losses and preserve their SEW, family firms are more willing to accept greater financial risks with respect to a reduced economic performance and thereby a greater probability of organization failure. However, this would impose agency costs for lenders as they will be confronted with a higher risk of wealth expropriation. Consequently, a SEW orientation of family firms might be interpreted as a negative signal by bank loan officers so that they will tend to ration credit for those firms. In a similar fashion, Kellermanns et al. (2012) propose that a family firm's SEW orientation might cause family-centric behavior, where "family firms place family needs above those of other stakeholders" (p. 1176), which would raise the risk of moral hazard and thereby the agency costs from the debtholders' perspective. In addition and by building upon the work of Cennamo et al. (2012) who proposed that the various FIBER dimensions cater different stakeholders ("family control and influence" and "renewal of family bonds" mainly target internal stakeholders with an instrumental motivation, "identification of family members with the firm" are majorly directed toward external stakeholders from an instrumental perspective while the dimensions "identification of family members with the firm", "emotional attachment of family members" and "binding social ties" are mainly focused on both internal and external stakeholders while being normatively motivated), Hauswald & Hack (in press) argue that family firms whose major reference point are the dimensions "family control and influence" and "renewal of family bonds" might behave negatively toward external stakeholders in cases when their SEW with respect to those two dimensions is at risk. They assert that this relationship might cause stakeholders' perception of a family firm's benevolence to be negatively influenced in cases when the family's SEW with respect to the dimensions "family control and influence" and "renewal of family bonds through dynastic succession" is at risk. As a consequence, loan officers might perceive the risk of moral hazard to be higher for those kinds of firms. Considering again the notion of

Gomez-Mejia et al. (2007) that SEW orientation is related to the level of family involvement in the business, it is possible that the level of family involvement will be negatively correlated with the loan officers' credit availability decision.

Furthermore, the RBV can also be used to develop hypotheses regarding the effect of family involvement on loan officers' judgment and decision making. As stated earlier, family business scholars propose that family firms develop complex, intangible, dynamic and idiosyncratic resources as a result of family involvement (see e.g. Habbershon & Williams, 1999; Eddleston et al., 2008; Sirmon & Hitt, 2003). These distinctive resources (often referred to as distinctive familiness) can be the source for sustainable competitive advantages for those firms (Naldi et al., 2008). In addition, Penrose (1959) notes that firms survive only by developing and employing competitive advantages. As a consequence, loan officers should favor firms with a high level of family involvement in terms of credit availability as the risk of default for those businesses is supposed to be lower.

In contrast to this perspective, Habbershon & Williams (1999) remark that a company's familiness, which arises from the involvement of the family, might also function as a constrictive resource so that negative consequence on the loan availability decision might be expected. Constrictive resources describe competitive disadvantages that are caused by the involvement of the family like e.g. family-induced conflicts, unqualified family managers that need to be employed due to the family tradition or a reduced capital stock as a consequence of excess flows of capital in the direction of the family (Sharma, 2008). Thus, the economic performance and the survival of the firm might be threatened by those constrictive resources. This would increase the risk of default which would cause loan officers to ration credit to firms with a high degree of family involvement.

Therefore, the RBV provides arguments for both the positive effect as well as the negative effect of family involvement on the loan officers' credit availability decisions. If family involvement is perceived to be a distinctive resource, a higher level of family involvement will be positively related to credit availability. Otherwise, if family involvement is perceived to be a constrictive resource, a higher level of family involvement will be negatively related to credit availability.

Tying the arguments from agency theory, the SEW approach and the RBV together, it has to be concluded that bank loan officers' might very well perceive family involvement to be either positive or negative with respect to their judgment and decision making. Thus, as the current literature is not sufficient to state a hypothesis with one clear direction, two hypotheses are proposed in order to capture this controversy. This way, the final direction has to be examined empirically. Hence, the following temporary hypotheses regarding the effect of family involvement are suggested:

> ***Temporary hypothesis TH1a:*** *The level of family influence within the business will be positively related to debt availability, i.e. the higher the degree of family involvement,*

the more positively bank loan officers will rate those companies in terms of the loan availability decision.

Temporary hypothesis TH1b: *The level of family influence within the business will be negatively related to debt availability, i.e. the higher the degree of family involvement, the more negatively bank loan officers will rate those companies in terms of the loan availability decision.*

At this point, these two hypotheses have to be further specified. As stated previously, not all family firms are the same. It is a very heterogeneous group where family influence can be manifested in many different ways. As a consequence, Astrachan et al. (2002) developed a framework which accounts for those differences by presenting a method for assessing the extent and identifying the type of family influence on an enterprise – the F-PEC scale. According to the F-PEC scale, the extent and quality of family influence on a business can be decomposed into the following three dimensions: (1) power, (2) experience and (3) culture. The power dimension captures the degree of legitimate authority that a family can exercise over a business via its ownership, governance and/or management involvement. The experience scale measures the extent of generational involvement in different areas of the business. Thereby, it accounts for the fact that a first generation family firm is different from e.g. sixth or seventh generation family firms. Finally, the cultural sub-scale describes the extent to which family values have been infused within the business and thus have influenced it.

Using the F-PEC scale, the temporary hypotheses could be further specified according to the various dimensions of family involvement. But due to the constraint of the method (conjoint analysis) that is ought to be used it is not possible to include all items from the F-PEC scale. However, this is not even necessary as some items can be excluded that are of minor interest for this study. Within the power dimension, the most relevant aspects of family involvement are ownership and participation within the company's management. The board function will be examined in the next paragraph. Thus, it is hypothesized

Hypothesis H1a: *The level of family influence within the business with respect to the ownership share will be positively related to debt availability, i.e. the higher the family ownership, the more positively bank loan officers will rate those companies in terms of the loan availability decision.*

Hypothesis H1b: *The level of family influence within the business with respect to the ownership share will be negatively related to debt availability, i.e. the higher the family ownership, the more negatively bank loan officers will rate those companies in terms of the loan availability decision.*

Hypothesis H2a: *The level of family influence within the business with respect to the participation in the management will be positively related to debt availability, i.e. the higher the domination of the family within the management, the more positively bank loan officers will rate those companies in terms of the loan availability decision.*

> ***Hypothesis H2b:*** *The level of family influence within the business with respect to the participation in the management will be negatively related to debt availability, i.e. the higher the domination of the family within the management, the more negatively bank loan officers will rate those companies in terms of the loan availability decision.*

It has to be mentioned that this study will not hypothesize and test the influence of the experience dimension on bank loan officers' judgment and decision making as it focuses on true family firms, i.e. exclude founder-run entities and first-generation family firms (see section 1.3 and Miller et al., 2007 or Brunninge & Melander, 2011 who distinguish between founder businesses and family firms). Because the intention of generational stability is given for all those firms, further information about the experience dimension of a family firm is expected to not influence loan officers' decision making. In addition, agency theory, the SEW approach and the RBV do not provide enough arguments to assume otherwise. Thus, there is no primary need to further investigate this dimension within this study.

In regards to the cultural dimension, it is hypothesized that the overlap between the family's and the company's value basis will influence loan officers' decision making. Arguments for this proposition were presented within this paragraph. Therefore, the next hypotheses can be stated as follows:

> ***Hypothesis H3a:*** *The level of family influence within the business with respect to the overlap between the families and the company's value basis will be positively related to debt availability, i.e. the higher the overlap between the family's and the company's value basis, the more positively bank loan officers will rate those companies in terms of the loan availability decision.*
>
> ***Hypothesis H3b:*** *The level of family influence within the business with respect to the overlap between the families and the company's value basis will be negatively related to debt availability, i.e. the higher the overlap between the family's and the company's value basis, the more negatively bank loan officers will rate those companies in terms of the loan availability decision.*

3.2.2 Board Function

Boards of directions can perform different functions within firms. The most common distinction of the boards' tasks is between the monitoring function - sometimes referred to as the control task - and the advising function - sometimes referred to as the service task (Minichilli et al., 2009; Forbes & Milliken, 1999).

According to agency theoretical considerations, lenders are concerned with the risk of moral hazard, i.e. the risk of wealth expropriation by shareholders as those might shift to risk seeking behavior once the credit has been granted (Jensen & Meckling, 1976; Stiglitz & Weiss, 1981). Consequently, a board of directors that supervises the work of the management and protects the interests of other stakeholders like e.g. lenders might be used as an appropriate agency mitigating tool (see e.g. Eisenhardt, 1989 or Bammens et al., 2011). It would reduce the risk associated with moral hazard and thus positively influence the loan officers' evaluation of the loan application as those will have fewer concerns when making the loan availability decision. Within the family business context and as stated earlier in this thesis, it has to be considered that family firms represent a unique set of agency problems like e.g. self-control problems which cannot be mitigated with higher interest rates or business collateral (see Steijvers & Voordeckers, 2009b). Thus, a monitoring board is of particular relevance for this type of business as it is exceptionally well suited to mitigate those kinds of problems.

Besides its monitoring role, the board can also perform an advising function. Within family firms, stewardship theory, the RBV, the resource dependence theory and stakeholder theory propose that an advising board does either (1) offer complementary expertise to the management and/or (2) mediates family conflicts (Bammens et al., 2011). This should serve as a positive signal to bank loan officers because (1) the ability to repay the loan will increase as the company will be able to generate higher cash flows (due to the additional expertise) and/or (2) the risk of default will be reduced as the risk of family induced conflicts decreases. Thus, family firms with an advising board should be preferred by loan officers in terms of credit availability in comparison to family firms without an advising board.

Reviewing empirical studies regarding the effect of the board function, it was found that scholars produced mixed empirical results when investigating the relationship between the composition or the task of the board of directors and their impact on the companies' performance (Dalton et al., 1998; Dalton et al., 1999; Johnson et al., 1996). However, available literature on the link between credit rating, availability and terms on the one hand and board composition and function on the other hand identified a positive effect of board independence and strength (Holder-Webb & Sharma, 2010; Ashbaugh-Skaife et al., 2006).

When comparing the effect of the monitoring and the service function, it is proposed that both functions will be positively related to credit availability. Nevertheless, it is assumed that the monitoring function will have a greater impact on credit availability as it directly reduces the risk for the borrower whereas an advising board only indirectly reduces any related risks. Therefore, the hypothesis regarding the effect of the board function is stated as follows:

> ***Hypothesis H4:*** *The monitoring function of the board of directors will be positively related to credit availability, i.e. the stronger the board of directors with respect to their monitoring function, the more positively bank loan officers will rate those companies in terms of the loan availability decision.*

3.2.3 Experience of the CEO

Literature found that the capability of the company's management is a critical factor that influences its performance and viability (see e.g. Dess & Picken, 1999). Thus, information about the quality of a loan applicant's management team might be an important variable for the loan officers' decision making process. Reviewing the empirical literature on this topic, it was found that the managements' capabilities are indeed an overly important factor in the loan officers' decision making process (see e.g. Jankowicz & Hisrich, 1987 or Fletcher, 1995). However, it has to be noted that management quality cannot be easily observed by external parties like e.g. loan officers (Bruns & Fletcher, 2008; Keasey & McGuinness, 1990). Therefore, loan officers might find it helpful to use proxies for the management' quality. Scholars demonstrated that loan officers tend to use information about the managements' experience or track record of managing the business (Jankowicz & Hisrich, 1987). Managers with little or no experience in managing a company will be associated with a higher risk of default as the uncertainty regarding their capabilities to cope with adversity will be perceived to be higher. Contrary, experienced managers are expected to be more capable of handling unexpected situations better and thus reduce the risk of default (Berger, 1997; Jankowicz & Hisrich, 1987). Other indicators for the quality of the management like e.g. formal education have shown to be only marginally related to the credit availability decision (Bruns et al., 2008). Therefore, the hypothesis regarding the influence of the managements' capabilities is formally defined as follows:

> ***Hypothesis H5:*** *The experience of the CEO will be positively related to credit availability, i.e. the more experience the CEO has in managing businesses and coping with adverse situations, the more positively bank loan officers will rate those companies in terms of the loan availability decision.*

3.2.4 Transparency

As discussed previously, one of the main problems of the lender-borrower relationship is informational asymmetry. In comparison to outsiders, managers generally have more and better information about the past, current and future condition of the business (Jensen & Meckling, 1976; Stiglitz & Weiss, 1981). External stakeholders like lenders receive, at best, noisy information regarding the company's financial and strategic situation which causes adverse selection problems and increases the risk of moral hazard. Lenders will try to assess the risk of default on the basis of the available information before granting a loan. Sengupta (1998) notes that the likelihood that the loan applicant withholds value-relevant negative information will be taken into account when calculating the risk of default. A company that withholds information will be penalized in terms of credit availability. Thus, the degree and quality of disclosure should be positively related to a firm's ability to borrow (Botosan, 1997; Botosan & Plumlee, 2002; Healy & Palepu, 2001; Mazumdar & Sengupta, 2005).

Empirical studies have typically confirmed this effect in the past. Yu (2005) showed that companies with higher AIMR disclosure ratings (this is a standard measure for the level of transparency; AIMR stands for Association for Investment Management and Research) tend to have lower credit spreads i.e. lower cost of debt. Similarly, Sengupta (1998) showed that companies with a higher level of disclosure enjoy lower costs of issuing debt.

As a consequence of the presented arguments, the hypothesis regarding the direct effect of the level of transparency on the loan availability decision is defined as follows:

> ***Hypothesis H6:*** *The level of transparency will be positively related to credit availability, i.e. the higher the level of transparency, the more positively bank loan officers will rate those companies in terms of the loan availability decision.*

3.2.5 Level of Attestation

As stated at the beginning of this chapter and according to the framework of the 5 C's of lending, loan officers take information about the prospective borrower's character into account when evaluating loan applicants, i.e. they try to gather information about the borrower's integrity and honesty. Guiral et al. (2010) argue that information about the applicant's character is one of the most important pieces of information as it affects the presentation and interpretation of all other information like e.g. financial information. So, when loan officers assess whether the presented financial information represents the true economic position of the business, they will need information about the borrower's integrity and honesty. In addition, information about the loan applicant's character will help loan officers to further verify the perception of the risk of moral hazard. In this context, an independent auditor's attestation might serve as an important source of information for the borrower's character. The level of attestation could signal the creditworthiness and especially trustworthiness of an applicant (Guiral-Contreras et al., 2007; Bamber & Stratton, 1997; Bandyopadhyay & Francis, 1995). It is argued that loan officers will perceive audited information as more credible than unaudited information and thus prefer borrowers that provide audited information in terms of credit availability.

Reviewing currently available literature on this topic, it has to be concluded that the gathered empirical evidence displays ambiguous results regarding the effect of auditor attestation on credit availability. Schneider & Church (2008), Guiral-Contreras et al. (2007), Kitindi et al. (2007) and Bandyopadhyay & Francis (1995) confirm the positive effect of the level of attestation on loan availability whereas Johnson et al. (1983), Wright & Davidson (2000) and Kim & Elias (2007) could not identify any significant relationship between an auditor's attestation and the availability of credit. However, even though Wright & Davidson (2000) couldn't confirm the effect of the level or type of auditor attestation (review or audit) on loan approval, they found evidence for the fact that the existence of any kind of attestation is perceived more positively in regards to the credit availability decision than no attestation at all. This finding is also in line with the other papers that couldn't find a significant effect. Kim & Elias (2007) and Waterston (1979) provide a potential explanation for this. They assume that loan officers may not understand the difference between the various levels of attestation, but perceive the existence of any kind of attestation as an indicator for the borrower's trustworthiness. Hence, the hypothesis regarding the effect of the level of attestation is defined as follows:

> ***Hypothesis H7:*** *The existence of an auditor's attestation will be positively related to credit availability regardless of the type of attestation, i.e. if the information from the loan applicant is audited from an independent auditor, bank loan officers will rate those companies more positively in terms of the loan availability decision.*

3.2.6 Independence of Collateral

Loan officers' decision making criteria are typically based on the 5 C's of lending, which also include collateral. The term collateral generally describes all types of alternative sources of loan repayment in case of a borrower's bankruptcy. Therefore, it serves as an instrument to mitigate agency related problems; both problems with adverse selection as well as issues regarding moral hazard (Steijvers & Voordeckers, 2009a; Coco, 2000). It is assumed that loan officers will consider information about collateral when making decisions of whether to approve or deny a loan request.

Information about collateral can be manifold as different types of collateral can be used like e.g. business collateral vs. personal collateral. Therefore, this study will concentrate on the independence of the offered collateral. If loan officers grant a loan for an investment, they typically use the underlying asset as a basis for the overall arrangement of the collateral package. In addition, they try to negotiate further collateral (Fabozzi, 2008). This might be independent from the success of the company (like e.g. property) or dependent (like e.g. receivables). It is assumed that loan officers will prefer additional independent collateral as it minimizes the risk in case of default. If a borrower goes bankrupt, the amount of assets like receivables will probably have been reduced during the months before officially announcing bankruptcy, so that the bank has to discount them (see e.g. Fabozzi, 2008).

On the basis of the presented arguments, the hypothesis regarding the impact of information about the independence of the additionally offered collateral is stated as follows:

> ***Hypothesis H8:*** *The independence of the additional collateral will be positively related to credit availability, i.e. the higher the independence of the additionally offered collateral, the more positively bank loan officers will rate those companies in terms of the loan availability decision.*

3.3 Moderating Effects

3.3.1 Similarity Bias

This study investigates whether the similarity between the loan officer and the loan applicant systematically influences bank loan officers' decisions. Therefore, the corresponding hypotheses are developed on the basis of the body of work surrounding the similarity effect. In the first step, the general theoretical foundation regarding the similarity effect will be presented. Afterwards, testable hypotheses are derived.

Aristotle (1934) was one of the first to observe the relationship between similarity and attraction when he noted that people "love those who are like themselves". Later, Lazarsfeld & Merton (1954) coined the term "homophily" to describe people's tendency to be attracted to others who have similar attitudes, beliefs, and personal characteristics. Similarly, Byrne (1971) defined the similarity-attraction or similar-to-me hypothesis stating that people tend to rate other people more positively the more similar they are to themselves. Three theories that are more general in scope support this hypothesis, namely (1) social identity theory, (2) self-categorization theory and (3) learning theory. According to social identity theory, individuals develop a social identity by categorizing themselves and others as members of different social groups and attaching a particular value to that membership. Assuming that people mainly aim to reach a positive social identity, the theory asserts that in-group favoritism emerges i.e. an individual's tendency to favor the in-group at the expense of the out-group (Tajfel & Turner, 1986). Likewise, self-categorization theory states that an individual's self-concept is generally based on social categories. As mentioned previously, people strive to build and maintain a positive self-concept which causes them to prefer people who are similar to themselves in regards to the social categories they identify with (Jackson et al., 1991; Tsui et al., 1992; Turner, 1988). Additionally, the theory suggests that no interaction is required for the categorization of others and thus for the similarity effect to occur. One should note that social identity and self-categorization theory are very similar to each other, but differ essentially in terms of explanatory scope and power (see Haslam, 2004 for a more detailed elaboration on the differences between those two theories). Drawing on learning theory and more specifically on operant conditioning, Byrne (1971) argues that evaluative responses represent reinforcing stimuli where similar attitudes are being perceived as rewarding and therefore function as positive reinforcements and dissimilarities as negative reinforcements. As a consequence, people learn to favor others who are similar to themselves.

Conversely to the presented similarity-attraction paradigm, Rosenbaum (1986) offers a different view on this topic by formulating the dissimilarity-repulsion hypothesis proposing that attitudinal dissimilarity causes repulsion and that similarity per se does not lead to attraction. However, Drigotas (1993) tested both theories and found empirical evidence supporting the similarity-attraction hypothesis by showing that subjects tend to first include similar others and then exclude dissimilar ones.

In addition, researchers distinguish between actual similarity, i.e. the degree to which individuals are objectively similar to each other and perceived similarity, i.e. the degree to which individuals think or belief others are similar to themselves. While some scholars argue that actual similarity is necessary to provoke attraction (Byrne, 1971; Duck & Craig, 1978), others assert that only perceived similarity causes attraction (Hoyle, 1993; Ptacek & Dodge, 1995; Orpen, 1984). Using meta-analysis techniques, Montoya et al. (2008) conclude that perceived similarity is a stronger predictor of attraction. Information processing models within behavioral sciences support those findings by arguing that people base their judgment and decision making on mental representations of reality. In that sense, Kahneman (2000) writes "Anyone who has taken a course in perception has learned [...] to distinguish both reality and stimulus from the mental representation that the observer eventually constructs" (p. xiv). Consequently and because this study pursues a behavioral approach, it focuses on perceived rather than actual similarity.

From an empirical perspective, scholars have produced tremendous evidence in support of the similarity-attraction hypothesis. In this regard, they tested numerous dimensions of similarity. So, Bleda (1974) investigated the effect of similarity regarding personality traits, Yeong Tan & Singh (1995) used attitudinal similarity, Werner & Parmelee (1979) discussed the similarity of hobby preferences, Homburg et al. (2002) examined the effect of interorganizational similarity and Murnieks et al. (2011) analyzed cognitive similarity as a potential dimension of similarity. In addition, the similarity bias could be confirmed in a variety of contexts. Besides the vast empirical evidence that exists for non-business situations (see e.g. Frank & Hackman, 1975 for an investigation of the similarity bias in the context of college admission judgments or Burleson & Denton, 1992 for an investigation of the phenomenon in regards to romantic relationships), some scholars applied the concept to the management field. So, Franke et al. (2006) and Murnieks et al. (2011) examined the effect of the similarity bias on venture capitalists evaluations of start-up teams and new venture deals. Moreover, scholars like e.g. Smith (1998) exploited on the similarity-attraction paradigm with respect to marketing issues studying the impact on buyer-seller relationships (see Lichtenthal & Tellefsen, 2001 for a review regarding the buyer-seller similarity). In addition, numerous scholars applied it to the field of human resource management (Strauss et al., 2001 on performance appraisals, Devendorf & Highhouse, 2008 on evaluations of employer attraction or Graves & Powell, 1995 on recruiters' evaluations of actual applicants).

All in all, the similarity bias is a widely confirmed phenomenon. Berger (1973) even claims that the similarity effect is "one of the most robust relationships in all of behavioral sciences" (p. 281). However, Haslam (2004) warns to make context-independent generalizations and argues that this bias only occurs in a limited set of circumstances. So, even though Bruns et al. (2008) examined the similarity-attraction hypothesis in the context of lending, demonstrating that the similarity between the loan officers' and the applicants' specific human capital is a significant indicator of loan approval, it is still not known whether this effect also causes differences in lending behavior toward family firms. Therefore, this study tests whether the similarity bias is prevalent within this specific context and thus could explain some of the heterogeneity in lending behavior toward family firms with different levels of family influence.

After reviewing the available literature on loan officers' decision making and discussing research with respect to the similarity bias in general, it is now time to apply those findings to the family firm context and develop testable hypotheses which might explain some of the heterogeneity in lending behavior toward firms with varying levels of family influence.

As mentioned previously, literature asserts that loan officers' judgment and decision making is biased by their perceived similarity between them and loan applicants. The more similar the bank loan officer perceives the loan applicant, the more favorable the decision outcome will be. In addition, it is argued that bank loan officers make generic associations with firms that they perceive as family firms i.e. are known to be family-owned, family controlled or show any other form of family involvement. Research has shown that people create simplified representations of reality as they are not able to fully process all of the environmental complexity (Kahneman, 2000; Tenenbaum & Land, 2009; depending on the research context, scholars refer to terms like stereotype or image point to those simplified, complexity-reducing constructions – see Banaji et al., 1993 or Banaji & Hardin, 1996). Within the field of family business research, scholars with a focus on marketing argue that customers make specific associations with the term family firm or family business (e.g. Carrigan & Buckley, 2008 or Presas et al., 2011). This suggests that family firm itself can be defined as a brand that holds a particular image and evokes stereotyping. So, Blombäck (2009) proposes that family business is perceived as a category brand which influences individuals' attitudes and behavior toward companies that use the reference of family involvement in their communication. Those generic associations are assumed to vary with respect to the degree of family involvement (see discussion above for a more detailed elaboration on this topic). Tying the parts together, the main broad hypothesis is specified as follows:

> ***Temporary hypothesis TH9a:*** *The loan officers' perceived similarity between them and family firms or their generic image of these moderates the relationship between family influence and the loan officers' credit availability decision. Specifically, higher perceived similarity between loan officers and family firms or their generic image of these will lead to a more positive effect of family involvement on their credit availability decision.*

In general, similarity is a broad and multidimensional concept. Scholars examined the effect on both rather superficial levels of similarity like e.g. age or sex congruence (see e.g. Franke et al., 2006 and Smith, 1998) as well as on deeper levels of similarity like e.g. cognitive similarity (Murnieks et al., 2011). Bank loan officers might also use a variety of indicators to evaluate the level of similarity between them and loan applicants. This study focuses on aspects that are characteristic for family firms as it aims to understand differences in lending behavior toward firms with varying levels of family involvement which automatically disqualifies dimensions that are unlikely to explain those differences like e.g. age or sex.

As stated above, family business research takes the position that SEW is one of the main factors that affects family firm behavior. According to Gomez-Mejia et al. (2007) and Berrone et al. (2012) it even is the most important differentiator of family firms. Scholars suggest that family firms are typically motivated by considerations regarding the preservation of their SEW. However, as not all family firms are the same, the emphasis a particular firm puts on SEW might vary. Thus, family firms can be classified with respect to how they prioritize issues relating to their SEW. Gomez-Mejia et al. (2007) argue that the higher the level of involvement of the family within the firm, the more likely the family firm is to strive to protect its SEW. Taking additionally into account that the loan officers' perceived similarity or dissimilarity depends on their generic image of loan applicants, it is assumed that the perceived similarity or dissimilarity with respect to SEW will represent an important source of influence. In particular, it is suggested that the loan officers' attitudes might also be coined in terms of SEW. Stockmans et al. (2010), for instance, noted that though the concept of SEW is typical to family firms, nonfinancial objectives might also influence judgment and decision making processes of non-family firm subjects. Thus, it is assumed that loan officers hold SEW related attitudes. So, they might also pursue noneconomic goals like e.g. the need for power or binding social ties. It is further proposed that loan officers are able to anticipate the importance applicants place on issues relating SEW on the basis of the information regarding the level of family influence and thereby evaluate the similarity between them and prospective borrowers. At this point, it has to be noticed that this process will probably happen automatically i.e. unconsciously. On the basis of those arguments, the initial hypothesis is refined as follows:

> ***Temporary hypothesis TH9b:*** *The loan officers' perceived similarity between them and loan applicants or their generic image of these with respect to SEW related attitudes moderates the relationship between family influence and the loan officers' credit availability decision. Specifically, higher perceived similarity between loan officers and family firms or their generic image of these with respect to SEW related attitudes will lead to a more positive effect of family involvement on their credit availability decision.*

Scholars generally allude to the fact that SEW is a multidimensional concept which in the context of family firms captures all aspects of affective endowment that a family has with regards to the business (Berrone et al., 2012; Gomez-Mejia et al., 2007; Cennamo et al., 2012). As mentioned, Berrone et al. (2012) broke down this concept into five dimensions that they labeled as FIBER. They consist of the dimensions (1) family control and influence, (2) family members' identification with the firm, (3) binding social ties, (4) emotional attachment and (5) renewal of family bond to the firm through dynastic succession. Unfortunately, Berrone et al. (2012) defined those dimensions with family firms in mind which makes it difficult to adopt them to the field of bank loan officers. However, because this study want to examine the perceived attitudinal similarity, it can investigate the loan officers' attitudes regarding the FIBER dimensions under the hypothetical case that they were part of a family firm. At this point it is assumed that loan officers hold attitudes regarding the FIBER dimensions in case they were in the situation of family firms. They know what would be important to them and sympathize with family firms who they perceive to think alike. A loan officer who would place much emphasis on dynastic succession and/or family control will probably perceive a higher degree of similarity with family firms that think alike in comparison to family firms that do not care so much about those issues.

As a consequence of refining the idea of SEW, the temporary hypothesis can be further narrowed down and formulated as the final hypothesis for the similarity effect with regards to SEW orientation on the individual level as follows:

> ***Hypothesis H9:*** *The loan officers' perceived similarity between them and loan applicants or their generic image of these with respect to the FIBER dimensions moderates*

the relationship between family influence and the loan officers' credit availability decision. Specifically, higher perceived similarity between loan officers and family firms or their generic image of these with respect to the FIBER dimensions will lead to a more positive effect of family involvement on their credit availability decision.

Besides individual level similarity i.e. similarity between the loan officer himself and loan applicants, organizational research has shown that individuals' decision making is also affected by organizational expectations, values, routines and doctrines (see e.g. Cyert & March, 1963; Schein, 1984; Trevino, 1986 or McNamara & Bromiley, 1997). McNamara & Bromiley (1997) e.g. showed that loan officers working for banks promoting a profit orientated philosophy make systematic errors when evaluating a borrower's risk. More specifically, they found that loan officers tend to underrate the risk of large loans in comparison to smaller ones as they associate large loans with higher absolute profits. Consequently, it is assumed loan officers to also be biased by their perceived organizational level similarity i.e. the similarity between the organization they work for and loan applicants. This study focuses on similarity with respect to (1) family background and (2) importance of SEW. So, loan officers working for family-owned banks are assumed to perceive a higher similarity with family firms than loan officers working for widely-held banks. In addition, private-family banks, public banks and cooperative banks are assumed to place a higher priority on issues related to SEW in comparison to private non-family banks as a result of their specific ownership and governance structure (see Hau & Thum, 2009 for an more detailed elaboration on the differences between those bank types). Thus,

Hypothesis H10: *The loan officers' perceived similarity between the company they work for and loan applicants or there generic image of these with respect to (a) family background and (b) SEW moderates the relationship between family influence and the loan officers' credit availability decision. Specifically, higher perceived similarity between loan officers and family firms or their generic image of these with respect to (a) family background and (b) SEW will lead to a more positive effect of family involvement on their credit availability decision.*

3.3.2 Framing Effect

Besides the investigation of the similarity effect, a further objective of this study is to examine whether variations in the framing of loan applications systematically influence the loan officers credit availability decision toward different kinds of family firms. In order to achieve this objective, this dissertation builds on the body of work surrounding the framing effect. In a first step, an abridgment of the general theoretical and empirical literature regarding the framing effect is presented. Afterwards, testable hypotheses with respect to the specific research question in focus will be derived.

In general, framing can be defined as the context within which information regarding a decision task is presented (Donovan & Jalleh, 1999). During the evolvement of research regarding behavioral economics, scholars found that decision makers are sensitive to variations in the framing of decision tasks. Tversky & Kahneman (1981) were one of the first to discover the so called framing effects, i.e. the people's tendency to systematically respond differently to objectively equivalent decision problems under altered frames. They defined decision frames as "the decision-maker's conception of the acts, outcomes, and contingencies associated with a particular choice" (p. 453) and further noted that "[the] frame that a decision-maker adopts is controlled partly by the formulation of the problem and partly by the norms, habits, and personal characteristics of the decision-maker" (p. 453). In their classical "Asian disease problem", Tversky & Kahneman (1981) demonstrated that the decision between a risky and a riskless option depends upon whether the options are described in positive or negative terms. More specifically, they asked two groups of students to image "that the U.S. is preparing for the outbreak of an unusual Asian disease, which is expected to kill 600 people" (p. 453) and that they had to choose between two alternative programs to combat the disease. The first group that was presented with a positively framed version of the task ("If Program A is adopted, 200 people will be saved." [p. 453] vs. "If Program B is adopted, there is 1/3 probability that 600 people will be saved, and 2/3 probability that no people will be saved." [p. 453]) predominantly selected the certain outcome, whereas the majority of students in the second group that were presented with a negatively framed version of the decision task ("If Program C is adopted, 400 people will die." [p. 453] vs. "If Program D is adopted, there is 1/3 probability that nobody will die, and 2/3 probability that 600 people will die." [p. 453]) chose the risky option. However, this shift in choices should not happen according to neoclassical approaches. A risk-averse decision-maker should always choose Program A or C whereas a risk-seeking decision-maker should prefer Program B or D. As per expected utility theory and its description invariance assumption, people should not make different decisions only because of variations in the presentation of the decision task as long as the decision task itself is not altered (Raiffa, 1968; Fishburn, 1970). Originally, Tversky & Kahneman (1981) explained framing effects on the basis of prospect theory. They theorized that framing effects occur because decision makers tend to encode information as positive or negative which determines their reference point on the psychological value function and thus influences the decision outcome (see Kahneman & Tversky, 1979 for more details regarding theoretical concept of prospect theory). However, subsequent studies advanced this original theory and provided further arguments for the existence and cognitive basis of faming effects – especially with regards to the different types of framing effect (see discussion below).

The discovery of framing effects has additionally questioned the adequacy of neoclassical theories to describe and predict actual judgment and decision making and evoked more research in the field of behavioral economics (see e.g. Edwards, 1996). In the course of the further research, scholars have examined the effect of different types of framing effects in various situations of decision making like e.g. health care, nutrition, gambling, financing and shopping (Schwartz et al., 2008; Brug et al., 2003; Levin et al., 1998; Kühberger, 1998). Despite or maybe as a result of the vast amount of studies regarding the framing effect, the use of the term "frame" became inconsistent within the literature (Druckman, 2001; Kühberger, 1998). Some use the term in order to refer to frames in communication whereas others use the term to refer to frames in thought. Frames in communication describe only the semantic manipulations of decision problems, i.e. the particular wording conveyed to subjects within experiments (Druckman, 2001). Kühberger (1998) refers to this approach as the strict definition of framing. In contrast, frames in thought describe the individuals' cognitive representation of a decision task (Druckman, 2001; Tversky & Kahneman, 1981). It refers to an individual's internal mental process of perceiving, organizing and interpreting a problem. In that sense the term "frame" represents a mental model of the decision problem (Johnson-Laird, 1983; Soman, 2007). Kühberger (1998) refers to this approach as the loose definition of framing as variations in the frame might be caused by a variety of aspects and not only by differences in wording. At this point, it has to be noted that the two definitions are inseparably connected to each other as semantic manipulations of a task are always processed by an individual and are thus subject to internal framing effects. This study will use the term framing in order to refer to manipulations in the wording of a decision task, which cause distinct mental representations of the decision task and result in the previously described framing effects.

In addition, research found various types of framing effects which all have unique characteristics in that they are caused by different underlying mechanisms and evoke distinct consequences (see Levin et al., 1998). Unfortunately, most of the research in this field treats those effects as a homogeneous group which causes some problems as scholars typically use a single theory - mostly prospect theory - and thereby have trouble to explain framing-related phenomena that deviate from this theoretical basis. When reviewing the available literature, various attempts to classify the diverse framing effects were found. So, Tversky & Kahneman (1981) differentiate in their original paper between framing of acts (refers to the question of whether to present a decision task in terms of its combined outcomes or in terms of its components), framing of contingencies (refers to the question of whether to present a decision task in an either conditional or unconditional form) and framing of outcomes (refers to the question of whether to present the outcome of a decision task as gains or losses). Rothman et al. (1993) typify framing effects with respect to their consequences. As a result they distinguish between same consequence and different consequence framing manipulations (refers to the question of whether to present the decision task in terms of different behavior and same consequences or same behavior and different consequences, thus either emphasizing variations in the decision's attributes or its outcome). Fagley (1993) identified pure framing effects in contrast to reflection effects (pure framing effects are based on mere variations in the description of the decision task, so that the decision outcomes are objectively equal; reflection effects do not have the same decision outcomes and thus do not fit the underlying definition of framing effects). Finally, Levin et al. (1998) provide a further classification system of framing effects, which is not exhaustive, but incorporates the most relevant framing effects that have been discovered. In addition, their approach is one of the most used taxonomy in the literature (see e.g. Gamliel & Peer, 2006; Piñon & Gambara, 2005 or McKenzie & Nelson, 2003). In particular, they distinguish between risky choice framing, attribute framing and goal framing. Within risky-choice framing, decision makers have to choose between different options that represent varying levels of risk whereby the options are described in alternative ways (typically positive vs. negative frame). The most prominent example of the risky choice frame is the previously described "Asian disease problem". In order to explain risky-choice framing effects, scholars usually use prospect theoretical arguments (see Tversky & Kahneman, 1981, Levin et al., 1998). Work on risky-choice framing has shown that risk attitudes change when frames are altered. In contrast, attribute framing is concerned with the effect of variations in the presentation of a single attribute on decision makers. In this context, scholars typically use a positive and a negative frame to present the attribute in focus and examine its effect on judgment and decision making results. Levin et al. (1998) suggest that due to its basic form, attribute framing is especially useful for investigating how descriptive valence affects a decision maker's processing of information. An example of the attribute framing effect is described in the "meat experiment" by Levin & Gaeth (1988). The authors found that the perception of the quality of ground beef within a private consumers buying context depends upon the presentation of the information regarding the level of fat of the beef. So, people rated the beef as better tasting when the product was labeled "75% lean" in comparison to "25% fat". Again this behavior is not consistent with the predictions of expected utility theory which postulates description invariance and thus demonstrates the relevance of framing in decision making. Levin et al. (1998) argue that attribute framing cannot be explained by prospect theory, as this particular theoretical concept is designed to rationalize changes in preferences for option with varying levels of risk as a result of altering decision frames. Hence, a different theoretical explanation is needed. Levin & Gaeth (1988) argue that information is encoded relative to its descriptive valence, so that positive descriptions of an attribute evoke favorable associations in memory, whereas attributes that are labeled negatively tend to cause an encoding that evokes unfavorable associations. In addition, Levin et al. (1985) propose that framing effects might be caused by stimulus-response compatibility effects, i.e. the people's tendency to solve tasks easier if the stimuli and response are similar to each other (see Kornblum et al., 1990 for more details on the stimulus-response compatibility effects). As a consequence, Levin et al. (1985) claim that a positive (negative) evaluation of a stimuli is more likely if the stimuli is positive (negative). Moreover, those arguments are basically in line with literature on priming effects as applied in the field of attitude and impression formation research. Scholars in this area of research state that priming is an unconscious and implicit remembering process in which the exposure to a particular stimulus influences the likelihood of a certain response by affecting the person's information processing and decision making (Higgins & King, 1981; Gilad & Kliger, 2008). Within experiments, scholars prime subjects with positive or negative stimuli which usually are unrelated to the main decision task and examine the effect of the independent stimuli on judgment and decision making outcomes. Typically, the empirical results show that people tend to evaluate a task more favorably (unfavorably) when previously presented with a positive (negative) prime (Herr et al., 1983; Higgins et al., 1985; Sherman et al., 1990). Gilad & Kliger (2008), for instance, found that financial professionals tend to be more risk-seeking when previously reading about task-independent stories of positive consequences of risky behavior and vice versa. As a consequence, attribute framing can be interpreted as a priming effect where the framed attribute functions as a prime which is part of the decision task and not peripheral to it as in traditional research about priming effects (Levin et al., 1998). However, it has to be noted that this type of framing and the underlying mechanisms are distinct from risky-choice framing. As a third category, Levin et al. (1998) defined goal framing effects, which occur because of differences in the description of the consequences of performing an act or choosing an option by stressing the positive or negative consequences of the alternative. In one of the mostly cited experiments regarding goal framing, Meyerowitz & Chaiken (1987) presented two groups of women information regarding the consequences of breast self-examination (BSE). The first group that was presented with a positively framed text that stressed the positive consequences ("Research shows that women who do BSE have an increased chance of finding a tumor in the early, more treatable stages of the disease." [p. 504]) was predominantly less apt to engage in BSE, whereas the majority of the women in the second group that were presented with information that stressed the negative consequences ("Research shows that women who do not do BSE have a decreased chance of finding a tumor in the early, more treatable stages of the disease." [p. 504]) chose to undertake BSE. Other research has confirmed the effect of goal framing i.e. that the loss frame which stresses negative consequences elicits a stronger reaction than a gain frame which stresses positive consequences (see e.g. Levin et al., 1998 for a review of studies that examine this effect). From a theoretical standpoint, most scholars use again prospect theory to explain goal framing effects (Levin et al., 1998). However, some authors question this approach as identifying the relative risks that are associated with each option in this type of framing is difficult (Rutte et al., 1987). Therefore, Meyerowitz & Chaiken (1987) propose a different theoretical perspective on the reasons for goal framing effects. They argue on the basis of research regarding the negativity bias which states that people pay more attention to negative rather than positive information (see also Haizlip et al., 2012; Peeters & Czapinski, 1990; Rozin & Royzman, 2001; Taylor, 1991).

From an empirical perspective, the existence of framing effects has been confirmed in the majority of studies (see e.g. Kühberger, 1998 or Levin et al., 1998). Scholars have empirically investigated different kinds of framing effects in a variety of contexts like e.g. health care (see e.g. Robberson & Rogers, 1988), gambling (see e.g. Tversky & Kahneman, 1981), financial decision making (see e.g. Roszkowski & Snelbecker, 1990) and consumer buying choices (see e.g. Levin & Gaeth, 1988). In addition, papers that have reviewed the empirical work on framing effects also conclude that framing does affect judgment and decision making processes (see e.g. Levin et al., 1998; Kühberger, 1998 or Maule & Villejoubert, 2007). However, Levin et al. (1998) note that framing effects are not a homogeneous set of phenomena. They differ in critical aspects and thus have to be considered independently in empirical studies. Otherwise, the empirical results will hold ambiguous conclusions. When considering each framing type separately (risky choice framing, attribute framing and goal framing), they found that the empirical results are substantially consistent. Later, Levin et al. (2002) confirmed these conclusions by performing power analysis on the three different types of framing. Besides the general existence of framing effects, it has to be questioned whether framing effects matter in real world situations as a substantial part of the research is built around experimental investigations. Reviewing studies that investigate framing effects in real world situations, Soman (2007) concludes that framing does indeed matter in real world situations. Hence, framing might be considered a profound process in humans' judgment and decision making which might also influence the loan officers' decision making process.

After reviewing the available theoretical and empirical literature on the framing effect in general, it is now time to to apply those findings to the family firm context and develop testable hypotheses which might explain some of the heterogeneity in lending behavior toward firms with varying levels of family influence as a consequence of framing effects.

In section 3.2.1, the effect of family involvement on loan officers' credit availability decisions has been mapped from a theoretical standpoint. But because of the janiform nature of family influence and the ambivalent consequences of such, it was not possible to develop a single unambiguous hypothesis of the direct effect of family involvement on loan officers' credit availability decision. Instead, two opposing hypotheses have been formulated. On the one hand, it was hypothesized that family influence is positively related to credit availability as it signals a positive behavior toward external stakeholders like lenders. This view is supported by agency theory, SEW and the RBV and typically argues that family involvement will be associated with longer investment horizons, risk-averse behavior, positive altruistic behavior from the lenders perspective, more PSE activities and stronger competitive advantages so that the risk of borrowing money to firms with a high level of family involvement will be lower than for firms with lower levels of family involvement (see section 2.2.2 and 3.2.1. for a more detailed elaboration of the individual arguments in favor of family involvement). On the other hand, it was hypothesized that family influence is negatively related to credit availability as it holds negative consequences for lending institutions. Again, agency theory, SEW and RBV were used to rationalize why loan officers will rather associate negative aspects of family involvement. It is argued that a high level of family involvement comes along with concentrated power and parental altruism which cause specific agency problems like e.g. self-control issues, free-riding and/or excessive compensation of family members. All those aspects would increase the risk of borrowing and thus cause loan officers to ration credit to firms with a high level of family involvement (see section 2.2.2 and 3.2.1 for a more detailed elaboration of the individual arguments in disfavor of family involvement). In addition, this ambiguity is largely supported by the currently available empirical results of studies that investigated the impact of family involvement on credit availability decisions. So, some authors found empirical evidence for the positive effect of family involvement on credit availability while others report that their data supports the notion that family involvement is negatively related to credit availability (see section 2.2.3).

At this point, it is argued that framing might explain some of the observed ambiguity in the effect of family involvement on loan officers' credit availability decisions. As argued earlier within this section of the thesis, research found that framing variations affect humans' judgment and decision making. According to literature on the attribute framing effect, positive frames evoke positive associations and thus more positive reactions, whereas negative frames evoke negative associations and thus rather negative reactions with respect to judgment and decision making (Levin et al., 1998). Tying the parts together, it is proposed that loan officers might perceive family involvement as more positive when presented with a positive frame in comparison to situations when presented with a negative frame. Because family involvement might be interpreted as both positive and/or negative, variations in framing should provoke a preferential treatment of one of those perspectives depending on the valence of the frame, i.e in favor of a higher level of family involvement when presented with a positive frame and in favor of a lower level of family involvement when presented with a negative frame. The proposed effect is based on the literature regarding the attribute framing effect, as it seems to be the most relevant framing effect with respect to this dissertation's leading research question. In addition, Levin et al. (1998) argue that this type of framing is especially useful to investigate how descriptive valence affects judgment and decision making. Hence, it is particularly useful for the current study as the goal is to examine the simple effect of framing variations on the influence of family involvement on loan officers' credit availability.

As a result of the previously presented arguments, the hypothesis regarding the moderating effect of framing variations on the relative importance of family involvement on loan officers' credit availability decisions is defined as follows:

> ***Hypothesis 11a:*** *Framing variations moderate the relationship between family influence and the loan officers' credit availability decision. Specifically, positive frames will cause loan officers to associate more positive characteristics with family influence and thus to prefer firms with higher degrees of family involvement. In contrast, negative frames will cause loan officers to associate more negative characteristics with family influence and thus to prefer firms with lower degrees of family involvement.*

3.3.3 Environmental Context Effect

Complementary to the previously described framing effect and based on the currently available literature within family business research, it is argued that loan officers might also be inversely, i.e. negatively affected by the valence of the environmental context, which can be interpreted as a particular type of frame. Previously it was argued that loan officers will recall more negative associations with strong family influence when evaluating loan applications under a negative frame. However, literature also allows for assuming an opposing effect, i.e. that loan officers will recall more positive associations with strong family influence when evaluating loan applications of family firms within a negative environmental context.

Based on the RBV, scholars argue that family firms can resort to family-related resources, like e.g. time, social networks or financial assets, when faced with a weak economic environment (Olson et al., 2003; Distelberg & Sorenson, 2009; Sirmon & Hitt, 2003). Sirmon & Hitt (2003) label those resources "survivability capital" which encompasses all of the pooled personal resources that family members are willing to contribute to the business. They state that this type of capital "can help sustain the business during poor economic times" (p. 343). In addition, the authors argue that the value and amount of survivability capital varies among family firms. So, family firms with high levels of family involvement will be more likely to transfer resources from the family to the business in comparison to family firms with lower degrees of family involvement due to the stronger connection between the two sub-systems and the importance of the firm's survival for the corresponding families (Sirmon & Hitt, 2003; Distelberg & Sorenson, 2009). Olson et al. (2003) found empirical support for this relationship, indicating that family firms tend to indeed transfer personal resources to the business in difficult economic times.

Moreover, literature on framing in general and goal framing in particular states that negative frames cause decision makers to focus on avoiding the negative consequences of their actions by minimizing potential losses. In this regard, Levin et al. (1998) remark that "due to loss aversion, negative wording that focuses on avoiding a loss may produce greater force than comparable positive wording that focuses on obtaining a gain" (p. 179). Most of this literature argues on the basis of the negativity bias (see discussion in the preceding section). Therefore, it can be assumed that loan officers will focus more strongly on risk-related factors when evaluating loans within a weak economic environment. This relationship is also supported by other streams with the research community, like e.g. by the literature on individual needs and their relationship to the environmental context (Maslow, 1954; Alderfer, 1972; Inglehart, 1971) which can be applied to the organizational context stating that lenders will focus more on lower order needs (focus on security which implies the avoidance of monetary losses) in weak economic environments.

When tying the parts together, it can be assumed that loan officers will prefer family firms with high levels of family involvement over firms with lower degrees of family involvement in times of a weak general economy. Within negative environments bank loan officers will be particularly concerned with avoiding any potential losses and thereby focus more strongly on risk-related factors. Due to the fact that family firms with strong family involvement will be more likely to rely on the personal resources of the family and given that loan officers perceive and value this additional survivability capital, they should prefer family firms with high levels of family involvement over firms with lower degrees of family involvement in times of a weak general economy as the risk of default will be perceived lower for those businesses. Thus, based on the previously presented arguments, the hypothesis regarding the moderating effect of the general economic environment on the loan officers' evaluation of family-related decision attributes within the loan availability decision is defined as follow:

> ***Hypothesis 11b:*** *Environmental context variations moderate the relationship between family influence and the loan officers' credit availability decision. Specifically, negative environmental contexts will cause loan officers to associate more positive characteristics with family influence and thus to prefer firms with higher degrees of family involvement.*

3.4 Interaction Effects

In addition to the eight main and the two moderating effects, it is likely that five important interaction effects will affect bank loan officers' judgment and decision making. In particular, it is argued that the five general decision attributes (hypotheses H4-H8) will be moderated by the level of family influence. In the following, the author will present various arguments and derive testable hypotheses regarding the related interaction effects.

3.4.1 Family Influence and the Board Function

Previously, it was hypothesized that the monitoring function of the board of directors will be positively related to credit availability. It was proposed that the stronger the board of directors with respect to their monitoring function, the more positively bank loan officers will rate those companies in terms of the loan availability decision (see section 3.4.1). At this point, this hypothesis is complemented by suggesting that the effect of the monitoring function of the board of directors will be moderated by the degree of family influence on the business, i.e. loan officers will rate the influence of the monitoring power of the board of directors differently for distinct kinds of family firms (distinct in terms of the level of family influence).

As argued earlier in this dissertation, family influence might be associated with a positive behavior toward external stakeholders. Cennamo et al. (2012), for instance, suggested that family firms with an increased priority on SEW tend to invest more in PSE activities as those hold a socioemotional reward for the family. In addition, part of the research on family firms and lending behavior that builds on agency theory provided additional evidence for the positive effect of family involvement regarding the risk of moral hazard. So, scholars argue that a higher degree of family involvement is related to e.g. longer investment horizons, a stronger tendency for risk-aversion and increased kinship as well as altruism (see discussion in section 2.2.2 and 3.2.1). Assuming that loan officers perceive an increased level of family involvement equivalently, they will consequently perceive a lower risk of moral hazard when evaluating those businesses. Because the risk of moral hazard is lower, bank loan officers will not need additional agency mitigating mechanisms regarding the risk of moral hazard. However, the monitoring function of the board performs exactly this function. It reduces the risk of moral hazard by supervising the work of the management and protecting the interests of external stakeholders like e.g. lenders. Hence, a monitoring board becomes obsolete or at least not that necessary from the bank loan officers' perspective in case of high family involvement. Any increase of the monitoring function of the board will have a greater effect on the credit availability of firms with a lower degree of family influence as those businesses do not benefit so much from the positive effect of the family with respect to the risk of moral hazard. Therefore, it follows:

> ***Hypothesis H12a:*** *The influence of the board function will decrease with a higher degree of family involvement, i.e. the higher the family influence, the lower the effect on the loan officers' credit availability decision with a stronger board of directors with respect to the monitoring function.*

Besides the positive associations loan officers can make, family influence might also be related to negative behavior toward external investors which would change the previously formulated hypothesis. According to Gomez-Mejia et al. (2007), family firms with a higher level of family influence (which is typically related to a stronger focus on SEW preservation), represent an increased risk of default as those firms are willing to accept a greater probability of organizational failure. Additionally, scholars relying on agency theory argue that family involvement also has a dark side from the perspective of lenders. A higher degree of family involvement raises the risk of moral hazard as the subsequent concentrated power makes it easier to expropriate wealth from external providers of money (Steijvers & Voordeckers, 2009b; Mueller & Inderst, 1999; Claessens et al., 2002). In addition, they state that family influence is positively related to e.g. self-control issues and excessive compensation of family members (see discussion in section 2.2.2 and 3.2.1). All of those factors make agency mitigating mechanisms that monitor the borrowers' behavior even more necessary, so that a board of directions with a strong monitoring function will be especially beneficial for firms with a high level of family influence from the bank loan officers' point of view. As a consequence of this line of arguments, the monitoring function of the board should have a greater effect on the credit availability of firms with a high level of family involvement. The mitigating effect for firms with a lower degree of family involvement should not be as strong as for family firms with a strong family background. Thus, it is alternatively hypothesized:

> ***Hypothesis H12b:*** *The influence of the board function will increase with a higher degree of family involvement, i.e. the higher the family influence, the higher the effect on the loan officers' credit availability decision with a stronger board of directors with respect to the monitoring function.*

In order to make it easier for the reader to understand the hypothesized effects, the previously developed hypotheses H12a and H12b are illustrated in Figure 4.

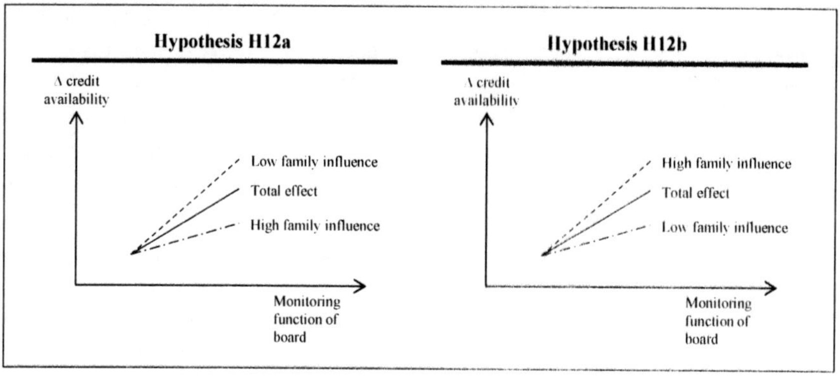

Figure 4: Hypotheses H12 - Family Influence x Board Function

3.4.2 Family Influence and the CEO's Experience

In section 3.2.3 it was hypothesized that the experience of the prospective borrower's CEO will be positively related to credit availability, i.e. the more experience the CEO has in managing businesses and coping with adverse situations, the more positively bank loan officers will rate those companies in terms of the loan availability decision. Within this section, it is argued that this main effect will be influenced by the level of family influence within a given company.

Drawing upon the RBV, numerous scholars within family business research argue that family firms create unique and valuable resources as a result of the entanglement and interactions between the family and the firm. As previously described, the research community typically uses the term "familiness" to refer to those family-related resources that create competitive advantages (Cabrera-Suárez et al., 2001; Habbershon & Williams, 1999). It has to be noted that familiness is related to the degree of family involvement. So, businesses that display a low level of family involvement are not as inherently connected to and do not interact as much with the family system (Minichilli et al., 2010; Zellweger et al., 2010). Within this area of research, authors claim that firms with a high level of family involvement are characterized by socially complex tacit knowledge that is diffused throughout the family firm and though it is not necessarily unique to those businesses, it is particularly prevalent among them (Barney, 1991; Tokarczyk et al., 2007; Reed & Defillippi, 1990). If loan officers perceive the involvement of the family similarly, they might value the CEO's experience differently for different types of family firms. Because a high level of family involvement creates familiness that functions as a distinctive resource and creates competitive advantages, the CEO might not need as much experience within this type of business as the company itself has resources like e.g. tacit knowledge that might enable it to deal with unexpected and adverse situations. In comparison, firms without this level of familiness will be more challenging to manage in case of an economic crisis as they do not have such unique resources. In those businesses, the management (personified by the CEO) needs to compensate for the lack of those resources with his knowledge and experience. Thus, the following hypothesis is formulated on the basis of this line of arguments:

> ***Hypothesis H13a:*** *The influence of the experience of the CEO will decrease with a higher degree of family involvement, i.e. the higher the family influence, the lower the effect on the loan officers' credit availability decision for loan applicants that have a CEO with a high level of experience.*

Besides this direction of the interaction effect, it is argued that the level of family influence might also have an opposing effect on the value loan officers attach to the information regarding the CEO's experience. Lubatkin et al. (2005), for instance, noted that family firms tend to restrict top management positions to family members. However, not considering external candidates would raise the risk of hiring low-quality employees as the potential pool of future employees is limited. Consequently, this would result in a higher likelihood of default as low-quality managers will struggle to deal with unexpected adverse situations. Loan officers might perceive this threat as particularly present when the family is eminently involved in the business and even more so when they know that the family is excessively active within the companies' management. Hence, loan officers that are faced with a borrower with a high level of family influence (particularly in regards to the family's involvement in the management) will value positive information about the CEO's experience higher-than-average as the risk of stumbling across a low-quality CEO is higher in such firms. Besides this line of arguments, Rüsen & Schlippe (2007) argue that a high level of family involvement raises the risk of family induced conflicts within the business which would cause higher agency costs from the lenders' perspective. It is assumed that experienced CEO's are better suited to handle those situations and cope with these specific conflicts. Thus, experienced managers might be an adequate instrument to mitigate the related risks. So, because firms with a low level of family involvement do not have an increased need for CEO's that are able to handle these family-induced conflicts, loan officers will not value the CEO's experience so much in those firms. On the other hand, positive information about the CEO's experience of a firm with a high level of family influence signals loan officers that these firms are not afflicted with higher agency costs. Therefore, the hypothesis regarding the opposing interaction effect between the level of family influence and the CEO's experience is defined as follows:

> ***Hypothesis H13b:*** *The influence of the experience of the CEO will increase with a higher degree of family involvement, i.e. the higher the family influence, the higher the effect on the loan officers' credit availability decision for loan applicants that have a CEO with a high level of experience.*

In addition, the hypotheses regarding the interaction effect of family involvement on the influence of the experience of the prospective borrower on the bank loan officers' credit availability decision is visualized in Figure 5.

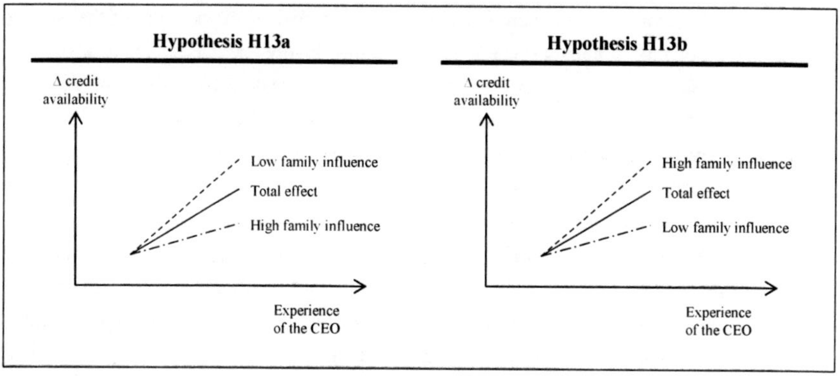

Figure 5: Hypotheses H13 - Family Influence x Experience of the CEO

3.4.3 Family Influence and the Level of Transparency

In general, the level of transparency is supposed to be positively related to credit availability, i.e. the higher the level of transparency of a prospective borrower, the more positively bank loan officers will rate those companies in terms of the loan availability decision (see section 3.2.4 for a more detailed elaboration on the corresponding hypothesized main effect, here hypothesis H6). Simultaneously, it is expected that this effect is moderated by the level of family involvement within the business.

One stream of research regarding family firms argues that family involvement is related to positive behavior toward external stakeholders. Those scholars typically conclude that family involvement leads to longer investment horizons, risk-aversion and altruistic behavior, which lowers the risk of moral hazard (see discussion in section 2.2.2 and 3.2.1). As a consequence, loan officers would not need as many information from those firms as from firms with lower levels of family involvement. Moreover, firms with a high level of family influence are able to build longer and more intense relationships with lenders as a result of their long-term orientation. Thus, loan officers would be able to generate much more information on their own without relying on the disclosed information of the company (see e.g. Steijvers & Voordeckers, 2009b). Consequently, it is suggested that loan officers will value an increased level of transparency less positively for firms with a high degree of family involvement as the amount of disclosed information will be interpreted as a substitute for high family influence where loan officers can generate information on their own over time. On the basis of this stream of research it is hypothesized that:

> ***Hypothesis H14a:*** *The influence of the level of transparency will decrease with a higher degree of family involvement, i.e. the higher the family influence, the lower the effect on the loan officers' credit availability decision for loan applicants that are characterized by a high level of transparency.*

Complementary, another line of family business research challenges the view of the positive impact of family involvement by claiming that family involvement is typically associated with negative consequences for external stakeholders like lenders (see e.g. Schulze et al., 2003; Mueller & Inderst, 1999; Lubatkin et al., 2005). According to this view, family involvement leads to e.g. self-control issues and excessive compensation of family members, which increases the risk of wealth expropriation. Consequently, bank loan officers have to require more information from those businesses in order to better monitor the borrowers' financial situation. In addition, Poutziouris (2001) reported that family firms tend to pursue a "keep it in the family" policy, which causes extra informational asymmetries between the parties. He found that this effect is especially severe when the level of family involvement is high as the need to communicate with outsiders is relatively low (see also Ali et al., 2007; Chen et al., 2008 and Daily & Dollinger, 1991). As a result, it is assumed that bank loan officers should react exceedingly positive to firms that on the one hand are highly interconnected with the family but on the other hand disclose information above average. Those firms signal that they do not pursue a "keep it in the family" policy and are willing to cooperate with lenders. This should cause loan officers to react more positively toward those family firms in comparison to loan applicants with lower levels of family involvement as the latter are typically not associated with particular moral hazard issues or informational problems and thus do not need to additionally signal their willingness to disclose above average information. So, though a higher level of transparency will be perceived positively by loan officers when evaluating firms with a low level of family involvement, the size of this effect will be smaller for those firms in comparison to firms with a high level of family involvement as loan officers will be particularly concerned with transparency problems when dealing with those kinds of borrowers. Hence, the following hypothesis can be derived from this line of research regarding the interaction effect between family influence and the level of transparency:

> ***Hypothesis H14b:*** *The influence of the level of transparency will increase with a higher degree of family involvement, i.e. the higher the family influence, the higher the effect on the loan officers' credit availability decision for loan applicants that are characterized by a high level of transparency.*

On the basis of hypothesis H14a and H14b, loan approvals are predicted to follow the pattern shown in Figure 6.

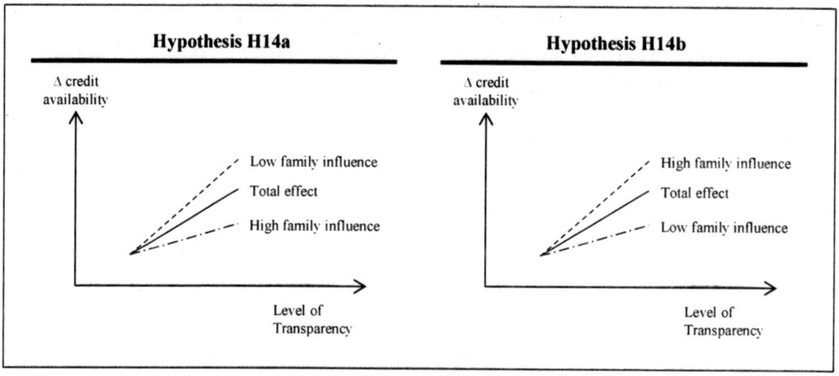

Figure 6: Hypotheses H14 - Family Influence x Level of Transparency

3.4.4 Family Influence and the Level of Attestation

The level of attestation is assumed to directly influence the loan officers' judgment and decision making. In particular, this study hypothesizes that the existence of an auditor's attestation will be positively related to credit availability regardless of the type of attestation, i.e. if the information from the loan applicant is audited from an independent auditor, bank loan officers will rate those companies more positively in the context of the loan availability decision (see section 3.2.5 for a more detailed discussion on this hypothesis – here hypothesis H7). On the basis of the currently available literature, this hypothesis is complemented within this section by proposing that the impact of the level of attestation will be moderated by the degree of family involvement within the firm. However, just as with the other interaction effect, the direction of this particular moderating effect is ambiguous which is why two separate sub hypotheses are formulated.

On the one hand and as previously mentioned several times, scholars within the field of family business research argue that family involvement is related to a positive behavior toward lenders. They argue that those firms have a different incentive structure as a result of their substantial investment in the firm which causes them to approach longer investment horizons and risk-averse strategies. Because of their long-term orientation, firms that show a high level of family involvement tend to build sustainable relationships with their stakeholders and therefore have only little incentives to cheat on external partners like e.g. lenders as this would damage their reputation and thereby their ability to survive over generations. Hence, loan officers are assumed to have a lower need for audited information from companies with high levels of family influence as the risk of misrepresentation or fraud will be lower within those types of businesses. Similarly, Cennamo et al. (2012) argue that family firms with an increased priority on SEW tend to invest more in PSE activities as those hold a socioemotional reward for the family. From the lenders perspective, this means that firms with a higher degree of family involvement will tend to anticipate their needs and act accordingly. This again would lower the risk of fraud and thus the need for audited information. Consequently, the first hypothesis regarding the interaction effect between family influence and the level of attestation can be formulated as follows:

> ***Hypothesis H15a:*** *The influence of the level of attestation will decrease with a higher degree of family involvement, i.e. the higher the family influence, the lower the effect on the loan officers' credit availability decision for loan applicants whose information are audited by an independent auditor.*

On the other hand, scholars argue that family involvement is associated with rather negative consequences for lenders. Typically, they argue that a higher degree of family involvement leads to concentrated power which makes it easier for those firms to pursue unfavorable policies from the lenders perspective (Gomez-Mejia et al., 2001; Mueller & Inderst, 1999; Claessens et al., 2002). Consequently, the risk of moral hazard would rise as loan officers had to fear that borrowers of that type will conceal important information or even manipulate them in order to expropriate wealth from them. In addition, Stockmans et al. (2010) presented evidence for such a behavior from a different theoretical perspective, namely the SEW concept. They demonstrated that the more importance private family firms attach to non-financial objectives, i.e. SEW, the more likely they will manage earnings upward when firm performance is poor. This means that firms with a high level of family involvement will try to manipulate their earnings reports if firm performance is weak in order to communicate a better economic situation to external stakeholders and thus not lose part of their SEW. At this point, it is assumed that loan officers will anticipate those upward earnings management policies by firms with a high level of family involvement and request audited information. As a consequence, loan officers will value a higher level of attestation more for those firms as it provides an additional and independent source of information that does not misrepresent the "true" current state of the prospective borrowers' financial situation. It is a useful method to reduce the specific risks that are associated with those companies, i.e. the risk of intentionally misrepresenting the current state of the businesses. The effect of the level of attestation should not be as strong for firms with a lower level of family influence as those are not especially affected by this type of risk. Hence, the following hypothesis regarding the interaction effect between family influence and the level of attestation can be derived on the basis of the currently available literature:

> ***Hypothesis H15b:*** *The influence of the level of attestation will increase with a higher degree of family involvement, i.e. the higher the family influence, the higher the effect on the loan officers' credit availability decision for loan applicants whose information are audited by an independent auditor.*

Finally, the effects of both developed hypotheses of this section are visualized in Figure 7.

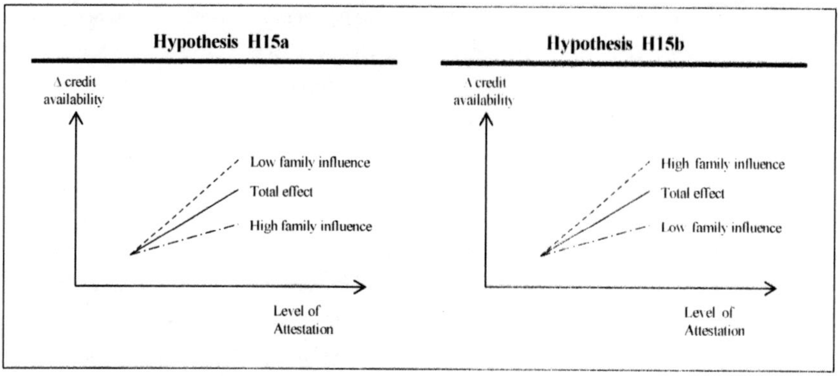

Figure 7: Hypotheses H15 - Family Influence x Level of Attestation

3.4.5 Family Influence and the Independence of Collateral

Previously, it was hypothesized that the level of independence of the additional collateral will be positively related to credit availability, i.e. the higher the independence of the additionally offered collateral, the more positively bank loan officers will rate those companies in terms of the loan availability decision (see section 3.2.6 for a detailed discussion regarding this main effect). Drawing upon the currently available literature, this effect is expected to be moderated by the level of family involvement within the firm. However, research in this field provides ambiguous insights with respect to the direction of this particular interaction effect which is why two opposing hypotheses regarding the moderating effect of family involvement on the value of information about the independence of additional collateral have been derived.

As already described several times in this thesis, one line of family business research claims that family involvement is associated with rather positive than negative behavior toward external stakeholder. So, scholars who take up this position typically argue that family involvement leads to longer investment horizons, higher degrees of risk-aversion and less selfish behavior (as a result of altruism and kinship). Similarly, Cennamo et al. (2012) argue on the basis of the SEW approach that the level of family involvement is positively related to PSE activities, i.e. positive behavior toward stakeholders. Therefore, agency problems or rather the risk of moral hazard should be perceived to be lower for firms with a high level of family involvement (see section 2.2.2 ad 3.2.1 for a more detailed elaboration on the effect of family involvement on the bank loan officers judgment and decision making). Because the associated risk is perceived to be lower, bank loan officers should ceteris paribus not require as many agency mitigating instruments from those firms in comparison to prospective borrowers that are characterized by a higher risk of moral hazard. Put differently, this means that loan officers will rate the value of additional agency mitigating tools for firms with high levels of family involvement not as much as they will for borrowers with lower levels of family involvement because family involvement itself can be seen as an agency mitigating instrument so that other tools are redundant and thereby dispensable. Therefore, this thesis hypothesizes the following interaction effect between the level of family influence and the independence of additional collateral as an agency mitigating tool:

> ***Hypothesis H16a:*** *The influence of the independence of additionally offered collateral will decrease with a higher degree of family involvement, i.e. the higher the family influence, the lower the effect on the loan officers' credit availability decision for loan applicants that offer additional independent collateral.*

Besides the positive effect of family involvement, some scholars argue that family influence has in total negative consequences for external stakeholders. It is suggested that concentrated power, parental altruism and kinship result in specific agency problems like e.g. self-control issues, free-riding and/or excessive compensation of family members (see e.g. Schulze et al., 2003; Lubatkin et al., 2005; Mueller & Inderst, 1999 and Claessens et al., 2002). Therefore, loan officers need to implement appropriate agency mitigating mechanisms to cope with those issues. As presented earlier in this thesis, collateral is such a device to reduce the associated risks – with independent collateral to even further minimize the risk of lending money (see section 3.2.6 for a detailed elaboration regarding this main effect). Therefore, it is assumed that loan officers will require collateral that is more independent of the firms' success from firms with high levels of family involvement as the risk of lending to those types of businesses will be more risky in comparison to firms with lower levels of family influence. Those companies are less likely to be affected by the specific family-related agency problems to the full extent. In other words, loan officers will value the independence of additional collateral more for firms with a high level of family influence as those are characterized by a higher level of specific family-related agency problems. Firms with high levels of family influence that offer highly independent collateral signal lower risks of moral hazard which is assumed to be prevalent among those types of businesses. Loan officers will greatly value this offer. On the other hand, firms with lower levels of family influence that offer highly independent collateral will not be able to reduce the associated risks to the same degree as firms with a high level of family involvement because they already have an overall lower risk level which reduces the benefits of the additionally offered highly independent collateral and causes loan officers to value this instrument less positively when faced with borrowers that display low levels of family involvement. In this regard, Steijvers & Voordeckers (2009b) found that loan officers require more personal collateral which is highly independent of the firms' success for firms with a high level of these specific family-related agency problems (which are related to the degree of family involvement). Tying together all of the presented arguments from this line of research, it is hypothesized that:

> ***Hypothesis H16b:*** *The influence of the independence of additionally offered collateral will increase with a higher degree of family involvement, i.e. the higher the family in-*

fluence, the higher the effect on the loan officers' credit availability decision for loan applicants that offer additional independent collateral.

In addition, the following figure (Figure 8) charts the hypothesized opposing effect of family influence on the value of information about the independence of the additionally offered collateral with respect to the credit availability decision.

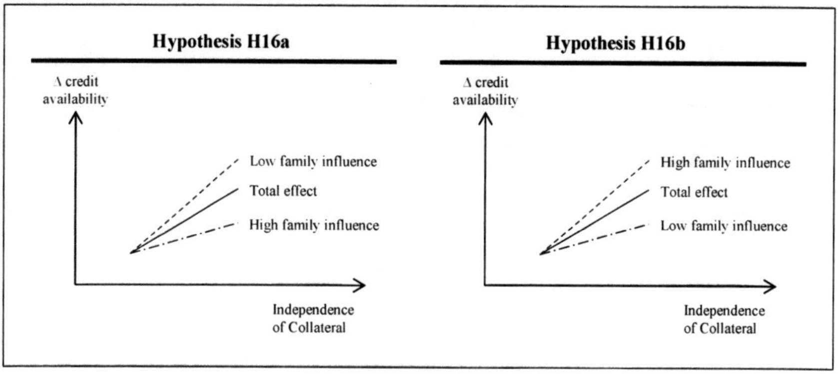

Figure 8: Hypotheses H16 - Family Influence x Independence of Collateral

3.5 Synopsis of the Hypotheses

At the end of this chapter, the hypothesized effects are visualized in Figure 9. In addition, Table 3 to Table 5 give an overview of all of the previously defined hypotheses which are to be tested empirically in the next section of this dissertation.

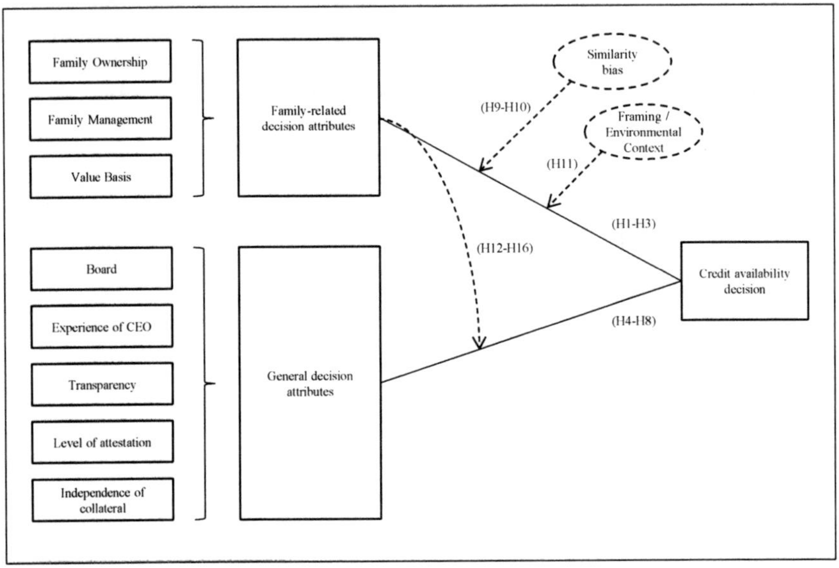

Figure 9: Synopsis of the Hypotheses

No.	Description	Effect Type	Theories
H1a	The level of family influence within the business with respect to the ownership share will be positively related to debt availability, i.e. the higher the family ownership, the more positively bank loan officers will rate those companies in terms of the loan availability decision.	Main effect	Agency perspective, SEW, RBV
H1b	The level of family influence within the business with respect to the ownership share will be negatively related to debt availability, i.e. the higher the family ownership, the more negatively bank loan officers will rate those companies in terms of the loan availability decision.	Main effect	Agency perspective, SEW, RBV
H2a	The level of family influence within the business with respect to the participation in the management will be positively related to debt availability, i.e. the higher the domination of the family within the management, the more positively bank loan officers will rate those companies in terms of the loan availability decision.	Main effect	Agency perspective, SEW, RBV
H2b	The level of family influence within the business with respect to the participation in the management will be negatively related to debt availability, i.e. the higher the domination of the family within the management, the more negatively bank loan officers will rate those companies in terms of the loan availability decision.	Main effect	Agency perspective, SEW, RBV

Table 3: Detailed Overview of the Developed Hypotheses (1/3)

No.	Description	Effect Type	Theories
H3a	The level of family influence within the business with respect to the overlap between the families and the company 's value basis will be positively related to debt availability, i.e. the higher the overlap between the family 's and the company 's value basis, the more positively bank loan officers will rate those companies in terms of the loan availability decision.	Main effect	Agency perspective, SEW, RBV
H3b	The level of family influence within the business with respect to the overlap between the families and the company 's value basis will be negatively related to debt availability, i.e. the higher the overlap between the family 's and the company 's value basis, the more negatively bank loan officers will rate those companies in terms of the loan availability decision.	Main effect	Agency perspective, SEW, RBV
H4	The monitoring function of the board of directors will be positively related to credit availability, i.e. the stronger the board of directors with respect to their monitoring function, the more positively bank loan officers will rate those companies in terms of the loan availability decision.	Main effect	Agency perspective
H5	The experience of the CEO will be positively related to credit availability, i.e. the more experience the CEO has in managing businesses and coping with adverse situations, the more positively bank loan officers will rate those companies in terms of the loan availability decision.	Main effect	Agency perspective, RBV
H6	The level of transparency will be positively related to credit availability, i.e. the higher the level of transparency, the more positively bank loan officers will rate those companies in terms of the loan availability decision.	Main effect	Agency perspective
H7	The existence of an auditor's attestation will be positively related to credit availability regardless of the type of attestation, i.e. if the information from the loan applicant is audited from an independent auditor, bank loan officers will rate those companies more positively in terms of the loan availability decision.	Main effect	Agency perspective
H8	The independence of the additional collateral will be positively related to credit availability, i.e. the higher the independence of the additionally offered collateral, the more positively bank loan officers will rate those companies in terms of the loan availability decision.	Main effect	Agency perspective
H9	The loan officers' perceived similarity between them and loan applicants or their generic image of these with respect to the FIBER dimensions moderates the relationship between family influence and the loan officers' credit availability decision. Specifically, higher perceived similarity between loan officers and family firms or their generic image of these with respect to the FIBER dimensions will lead to a more positive effect of family involvement on their credit availability decision.	Moderating effect	Similarity bias, SEW
H10	The loan officers' perceived similarity between the company they work for and loan applicants or there generic image of these with respect to (a) family background and (b) SEW moderates the relationship between family influence and the loan officers' credit availability decision. Specifically, higher perceived similarity between loan officers and family firms or their generic image of these with respect to (a) family background and (b) SEW will lead to a more positive effect of family involvement on their credit availability decision.	Moderating effect	Similarity bias; SEW
H11a	Framing variations moderate the relationship between family influence and the loan officers' credit availability decision. Specifically, positive frames will cause loan officers to associate more positive characteristics with family influence and thus to prefer firms with higher degrees of family involvement. In contrast, negative frames will cause loan officers to associate more negative characteristics with family influence and thus to prefer firms with lower degrees of family involvement.	Moderating effect	Framing effects, Agency theory, SEW, RBV
H11b	Environmental context variations moderate the relationship between family influence and the loan officers' credit availability decision. Specifically, negative environmental contexts will cause loan officers to associate more positive characteristics with family influence and thus to prefer firms with higher degrees of family involvement.	Moderating effect	Framing effects, Agency theory, SEW, RBV

Table 4: Detailed Overview of the Developed Hypotheses (2/3)

No.	Description	Effect Type	Theories
H12a	The influence of the board function will decrease with a higher degree of family involvement, i.e. the higher the family influence, the lower the effect on the loan officers' credit availability decision with a stronger board of directors with respect to the monitoring function.	Interaction effect	Agency perspective, SEW
H12b	The influence of the board function will increase with a higher degree of family involvement, i.e. the higher the family influence, the higher the effect on the loan officers' credit availability decision with a stronger board of directors with respect to the monitoring function.	Interaction effect	Agency perspective, SEW, RBV
H13a	The influence of the experience of the CEO will decrease with a higher degree of family involvement, i.e. the higher the family influence, the lower the effect on the loan officers' credit availability decision for loan applicants that have a CEO with a high level of experience.	Interaction effect	Agency perspective, SEW, RBV
H13b	The influence of the experience of the CEO will increase with a higher degree of family involvement, i.e. the higher the family influence, the higher the effect on the loan officers' credit availability decision for loan applicants that have a CEO with a high level of experience.	Interaction effect	Agency perspective, SEW, RBV
H14a	The influence of the level of transparency will decrease with a higher degree of family involvement, i.e. the higher the family influence, the lower the effect on the loan officers' credit availability decision for loan applicants that are characterized by a high level of transparency.	Interaction effect	Agency perspective, SEW, RBV
H14b	The influence of the level of transparency will increase with a higher degree of family involvement, i.e. the higher the family influence, the higher the effect on the loan officers' credit availability decision for loan applicants that are characterized by a high level of transparency.	Interaction effect	Agency perspective, SEW, RBV
H15a	The influence of the level of attestation will decrease with a higher degree of family involvement, i.e. the higher the family influence, the lower the effect on the loan officers' credit availability decision for loan applicants whose information are audited by an independent auditor.	Interaction effect	Agency perspective, SEW, RBV
H15b	The influence of the level of attestation will increase with a higher degree of family involvement, i.e. the higher the family influence, the higher the effect on the loan officers' credit availability decision for loan applicants whose information are audited by an independent auditor.	Interaction effect	Agency perspective, SEW, RBV
H16a	The influence of the independence of additionally offered collateral will decrease with a higher degree of family involvement, i.e. the higher the family influence, the lower the effect on the loan officers' credit availability decision for loan applicants that offer additional independent collateral.	Interaction effect	Agency perspective, SEW, RBV
H16b	The influence of the independence of additionally offered collateral will increase with a higher degree of family involvement, i.e. the higher the family influence, the higher the effect on the loan officers' credit availability decision for loan applicants that offer additional independent collateral.	Interaction effect	Agency perspective, SEW, RBV

Table 5: Detailed Overview of the Developed Hypotheses (3/3)

4 Research Methodology

In order to test the previously derived hypotheses, an experiment with a total of 90 loan officers working for different banks in Germany was conducted. The experimenter collected data on (1) bank loan officers' decision making strategies using a conjoint approach, (2) participants orientation toward SEW using a post-experimental questionnaire and (3) other controls like e.g. family background or education on the level of loan officers and their employers. In a first step, the conjoint experiment was conducted before collecting the other data in order to minimize the potential threat of response bias. Data was then analyzed with a HLM approach. In the following, the distinct methodological components will be discussed in more detail.

4.1 Experimental research in general

There are two general approaches for discovering causality – the non-experimental and the experimental method (Cozby, 2009). When pursuing the non-experimental approach, scholars are studying relationships among variables by interviewing respondents or observing what is currently happening or has happened in the past. With this approach, a relationship is assumed when different variables vary together (Cooper & Schindler, 2008). In contrast, when pursuing the experimental approach, scholars are able to directly manipulate and control the variables of interest. Thus, experiments involve the intervention of the researcher, typically by manipulating some variable in a particular setting and observing how it affects the dependent variable, which - in the context of social science - is typically the humans' behavior (Cooper & Schindler, 2008). With this approach, a relationship is not assumed on the basis of the mere observation of different variables varying together. Rather, one variable is introduced first to test whether it influences another variable, i.e. the dependent variable in focus (Cozby, 2009). This aspect is a key differentiating factor between the two general empirical approaches and emphasizes the basic differences of how causality is examined. In this regard, Antonakis et al. (2010) argue that experiments are better suited to examine causal relationships. Moore & McCabe (1993) even state that the "best method - indeed the only fully compelling method - of establishing causation is to conduct a carefully designed experiment in which the effects of possible lurking variables are controlled. To experiment means to actively change x [independent variable] and to observe the response in y [dependent variable]" (p. 202). Similarly, Cooper & Schindler (2008) note that though both experimental and non-experimental approaches are not able to prove causality with certainty, experiments come closer to accomplishing that goal as the probability that changes in the dependent variable are a function of the independent variable increases. This is a major advantage of experimental methods in comparison to non-experimental ones. Other advantages include aspects like the possibility to better control for contamination by extraneous variables, advantages in the convenience and cost of conducting a research project in comparison to other methods and the general ability to replicate experiments with alternative subjects, under varying conditions and even at different times in order to further verify the discoveries (Cooper & Schindler, 2008).

Despite their advantages, experiments also have some disadvantages. Scholars typically mention the artificiality of the laboratory setting as their primary disadvantage. However, this negative aspect can be alleviated by either conducting a field experiment or investing in the experimental facilities. In addition, scholars criticize that experiments are typically carried out with students while the corresponding results are generalized to the behavior of experienced managers and executives. This critique can be tackled by conducting the experiment with practitioners. Overall, literature remarks that the approach's desire to control for all potential types of contamination in the variables typically results in simplistic designs and might jeopardize the external validity of the corresponding results (Cooper & Schindler, 2008; Cozby, 2009; Howe, 2004). Furthermore, scholars argue that experiments hold some specific threats to internal validity. In particular, the following seven threats to internal validity are typically discussed within literature: (1) history (events that occur between the time of the treatment and the time the dependent variable is measured), (2) maturation (changes that occur within subjects that are not related to the treatment, like e.g. that subjects get tired or hungry), (3) testing (refers to learning effects during or between experiments that influence subjects' behaviors and thereby the study's results), (4) instrumentation (changes in observations as a result of changes of the measurement instrument or the observer), (5) selection (refers to the problems that arise because of differences between the experimental and the control group), (6) statistical regression (refers to the problems that arise when the measurement of the dependent variable is not perfectly reliable) and (7) experimental mortality (problems that occur because of changes in the composition of the groups during the tests) - (see e.g. Cooper & Schindler, 2008; Campbell et al., 1963 or Kirk, 1995 for a more detailed elaboration of these aspects).

As mentioned, experiments are one scientific approach. However, there are also different types of experiments. On an overall level, we can distinguish between true experiments and quasi-experiments. In true experimental designs, subjects are randomly assigned to the treatment conditions, i.e. to the different levels of independent variables. With this approach, the experimenter is able to control for extraneous variables and perfectly manipulate the experimental treatments. This enables scholars to examine actual cause-and-effect relationships with a high degree of certainty. In cases where the experimenter cannot control for extraneous factors and manipulate the experimental treatments as good as in true experiments, quasi-experimental approaches are conducted. Quasi-experimental approaches lack important features of true experimental designs like e.g. the random assignment to treatment conditions. Those methods are typically used when conducting experiments under field conditions as it is difficult to meet all of the requirements of true experiments in these circumstances. Therefore, quasi-experiments are on the one hand easier to implement but on the other hand are inferior to true experiments as it is more difficult to make causal inferences on the basis of this methodological approach. In addition, some authors mention a further overall category of experimental designs, namely pre-experimental designs. However, those are very weak in their

power to make causal claims as they completely fail to control for all of the previously listed threats to internal validity (see e.g. Cooper & Schindler, 2008 or Tuckman, 1999).
Within this study, a particular experimental method was used, namely conjoint experiments (also called conjoint analysis). This approach is typically conducted in a quasi-experimental-setting (Neubauer, 2003), but has its own characteristics and will therefore be discussed in the next section on a rather general level before describing the design specifics of the current study.

4.2 Conjoint Analysis as a Research Method

Conjoint analysis is the general term that refers to all decompositional methods for studying human decision making processes (Louviere, 1988; Green & Srinivasan, 1990). Originally, the basic method for conjoint analysis was developed by Luce & Tukey (1964). Later, numerous authors have refined and modified it. But even though several types of conjoint methods have been developed over time, the underlying mechanism is always the same. Typically, all of those techniques require respondents to make a series of judgments based on a set of predefined attributes. These judgments are made on a number of profiles which display different levels of the various attributes (e.g. green product vs. red product vs. yellow product or high product reliability vs. low product reliability). From there on scholars can investigate the underlying structure of the participants' cognitive system by decomposing the various judgments into part-worth utilities (this is also the reason why conjoint methods are called decompositional). So, this method enables researchers to examine the respondents' underlying preference structure with respect to the presented attributes and thus uncover actually used decision rules (Shepherd & Zacharakis, 1999). Because conjoint analysis is a real time method, it is possible to overcome many of the potential research biases associated with post-hoc research instruments. So, post-hoc methods collect data about a decision after it has been made, typically asking decision makers to self-report their decision rules and policies with respect to past events. Unfortunately, those methods face serious problems with regards to e.g. humans' limited ability to recall past events or the social desirability bias i.e. the respondents' tendency to answer questions in a manner that they think is expected or will be viewed positively by others. Conjoint analysis transcends most of those problems as it does not rely on participants' self-reported decision policies but rather derives a person's decision rules on the basis of actual, though hypothetical and mostly simplified, decisions. Research in this field emphasizes that real-time methods like conjoint analysis are better suited for uncovering a person's actual decision policies (Shepherd & Zacharakis, 1999; Lohrke et al., 2010). Due to this advantage in examining judgment and decision making, conjoint methods have been applied to a wide range of areas. Besides the commercial use of those methods (see Wittink & Cattin, 1989 and Wittink et al., 1994), conjoint analysis became particularly popular across researchers from diverse areas of expertise. At the beginning, primarily marketing scholars used the tool to find out what product attributes are important for customers during the buying process

(Orme, 2010). Later, it was applied to other fields as well. Reutterer & Kotzab (2000) applied conjoint analysis to supply chain management to measure preferences in supply chain design. Shepherd & Zacharakis (1999) started to use conjoint methods for studying venture capitalists' decision policies for evaluating new start-ups. Even researchers in the area of health care have adopted conjoint analysis in order to elicit preferences for different aspects of care (see e.g. Ryan & Farrar, 2000).

In general, the process of undertaking a conjoint experiment involves the following four main steps: (1) designing the conjoint experiment, (2) collecting the data, (3) analyzing the generated data and (4) interpreting the results. Within this process, the design stage is of major importance, as mistakes cannot be corrected in retrospect. Pocock (1984) underlines this importance by writing: "To propose that poor design can be corrected by subtle analysis techniques is contrary to good scientific thinking" (p. 58). Therefore, important general aspects of designing conjoint experiments will be discussed in the following. This will help us to better understand the decisions that have been made with respect to the design of this particular experiment.

In general, the design stage of conjoint analysis involves five sub tasks which can be classified into (1) definition of dependent variables, attributes and attribute levels, (2) decision upon the stimuli presentation method, (3) decision upon the question type, (4) definition of the experimental design and (5) decision upon the data collection instrument.

Conjoint analysis requires the researcher to define the relevant drivers of the participants' decision making process in advance. This includes the exact specification of the decision task, the attributes that influence the subjects' decisions and the different levels of each attribute that are examined. The decision making process can only be examined with respect to the included variables. So, including and excluding decision variables is a critical step in conjoint analysis (Hair et al., 1995). Shepherd & Zacharakis (1999) argue that it requires theory to define the relevant decision attributes that have to be included in the conjoint experiment. However, it is not possible (not even necessary) to include all potential decision attributes in the decision task. Shepherd & Zacharakis (1999) outline that the maximum number of attributes to be included in a conjoint experiment is eight, with many studies using only three to five attributes. Please note that though newer methods made it possible to include some more attributes (like e.g. adaptive methods), they still reach limits. Attributes are then operationalized by assigning different values to each attribute (typically two to four levels per attribute). This can be done by relative (high vs. low) or absolute values (1.000 EUR vs. 100.000 EUR). When defining the decision task, the attributes and the attribute levels, the researcher should keep the actual decision environment in mind and try to simulate it in order to maintain response validity. It is necessary to define a common context of the decision task in order to control respondent variation and thereby avoid contaminated results (Shepherd & Zacharakis, 1999).

The second design question of conjoint analysis is how to present the stimuli to respondents. Literature typically differentiates between full-profile and partial-profile approaches (Green & Srinivasan, 1978; Breidert et al., 2006; Johnson, 1974). The full-profile approach includes the complete set of attributes in each profile, so that participants have to take all attributes into account when making their decision. A model containing M attributes and L levels per attribute produces a maximum number of $L_1 \times L_2 \times \ldots \times L_M = L^M$ different stimuli combinations (this equals the number of different profiles) which can be presented to the respondent. By including all of the previously defined attributes in the decision task, the full-profile approach creates a more realistic description of the stimuli on the one hand, but on the other hand might cause problems with information overload due to the more complex task. Nonetheless, Wittink & Cattin (1989) report that the full-profile approach is the most commonly used method. Partial-profile methods require respondents to make decision on profiles which consist of only a fraction of the previously defined attributes (Green & Srinivasan, 1978). Thereby, the experimenter reduces the risk of information overload on the part of the respondent by simplifying the decision task. However, this approach displays serious limitations. So, by further decomposing the decision task, there is a sacrifice in realism as judgments and decisions in reality are affected by numerous factors and are typically not broken down into decisions between a partial set of attributes. In addition, though the complexity of a single decision task is reduces, the total number of decisions a respondent makes increases as the experimenter still needs to examine all attributes which causes problems of its own (see Green & Srinivasan, 1978 for further details on this topic). Besides the decision about the scope of stimuli presentation, the experimenter has to choose between one of the two following general stimuli presentation methods: (1) fixed method or (2) adaptive method. Within the fixed approach, the order in which the profiles are presented to the participant is fixed, i.e. predefined by the experimenter. It will not be changed during a survey. The adaptive method, which was initially developed by Richard M. Johnson (1987), works differently. It is an interactive approach that uses the respondents' actual decisions to calculate which stimuli combination to present next in order to decompose the underlying decision rules most efficiently. It is usually used with the partial-profile approach, so that a respondent will not see all attributes on one profile. In addition, this method has to be used with a computer-based survey instrument due to the continuous analysis of the already made decisions and the flexible creation of new stimuli combinations. The adaptive method is primarily used when the number of attributes is high. Green & Srinivasan (1990) recommend the use of an adaptive method when the number of attributes is higher than ten. Otherwise, they recommend the use of the fixed method and if feasible a full-profile approach. In addition to the scope of the stimulus presentation and the general stimulus presentation method, the researcher has to decide upon the attribute presentation style. The design question is whether to present the attributes in a verbal or pictorial style? A pictorial presentation of the stimulus might, for instance, increase realism (Shepherd & Zacharakis, 1999). However, as this question is of particular interest to marketing scholars and not that relevant to the present study, it will not be further elaborated within this thesis. Within this study, a verbal presentation is used as bankers typically rely on verbal reports.

Moreover, a question type has to be chosen. The three most frequently used question types in conjoint analysis are (1) ranking questions, (2) paired comparisons and (3) rating questions (Louviere, 1988; Lohrke et al., 2010). The ranking method asks respondents to rank the presented stimuli with respect to their individual preferences. This method is particularly useful when the number of attributes in an experiment is low, as it is more reliable and valid in comparison to the rating-based methods (Krosnick & Alwin, 1988; Russell & Gray, 1994). But if the number of attributes is high, respondents might be overwhelmed with the decision task which makes this approach unfeasible. In this case, a paired comparison might be appropriate. Respondents are confronted with only two profiles at the same time from which they have to choose the one they prefer. This reduces the cognitive load of a single decision task significantly. Nevertheless, with an increase size of different profiles, the amount of decisions the respondent has to make rises as well, which again might cause problems regarding information overload (Malhotra, 1982). The third alternative of constructing conjoint questions is the rating-based method. Using this method, respondents receive profiles which they have to rate individually without considering other potential stimuli combinations (Green & Srinivasan, 1990). Therefore, experiments typically use 7-point, 9-point or 11-point scales (see e.g. Bruns et al., 2008; Patzelt & Shepherd, 2009; Shepherd et al., 2000; Choi & Shepherd, 2004; Murnieks et al., 2011 and Preston & Colman, 2000 for a discussion on the optimal number of response categories in rating scales). A question might e.g. be "How would you rate the likelihood of buying the product with the following features? Please rate on a scale from '1' (Not at all likely) to '5' (Very likely)." A potential downside of this method is the possibility, that respondents rate all profiles identically without using discriminant decision rules (see e.g. Krosnick & Alwin, 1988; Russell & Gray, 1994). Despite this threat, rating methods are the most commonly used method in conjoint analysis (Wittink & Cattin, 1989; Shepherd & Zacharakis, 1999). All in all, the final choice of the response type is largely situation-specific and depends on the design of a specific experiment. In addition to the response type, the experimenter has to decide upon how to phrase the questions semantically so that the to-be-tested construct is captured appropriately (difference between e.g. asking about which product they would rate better vs. asking about which product they would buy).

The next step in designing a conjoint experiment is to define an experimental design. Here, the main question is how many stimuli combinations to include in the experiment. If the experimenter chooses a full factorial design, the survey instrument contains all possible combinations of attribute levels. Thus, a full-profile experiment with e.g. six attributes at two levels would require 2^6=64 different profiles which had to be rated by the participant. Fortunately, experimental theory demonstrated that it is not necessary to adopt a full factorial design with all possible attribute level combinations in order to estimate main effects and first-order interactions appropriately. It is possible to design a fractional factorial design, i.e. include only a limited number of all possible profiles while still maintain orthogonality (absence of correlation) among the partial utility estimates (Green, 1974; Shepherd & Zacharakis, 1999; Box et al., 2005). But the higher the degree of reduction with respect to the possible attribute level combinations, the less interaction effects can be modeled. Hence, researchers have to make a trade-off when selecting a fractional factorial design. They have to weigh the benefits of using a particular fractional factorial design against the losses in precision when using such a design. However, the losses in precision should be of no significant consequence. According to Louviere et al. (2000), main effects typically account for 70 to 90 percent of the explained variance, two way interactions for 5-15 percent and higher order interaction for the remaining variance. Therefore, it is not surprising that most scholars are only interested in examining main effects and at most first-order interactions. Now, coming back to the initial example, it is possible to reduce the amount of needed profiles from $2^6=64$ to 32, 16 or even 8 (with 8 profiles causing some serious problems in the estimation of the main effects). Different types of fractional factorial designs can be found in the literature (Hahn & Shapiro, 1966; Addelman, 1962; Box et al., 2005). Nevertheless, the use of a particular type of design largely depends on the purpose of the study. Besides the use of fraction factorial designs, literature also discusses other topics on the experimental design of conjoint experiments, like e.g. the use of Pareto-optimally designed stimulus sets (Huber & Hansen, 1986; Moore & Holbrook, 1990) or the use of random sampling for creating stimulus descriptions (Green & Srinivasan, 1978). But as those aspects are only of minor importance for this study, it will not further elaborate on them but refer to literature on this topic.

The final important design question of conjoint analysis is what survey medium to use. The experimenter can generally choose between personal interviews, phone interviews, computer or internet-based surveys and paper-based surveys. Even though this decision might seem to be of minor relevance, it can help to ensure a smooth experimental procedure and an increased validity of the results. Depending on the decision situation, it might be useful prefer one medium over another. A conjoint experiment examining e.g. online purchase decisions of teenagers should use an online-based survey instrument in order to enhance realism. On the other hand, bank loan officers typically work with paper-based loan forms and applications (see e.g. Bruns et al., 2008), so that a paper-based method would seem appropriate in this context. In addition, the decision regarding the survey medium affects the time and thus costs of conducting such an experiment. Some types of conjoint analysis, like e.g. the adaptive conjoint approach, necessitate computer or internet-based surveys. Thus, researchers should choose a survey medium with deliberation (Shepherd & Zacharakis, 1999).

4.3 Conjoint Specifications of the Current Study

After having briefly outlined the important aspects of experiments in general and conjoint analysis as a particular experimental approach, this section will discuss the design specifications and the procedure of this study's conjoint experiment which was used to gather the necessary data for testing the previously developed hypotheses.

4.3.1 Participants

The experiment was conducted with a sample of 90 loan officers (12 female and 78 male) from 45 different German banks that were actively and regularly involved in both loan availability and loan contract term decisions at the time of the study. Initially, 152 loan officers were contacted which represents a positive response rate of 59.2% percent.

In addition, the sample was required to capture loan officers working for different types of banks as one goal of this study was to examine the effect of organizational level similarity. In Germany, the banking system is based upon three pillars: (1) private banks, (2) public banks and (3) cooperative banks. All differ in terms of ownership structure and represent different sets of goals, values and organizational cultures. Public and cooperative banks are not family influenced (i.e. family owned, family controlled or show any other form of significant family involvement) but are typically associated with the above discussed family related attitudes (see e.g. Hau & Thum, 2009 for a more detailed elaboration on the differences between those bank types). Within the group of private banks, this study differentiates between family-influenced banks and banks that are widely held because it is assumed that loan officers perceive them differently in terms of organizational level similarity. Family-influenced firms will be associated with a strong family background and distinct family-related attitudes if the loan officer perceives them as a family bank. Private widely held banks are supposed to not be associated with any form of family background nor with strong family related attitudes. Therefore, the sampling frame was organized according to those four distinct categories. Each stratum was then sampled independently in order to avoid any kind of sampling bias (like e.g. all participants from cooperative banks are younger than 30 years and participants from public banks are older than 40 years). The current sample contained 16 loan officers working for private family-controlled banks, 33 loan officers working for private widely held banks, 19 loan officers working for public banks and 22 loan officers working for cooperative banks.

Furthermore, the sample captures loan officers with a wide range of age and experience. The participants' age ranged from 24 to 62 years (mean=42.7, SD=8.7) and their experience in commercial lending ranged from 1 to 37 years (mean=15.2, SD=7.6). All of the subjects worked primarily with small and medium sized companies. The mean loan value per credit application within the last year was about 1,575,556 EUR (SD=2,879,215). Participants assessed on average about 11.6 loan applications per months (SD=12.6). This study does not investigate large loan applications as those are typically handled by a consortium of banks with separate departments in charge. Table 6 gives an overview regarding the construction of the sample.

Variable	Mean	SD
Age	42.78	8.65
Sex (dummy; 1 - male)	87%	-
Duration of Employment with Current Employer (in years)	14.15	10.10
Experience as Loan Officer (in years)	15.23	7.60
Avg. Frequency of Credit Application Evaluation (applications/month)	11.57	12.56
Avg. Amount of Credit Application Evaluation (in EUR)	1,575,556.00	2,879,215.00
Education - Secondary School (dummy)	10%	-
Education - A-Levels (dummy)	28%	-
Education - University Degree (dummy)	62%	-
Education - Ph.D. (dummy)	0%	-
Education - Postdoctoral Lecture Qualification (dummy)	0%	-
Family Status - Unmarried (dummy)	26%	-
Family Status - Married (dummy)	69%	-
Family Status - Widowed (dummy)	0%	-
Family Status - Divorced (dummy)	6%	-
Children (dummy; 1 - yes)	67%	-
Grandchildren (dummy; 1 - yes)	1%	-
Prior Family Business Experience (dummy; 1 - yes)	14%	-
Member of Family Business (dummy; 1 - yes)	8%	-

Table 6: Descriptive Statistics of the Total Sample (N=90)

4.3.2 Data Collection Procedure

Each loan officer received a paper-based survey package which included a short description of the study, detailed instructions for participation, the conjoint experiment and a post-experimental survey.

Within the conjoint experiment, loan officers were asked to evaluate a series of hypothetical medium-sized family firms with regards to the likelihood that they would support the loan application. The presented hypothetical profiles varied across eight attributes (see section 4.3.4 for a detailed description of those parameters). In order to avoid any unwanted context or framing bias, several aspects were explicitly held constant across all hypothetical companies. In addition, not keeping several parameters constant would only increase the complexity of this study probably without significantly enhancing its explanatory power. Therefore, loan officers were instructed to assume the following information to be equal for all of the subsequent hypothetical loan applications. All of the presented companies are mid-sized, second generation family firms applying for credit. They have about 80 employees and generate revenues of 10 million EUR per year. In addition, the companies have a medium sized product range with not more than 10 different products. The firms have a market share of about 10% in their markets where competition is neither intense nor weak or dull.

The financial situation of the hypothetical family firms (e.g. liquidity, profitability and capitalization) was also assumed to be identical across all profiles. Those factors have shown to always significantly influence the lending decision (see e.g. Ulrich & Arlow, 1981 or Fletcher, 1995). According to Beaulieu (1994), lenders only use information about character (which includes information about family background) when financial information is positive. Negative financial information is a deal breaker. Therefore, the current financial situation of all applications was defined as normal, i.e. either too bad to directly deny the loan nor too good to be able to grant the loan without further checking soft information.

All of the organizations apply for a loan to finance the growth of their company. More specifically, they want to finance new long-term assets i.e. property, plant and equipment. The expected return for this particular new investment can be regarded to be in line with typical market returns in this sector. All firms apply for a loan of about 500.000 EUR with a typical maturity for such investments.

Loan officers were not given any further specific information regarding the profiles. But they were explicitly advised to consider all other variables that were not included in the task description to be constant across the hypothetical profiles. Thereby, it was possible to control for other potentially confounding factors. In addition, they were asked to assume that the loan applicants represent family firms they typically assist in their day-to-day business.

In order to assure the appropriateness of the construct, a pre-test with five loan officers was conducted. The results and comments confirmed that the decision tasks and conjoint profiles were clear and appeared realistic. In order to avoid problems during the experiment, the experiment used the first decision task for practice. However, this test profile was not included in the analysis. Thereby participants did not encounter any problems in assessing the hypothetical sets of loan application profiles during the experiment.

4.3.3 Measurement of Loan Officers' Decision Making

As described previously, bank loan officers were presented with a series of hypothetical sets of experimentally controlled conjoint profiles. In order to measure the loan officers' decision making, they were asked to answer the following question: "How would you rate the probability that you would support this credit request when presented with it in your day-to-day job?" The present study used a rating-based approach to measure loan officers' decision making. In particular, loan officers had to answer the presented question on a 9-point scale anchored by "Not at all Likely" (corresponding to the score "1") and "Very Likely" (corresponding to the score "9"). Using this approach, the participants were basically asked for their behavioral intentions with respect to the lending decision which allowed making inferences regarding their actual behavior in such circumstances. In this context, Ajzen (1991) asserts that humans' behavioral intentions are the immediate antecedent of their behavior so that the measure of the loan officers' decision making within this study should be appropriate to capture the loan officers' actual decision making strategies (see Ajzen, 1985 for a more detailed elaboration on the relationship between behavioral intentions and behavior). Thus and by using the presented approach, it was possible to calculate the loan officers' implicit decision rules and thereby measure their decision making.

4.3.4 Decision Attributes

The participating loan officers were presented with loan applications which varied across eight specific decision attributes. The first three attributes were related to the degree of family influence. At this point, the F-PEC scale from Astrachan et al. (2002) was used as a reference to model the degree of family influence. According to this concept, family influence depends upon the three pillars of power, experience and culture. As the study held the generational dimension constant (all of the presented hypothetical companies were second generation family firms), it needed to include variables for power and culture. Thus, the following three family-related decision attributes were included in the conjoint profiles:

1. *Family ownership:* High (coded 0.5) – the family is the majority shareholder of the company with an ownership of more than 50% while the rest is widely held by private investors. Low (coded -0.5) – the family is a minority shareholder of the company with an ownership of not more than 25% while the rest is widely held by private investors.
2. *Family management:* High (coded 0.5) – Family members are part of the management team of the company. In addition, a family representative holds the CEO position. Low (coded -0.5) – Family members are not part of the management team of the company. Thus, the company is represented by a non-family CEO.
3. *Overlap between family values and business values:* High (coded 0.5) – The organization's culture is based on family values and guidelines. Core family values are the basis for most business operations. Low (coded -0.5) – The organization's culture is independent from family values and guidelines. Family values are not the basis for the company's operations.

Besides those three family-related decision attributes, the constructed conjoint profiles contain five general decision attributes, which have shown to be important for the loan officers' loan availability decision (see sections 3.2.2 to 3.2.6 for a more detailed elaboration on the corresponding hypotheses). Those general factors were varied as follows:

4. *Monitoring function of the board:* High (coded 0.5) – The organization's board supervises the work and the decisions by the managements. They ensure the economic interests of all investors (incl. debtholders). Low (coded -0.5) – The business does not have a board who ensures the economic interests of the investors.
5. *Experience of the CEO:* High (coded 0.5) – The CEO has above average experience in managing the company. He has shown to perform under adverse conditions. Low (coded -0.5) – The CEO has below average experience in managing the company. He did not have the chance to show that he is capable of performing under adverse conditions.
6. *Transparency:* High (coded 0.5) – The firm discloses a lot of information about the current situation of the company. The amount of disclosed information is above average in comparison to other companies in this industry. Low (coded -0.5) – The firm discloses only little information about the current situation of the company. The amount of disclosed information is below average in comparison to other companies in this industry.

7. *Level of attestation:* High (coded 0.5) – All of the disclosed financial information has been prepared and audited by independent auditors. Low (coded -0.5) – All of the disclosed financial information has been prepared by the prospective borrower and was not audited by independent auditors.
8. *Independence of collateral:* High (coded 0.5) – The company offers additional collateral that is independent of the firm's success or failure, like e.g. personal guarantees or private property. Low (coded -0.5) – The company offers additional collateral that is dependent of the firm's success or failure, like e.g. receivables or floating charges.

4.3.5 Operationalization of the Similarity Effect

The similarity between loan officers and the hypothetical loan applicants was measured at two levels, namely the individual and the organization level.

On the individual level, similarity was previously defined as the congruence between the loan officers' and the family firms' orientation toward SEW. It was hypothesized that the higher the similarity between bank loan officers and loan applicants with regards to SEW, the more likely loan officers will prefer those applicants (see section 3.3.1 for a more detailed elaboration on the hypotheses that have to be tested). Unfortunately, SEW cannot be easily measured directly as it is an multidimensional concept that captures all aspects of affective endowment that a family has with regards to the business, including aspects like the family's desire to exercise authority and control, maintain family dynasty or retain a strong family identity (Berrone et al., 2012; Gomez-Mejia et al., 2007; Stockmans et al., 2010). Most prior research relying on the SEW concept has used simplified measures of SEW, like e.g. percentage of ownership or amount of family members in the management or the board (see e.g. Gomez-Mejia et al., 2007 or Stockmans et al., 2010). As a consequence, Berrone et al. (2012) anatomized this all-encompassing concept and proposed that SEW consists of five major dimensions, which they labeled as the FIBER dimensions. As discussed previously, those are (1) family control and influence, (2) family members' identification with the firm, (3) binding social ties, (4) emotional attachment and (5) renewal of family bond to the firm through dynastic succession. In addition to defining the FIBER dimensions, Berrone et al. (2012) specified a set of items to capture the different dimension of SEW. In particular, they created a list of 27 items, which was used within this study to measure the similarity between loan officers and loan applicants with respect to the relevance of SEW. Unfortunately, the original list of items is intended to be used for surveying family members which are seen as the unit of analysis for this construct, which causes problems when trying to use it with bank loan officers as the items are family specific like e.g. "In my family business, nonfamily managers and directors are named by family members". Therefore, the question of how to rate those items had to be reframed. This was accomplished by asking loan officers to rate each item with the following question in mind: "How important would you consider the following statements if you were the owner of a family firm?" The answers were measured on a 6-point Likert scale anchored by "Not at all Important" (score 1) and "Very Important" (scored 6). This study used a 6-point scale in order to have respondents think about their preference and thus commit to one side of the scale. As rating some of the presented items requires some time, some participants might have shortened the answering process when provided with the option of using a neutral choice which would have caused a bias in the results. Hence, the author decided to use a 6-point Likert scale and to not give participants a neutral choice option. Table 7 shows all of the used items to measure the FIBER dimensions.

Dimension	No.	Item
FIBER 1: *Family Control and Influence*	(1)	The majority of the shares in my family business are owned by family members.
	(2)	In my family business, family members exert control over the company's strategic decisions.
	(3)	In my family business, most executive positions are occupied by family members.
	(4)	In my family business, nonfamily managers and directors are named by family members.
	(5)	The board of directors is mainly composed of family members.
	(6)	Preservation of family control and independence are important goals for my family business.
FIBER 2: *Identification of Family Members With the Firm*	(1)	Family members have a strong sense of belonging to my family business.
	(2)	Family members feel that the family business's success is their own success.
	(3)	My family business has a great deal of personal meaning for family members.
	(4)	Being a member of the family business helps define who we are.
	(5)	Family members are proud to tell others that we are part of the family business.
	(6)	Customers often associate the family name with the family business's products and services.
FIBER 3: *Binding Social Ties*	(1)	My family business is very active in promoting social activities at the community level.
	(2)	In my family business, nonfamily employees are treated as part of the family.
	(3)	In my family business, contractual relationships are mainly based on trust and norms of reciprocity.
	(4)	Building strong relationships with other institutions (i.e., other companies, professional associations, government agents, etc.) is important for my family business.
	(5)	Contracts with suppliers are based on enduring long-term relationships in my family business.
FIBER 4: *Family Members*	(1)	Emotions and sentiments often affect decision-making processes in my family business.
	(2)	Protecting the welfare of family members is critical to us, apart from personal contributions to the business.
	(3)	In my family business, the emotional bonds between family members are very strong.
	(4)	In my family business, affective considerations are often as important as economic considerations.
	(5)	Strong emotional ties among family members help us maintain a positive self-concept.
	(6)	In my family business, family members feel warmth for each other.
FIBER 5: *Through Dynastic Succession*	(1)	Continuing the family legacy and tradition is an important goal for my family business.
	(2)	Family owners are less likely to evaluate their investment on a short-term basis.
	(3)	Family members would be unlikely to consider selling the family business.
	(4)	Successful business transfer to the next generation is an important goal for family members.

Table 7: Items to Measure the FIBER Dimensions

In order to test the appropriateness of the used questionnaire, an exploratory factor analysis (EFA) with principal component analysis (PCA) was conducted on the 27 items using orthogonal rotation (varimax). Before conducting the actual EFA, it was tested whether the underlying data could be appropriately analyzed with PCA. In this context, the Kaiser-Meyer-Olkin (KMO) measure verified the sampling adequacy. It yielded a value of 0.72, which is good according to Kaiser (1974) and Hutcheson & Sofroniou (1999). Thus, the sample size and data should be adequate for factor analysis. In addition, Bartlett's test of sphericity revealed that correlations between items were sufficiently large for a satisfactory factor analysis, i.e. that different items are loading different factors; χ (351) = 1087, $p < 0.001$.

In a first step of the actual EFA, the eigenvalues for each component in the data were calculated in order to explore the underlying factor structure. Seven factors had eigenvalues over Kaiser's criterion of 1 explaining 66% of the variance. However, the screen plot was slightly ambiguous suggesting five to seven factors. As a consequence, parallel analysis was run to gain further confidence regarding the number of factors to extract (Horn, 1965). In this context, Hayton et al. (2004) write that "parallel analysis is one of the most accurate factor retention methods while also being one of the most underutilized in management and organizational research" (p. 191). The results of Horn's parallel analysis suggest that the number of factors within the data is five. Thus and because the FIBER construct consists of five dimensions, five factors were extracted, explaining 57% of the observed variance. Table 8 shows the factors loadings after rotation. The values of the individual items suggest that factor 1 represents the dimension of "Identification of Family Members With the Firm", factor 2 the dimension of "Emotional Attachment of Family Members", factor 3 the dimension of "Family Control and Influence", factor 4 the dimension of "Binding Social Ties" and factor 5 the dimension of "Renewal of Family Bonds Through Dynastic Succession". Hence, the questionnaire seems to appropriately measure the loan officers' attitudes toward the FIBER dimensions and therefore toward issues that are related to SEW.

In addition, the subscales of the FIBER dimension were tested for reliability. The results of this analysis suggest that all of the subscales are reliable. The Cronbach's alpha was 0.80 for the first dimension (Family Control and Influence), 0.82 for the second dimension (Identification of Family Members With the Firm), 0.67 for the third dimension (Binding Social Ties), 0.83 for the fourth dimension (Emotional Attachment of Family Members) and 0.67 for the fifth dimension (Renewal of Family Bonds Through Dynastic Succession) – see Table 8. In general, scholars remark that values greater than 0.7 indicate reliable scales (Field et al., 2012). However, Kline (1999) notes that values below 0.7 might also be acceptable, depending on the domain of research and novelty of the constructs. Thus, the used subscales within this study can be regarded to be reliable – especially when considering its exploratory character.

Having generated data about the loan officers perceived importance of the five most relevant SEW dimensions, it was feasible to derive a similarity score as a proxy to the loan officers perceived similarity. Within this study it is assumed that the higher the loan officers' perceived importance with respect to the FIBER dimensions, the higher the perceived similarity between the loan officer and family firms. Thus, the FIBER score is used as a proxy for the perceived similarity on the individual level.

Item	Varimax rotated factor loadings FIBER2	FIBER4	FIBER1	FIBER3	FIBER5
Family members feel that the family business's success is their own success.	**0.79**	-0.03	0.17	0.12	0.11
Family members have a strong sense of belonging to my family business.	**0.74**	0.11	0.19	0.01	0.18
My family business has a great deal of personal meaning for family members.	**0.73**	0.14	-0.06	0.38	0.21
Family members are proud to tell others that we are part of the family business.	**0.68**	0.20	-0.05	0.17	0.12
Customers often associate the family name with the family business's products and services.	**0.61**	0.04	0.21	0.19	0.04
Being a member of the family business helps define who we are.	**0.54**	0.25	0.13	-0.07	0.12
In my family business, affective considerations are often as important as economic considerations.	-0.03	**0.79**	0.06	-0.11	0.02
Protecting the welfare of family members is critical to us, apart from personal contributions to the business.	0.18	**0.71**	0.15	-0.12	-0.01
In my family business, family members feel warmth for each other.	0.27	**0.70**	-0.02	0.17	0.05
In my family business, the emotional bonds between family members are very strong.	0.33	**0.69**	0.11	0.06	0.20
Emotions and sentiments often affect decision-making processes in my family business.	-0.12	**0.69**	0.28	-0.03	0.13
Strong emotional ties among family members help us maintain a positive self-concept.	0.22	**0.64**	0.02	0.39	0.15
In my family business, family members exert control over the company's strategic decisions.	0.37	0.17	**0.72**	-0.12	0.12
In my family business, nonfamily managers and directors are named by family members.	0.09	-0.17	**0.68**	0.17	0.00
The board of directors is mainly composed of family members.	-0.02	0.37	**0.64**	-0.11	-0.03
In my family business, most executive positions are occupied by family members.	0.15	0.32	**0.63**	-0.19	-0.02
The majority of the shares in my family business are owned by family members.	0.22	0.23	**0.53**	0.21	**0.44**
Preservation of family control and independence are important goals for my family business.	0.11	0.33	**0.49**	0.21	**0.43**
In my family business, contractual relationships are mainly based on trust and norms of reciprocity.	-0.04	0.03	0.31	**0.69**	0.14
Building strong relationships with other institutions (i.e., other companies, professional associations, government agents, etc.) is important for my family business.	0.03	-0.06	-0.05	**0.67**	0.10
In my family business, nonfamily employees are treated as part of the family.	0.19	0.00	-0.11	**0.62**	-0.35
Contracts with suppliers are based on enduring long-term relationships in my family business.	0.21	0.10	0.15	**0.58**	0.04
My family business is very active in promoting social activities at the community level.	0.13	-0.02	-0.25	**0.55**	-0.02
Successful business transfer to the next generation is an important goal for family members.	0.14	0.06	-0.13	0.05	**0.76**
Family members would be unlikely to consider selling the family business.	0.10	0.14	0.31	-0.08	**0.70**
Continuing the family legacy and tradition is an important goal for my family business.	0.35	0.10	-0.06	-0.04	**0.66**
Family owners are less likely to evaluate their investment on a short-term basis.	0.15	-0.04	0.34	0.29	**0.41**
Eigenvalues	3.63	3.62	2.97	2.67	2.43
Proportion of variance	0.13	0.13	0.11	0.10	0.09
α	0.80	0.82	0.67	0.83	0.67

Table 8: Results of the Exploratory Factor Analysis for the FIBER Questionnaire (N=90)

On the organizational level, it was hypothesized that the bank loan officers' perceived similarity between the company they work for and loan applicants with respect to the SEW orientation will be positively related to debt availability. To test this hypothesis, the present study used a rough proxy for the organizational level similarity in the form of the bank type. As stated earlier in this thesis, loan officers from four different types of banks participate in this study. It is suggested that loan officers working for private family-owned banks will perceive a high level of organizational similarity, while loan officers from widely held private banks will perceive a low organizational level similarity and thus disfavor firms with a high family influence. Public and cooperative banks are assumed to show a high level of similarity with family firms in regards to their SEW orientation as a result of their specific ownership and governance structure (see Hau & Thum, 2009 for a more detailed elaboration on the differences between those bank types). Therefore, a dummy variable was introduced to account for potential differences in similarity between those two organizational groups, i.e. widely held private banks with a low SEW orientation (group 1 – coded '1') vs. private family-owned banks, public banks and cooperative banks who show a high SEW orientation (group 2 – coded '0'). The use of this proxy was reassured by extensive consultation with various loan officers and academics.

4.3.6 Operationalization of the Framing and Environmental Context Effect

In order to test the research hypotheses presented in section 3.3.2, it is necessary to examine loan officers' credit availability decisions under different frames, namely a positive and a negative one. Within this experiment, the general economic environment was used as a framing instrument as it allowed to efficiently test both the hypothesis regarding the framing effect as well as the one regarding the environmental context effect proposed in section 3.3.3. Therefore, 46 loan officers (representing 51.1% of the total sample) were told that the current economic environment is positive. Consequently, they were supposed to evaluate the series of hypothetical family firms under the assumption that the national economy booms, the unemployment rate declines, the bankruptcy rate is at a relatively low level and that this situation will last for the next 24 months. All other participants (44 loan officers) received a negatively framed survey package which asked them to assess the hypothetical businesses under the assumption that the national economy stagnates, the unemployment rate rises, the bankruptcy rate is at a relatively high level and that this situation will last for the next 24 months. The positive scenario was coded 0.5, whereas the negative scenario was coded -0.5 (see sections 3.3.2 and 3.3.3 for more information about the hypothesized effects of framing and the environmental context).

All other parameters were held constant across both scenarios. Therefore, loan officers' should not rate the families' influence of the prospective borrower differently in relative terms if they are rational decision makers in a neoclassical sense. Hence, any deviation between the positively and negatively framed groups would reveal the hypothesized framing, respectively environmental context effect.

4.3.7 Control Variables

Several general control variables were included in the analysis in order to account for other potential sources of variance in the loan officers' decision making. In the following, those factors will be described briefly:

1. *Sex:* Bellucci et al. (2011) report that male and female loan officers decide differently. So, they argue that male loan officers exhibit higher risk tolerance and overconfidence while female loan officers are more inclined to process soft information like e.g. information about family background. Hence, gender might explain some of the observed variance which made it necessary to control for this factor. Within the study, a dummy variable for gender was used. Male loan officers were coded '1'; female loan officers were coded '0'.
2. *Age:* Andersson (2004) argues that loan officers' experience influences their decision making. He points to the possibility that the effect might be related to age rather than years of lending experience. Therefore, the demographic variable age is included as a control.
3. *Family status:* As pointed out earlier in this thesis, the similarity between the loan officer and the applicant might play an important role in the loan officers' decision making. Therefore, the loan officers' family status was included in the analysis as e.g. unmarried loan officers might perceive a lower similarity with family firms than married ones. It has to be mentioned that family status was only used as a control variable and not as a measure for similarity because the family status does not provide sufficient information regarding the loan officers' perceived similarity with respect to the importance of SEW. A loan officer might very well perceive himself as a family person and have a high preference for SEW while not being married. Thus, dummy variables for unmarried, married, widowed and divorced loan officers were included in the study to control for any potential variance. However, the econometric analysis only used the dummy variable for married loan officers to account for differences in the family status. The other related dummy variables were not used because of the composition of the sample, which made the inclusion of variable like e.g. the one for widowed loan officers useless (26% unmarried, 69% married, 0% widowed and 6% divorced; see descriptive statistics in Table 6).
4. *Children:* Since the fact that loan officers have children might cause them to perceive a higher level of similarity (though at a superficial level like their family status), a control variable was included in the current study. Hence, loan officers having children were coded '1' while loan officers without children were coded '0'.
5. *Grandchildren:* A control variable for loan officers' having grandchildren was also included in the study. This again results from the consideration that loan officers' with

grandchildren might value SEW more than those without grandchildren and thus perceive a higher similarity with family firms that have a high level of family involvement. Nevertheless, just like with the previous two control variables, loan officers' grandchildren are a vague proxy for the perceived similarity with regards to SEW, which is why it was only used as a control variable.

6. *Education:* Cohen & Cohen (1983) suggest that people with a greater level of education in an applicable field have a broader base of articulable knowledge and thus possess greater skills with respect to communication and problem-solving. In addition, Camerer & Johnson (1991) demonstrated that experts tend to use more contingent decision rules, i.e. considering interactions between different decision cues. As education is a very general aspect of expertise or human capital, which might explain some of the observed variance of the current study, it was included as a control variable. From a technical perspective, dummy variables for secondary school level, A-levels, university degree, PhD and postdoctoral lecture qualification were included in the post experimental survey. In addition, the participants were given the chance to specify another educational background that wasn't initially thought of by including the field "other education". The appraisal of the data showed that all answers in the field "other education" could be assigned to the category "university degree" (those loan officers attended a bank-owned and bank-specific college). Within the econometric analysis of the empirical material, the dummy variable "Higher Education" (i.e. at least a university degree) was used to account for differences in human capital. The other dummy variables for the factor of education were not used because of the composition of the sample, which made the inclusion of e.g. the variable for a Ph.D. superfluous (10% secondary school, 28% A-levels and 62% university degree; see descriptive statistics in Table 6).
7. *Experience as a loan officer:* As discussed in the last paragraph, expertise might significantly influence loan officers' decision making and therefore explain some of the observed variance. The participants' experience in the position of a loan officer is a proxy for their specific knowledge and thus human capital. Bruns et al. (2008) even found evidence that specific human capital is more important in explaining lending behavior than general human capital like e.g. education. Hence, the lending experience of the loan officers was included as a control variable in the present study. It is measured by the years that the participant is working as a loan officer. In addition, variables for the average amount of loan applications that loan officers have to assess and the average loan size that they process were included. Those are additional indicators for the loan officers' experience in lending.
8. *Prior employment with family firms:* Loan officers who previously worked for family firms might be biased in their decision making. They are assumed to have stronger beliefs about family firms and the attributes related to those types of businesses. Thus, a

dummy variable for the loan officers' prior employment by a family firm was included in the study. It was coded '1' if the loan officer was previously employed by a family firm (current employer not included) and '0' if the loan officer did not work for a family firm prior to his current employment.

9. *Member of a family firm:* Finally, the dummy variable "member of a family firm" was included. It was coded '1' if the loan officer is a member of a family business and '0' if the loan officer is not involved in a family firm. It was assumed that loan officers who are part of a family firm have stronger beliefs about such businesses and thus rate them differently. Hence, this study had to control for this factor in order to minimize the bias or error term within the analysis.

4.3.8 Experimental Design

The hypothetical company profiles that had to be evaluated by bank loan officers within this study alter across eight attributes with each attribute varying at two levels – high and low. Thus, a full factorial design for this study would comprise $2^8=256$ hypothetical profiles representing different parameter combinations every participant would have had to appraise. Besides the fact that assessing that many profiles would be an overwhelming task for all participants (Green & Srinivasan, 1990), such a design causes other problems like e.g. a bias toward non-compensatory decision rules which would distort this study's results (see e.g. Biggs et al., 1985). Consequently, this study does not use a full factorial design, but rather a fractional factorial design. More specifically, an 8_{IV}^{8-4}-design was employed in order to minimize the necessary profiles loan officers had to assess while at the same time being able to test all of the previously defined hypotheses (Box et al., 2005). This approach reduced the number of distinct profile combinations to 16. Choosing a design with a resolution of IV makes it possible to test each main effect and selected two-way interactions. In such a design, no main effects are aliased with any other main effect or two way interaction, but two factor interactions might be confounded with other two way or higher order interactions (see Montgomery, 2009). Therefore, non-hypothesized higher order effects should not bias this study's estimated effects (Louviere, 1988).

In addition, the 16 unique loan application profiles were replicated resulting in a total of 32 profiles that had to be evaluated by each loan officer. Duplicating the original profiles allowed estimating the individuals' decision consistency and thus using an additional measure of reliability within the final statistical analysis (Shepherd, 1999; Shepherd et al., 2000; Bruns et al., 2008). The resulting 32 profiles were randomly assigned for every participant in order to avoid any order effects which might have biased the loan officers' assessments. Finally, a practice case was included at the beginning of the conjoint section which familiarized loan officers' with the format and the evaluation task. It was not included in the subsequent analysis.

In effect, this experimental design allowed to effectively test the previously developed hypotheses without wasting resources as would have been the case with a full factorial design or a fractional factorial design with a higher resolution.

4.4 Data Analysis

According to Shepherd & Zacharakis (1999), data from conjoint based methods can be analyzed by two statistical methods, namely regression analysis and analysis of variance (ANOVA). However, the generated 90 x 32 = 2,880 data points are not independent from each other as every 32 decisions are nested within one individual. These might differ from other individuals' decisions as those might hold different experiences, values and/or mental models. Due to this circumstances, it is likely, that the generated data is characterized by autocorrelation, i.e. individual-level variance (Patzelt et al., 2011), which makes it difficult to apply standard OLS regression as proposed by Shepherd and Zacharakis (see also Monsen et al., 2010). As a consequence, scholars that currently conduct conjoint experiments tend to use HLM to analyze the generated data sets as this approach allows for an appropriate assessment of data that is subject to autocorrelation and to some extent heteroscedasticity, i.e. differences in variability between different individuals (see e.g. Bruns et al., 2008; Shepherd, 1999 or Patzelt & Shepherd, 2009). Patzelt et al. (2011) even note that HLM is the "state-of-the-art method to evaluate conjoint data" (p. 810). Nevertheless, Field et al. (2012) remark that scholars should not automatically rely on HLM but rather assess the need for it in the first place in order to avoid unnecessary steps and complexity within the analysis of the empirical data as standard general linear models (e.g. OLS, ANOVA) are much easier to handle than a HLM approach. In order to evaluate the need for a HLM model to accurately analyze the data set at hand, the fit of a general least squares model (model1.01 and model1.02) was compared to that of a multilevel linear model (model1.11 and model1.12) with respect to the underlying data. In particular, the intercept only models (model1.01 vs. model1.11) were compared to each other as well as the main effects models (model1.02 vs. model1.12). The results are shown in Table 9. In both cases, the Akaike information criterion (AIC) and the Bayesian information criterion (BIC), which represent measures of the relative goodness of fit of a statistical model, improve when using a multilevel linear model. In addition, this improvement is statistically highly significant ($p < 0.0001$). Hence, it is advisable to use a HLM approach to analyze the generated data.

Name	Model	df	AIC	BIC	logLik	Test	L.Ratio	p-value
model1.01	1	2	11,990.30	12,002.23	-5,993.15			
model1.11	2	3	11,739.74	11,757.63	-5,866.87	1 vs 2	252.56	<.0001
Name	**Model**	**df**	**AIC**	**BIC**	**logLik**	**Test**	**L.Ratio**	**p-value**
model1.02	1	10	10,093.47	10,153.13	-5,036.74			
model1.12	2	11	9,347.61	9,413.23	-4,662.81	1 vs 2	747.86	<.0001

Table 9: Comparison between the General Linear Model and the Multilevel Model

For reference, the hierarchical data of the present study consists of two levels. The first level (level-1) includes the individuals' decisions while the second level (level-2) describes the characteristics of the individuals, i.e. e.g. their age, family status and the type of employer. Consequently, the hypotheses regarding the main effects and the interaction effect will be tested on the basis of level-1 while level-2 will be incorporated to test the other hypotheses and control for any other effects.

Before modeling the observed decision policies on an aggregated level, regression analysis was used to examine each loan officer's decision policies in order to ensure the reliability of the used construct to measure their preferences. In this regard, test-retest checks of the individual decision policies were conducted by comparing the participants' decisions on the 16 original with the 16 replicated profiles computing Pearson R correlations. This helped to test whether the participants performed the decision tasks consistently. In case of the present experiment, the large majority of the individual assessments (representing 94.4 percent) were statistically significant ($p < 0.001$) with a mean R^2 of 0.83. This is generally in line with other comparable studies that used this approach like e.g. Bruns et al. (2008) who had a sample with 90.4% of individual statistically significant models and a mean R^2 of 0.83, Patzelt & Shepherd (2008) who looked at data where 97% of the individual assessments were statistically significant and had a mean R^2 of 0.85 or others (see Choi & Shepherd, 2004; Shepherd, 1999). In addition, 99 percent of the loan officers (equals 89 loan officers) were significantly reliable in their responses ($p < 0.05$). The overall mean test-retest Pearson R-correlation for the collected sample was 0.82, which again is consistent with the calculated values that have been published in recent similar studies (see e.g. Patzelt & Shepherd, 2008; Choi & Shepherd, 2004; Shepherd, 1999; Bruns et al., 2008; Monsen et al., 2010). This finding indicates that loan officers performed the decision tasks across the conjoint profile consistently and that their decisions represent a high explanatory ability.

Furthermore, it has to be mentioned that all level-2 variables have been centered, i.e. transformed into deviations around a fixed point. In this case, the grand mean of the respective variable was used as the centering point, so that the overall mean of a particular variable was subtracted from each individual score of that variable. This procedure is called grand mean centering and aims to (1) facilitate interpretation of the results and (2) reduce the amount of multicollinearity among the covariates with the associated fixed effects, i.e. main effects, in the model in order to ensure unbiased estimates of the level-1 estimates (Hofmann & Gavin, 1998; Field et al., 2012; for a more detailed review on the topic of centering see e.g. Enders & Tofighi, 2007; Kreft et al., 1995 or Kreft & Leeuw, 1998). Moreover, Field et al. (2012) note that multilevel models with centered predictors tend to be more stable and that the calculated estimates can be treated as essentially independent from each other. Further, Enders & Tofighi (2007) recommend using grand mean centering if the focus of a study is to examine level-2 variables while controlling for level-1 covariates which is an essential part of this study (see similarity and framing effects). Hence, the analysis of the gathered data is based on grand mean centered level-2 variables.

5 Results

Within this chapter, the empirical results of the previously described conjoint-experiment will be presented. However, it has to be noted that this part of the thesis will focus only on results that relate to the leading research question and to the to-be-tested hypotheses in order to ensure clarity and to not lose the plot of this study. In addition, this section only includes a description of the generated results. The discussion of the results will follow in the next chapter.

5.1 Main Effects

The results of the analysis regarding the main effects are presented in Table 10. For each of the included decision attributes, the tables present the standardized coefficients, the corresponding standard error, the t-ratio and the level of significance which is indicated by asterisks or a dagger ("†" if $p < 0.1$; "*" if $p < 0.05$; "**" if $p < 0.01$ and "***" if $p < 0.001$). The computed results reveal that all of the main decision attributes are positively and significantly related to the loan officers' credit availability decisions ($p < 0.001$). In other words, the higher the (1) family ownership, (2) family involvement within the firms' management, (3) connection between the family values and the business values, (4) the monitoring function of the board, (5) the experience of the loan officer, (6) the level of transparency, (7) the level of attestation and (8) the independence of the additionally offered collateral, the more positively loan officers rate those companies in terms of the loan availability decision. Hence, the hypotheses H1a, H2a, H3a, H4, H5, H6, H7 and H8 are generally supported by the empirical material. On the other hand, the hypotheses H1b, H2b and H3b which predicted a negative relationship between the level of family involvement and the loan officers' credit availability decisions could not be supported and are thus to be rejected. This is not surprising as H1b, H2b and H3b were defined as complements to H1a, H2a and H3a, so that only one set of hypotheses could hold true. In case of this particular study, with its previously described sample, the underlying data suggests that loan officers tend to associate rather positive characteristics with family influence than negative ones. However, the effect size of family-related decision attributes tends to be lower than the effect size of the general decision attributes i.e. the monitoring function of the board, the experience of the CEO, the level of transparency, the level of attestation and the independence of the collateral. Only the effect of the monitoring function of the board ($\beta = 0.3979$) is found to be relatively low in comparison to the level of family involvement in terms of ownership ($\beta = 0.6479$) and management ($\beta = 0.4688$). The connection between the family values and the business values has the lowest impact on loan officers credit availability decisions ($\beta = 0.3535$).

Evaluation Criteria	Coefficient	Std.Error	t-ratio	
Intercept	5.1399	0.0685	75.0139	***
Main effects				
Family Ownership	0.6479	0.0438	14.8011	***
Family Management	0.4688	0.0438	10.7082	***
Family-Based Values	0.3535	0.0438	8.0748	***
Monitoring Board	0.3979	0.0438	9.0901	***
Experience of the CEO	1.4715	0.0438	33.6158	***
Transparency	1.3368	0.0438	30.5382	***
Level of Attestation	1.0271	0.0438	23.4628	***
Independence of Collateral	1.1688	0.0438	26.6991	***
("†" if p < 0.1; "*" if p < 0.05; "**" if p < 0.01 and "***" if p < 0.001)				

Table 10: Results of the Main Effects

5.2 Moderating Effects

In section 3.3, it was proposed that the loan officers' decision making process and the related main effects are moderated by (1) the loan officers' perceived similarity on an individual level, (2) the loan officers' perceived similarity on an organizational level and (3) the type of frame respectively environmental context under which the loan officer makes his or her decisions. The corresponding results regarding those moderating effects are presented in Table 11. The loan officers perceived similarity between them and loan applicants was assumed to depend on the loan officers' attitude toward the FIBER dimensions under the hypothetical case that they would be part of a family firm. Based on the gathered data, it can be concluded that the loan officers' attitudes regarding the first four FIBER dimensions (family control and influence, family members' identification with the firm, binding social ties and emotional attachment) have no significant direct effect on their credit availability decisions (see FIBER1 to FIBER4 in Table 11). Nevertheless, the fifth FIBER dimension, i.e. the importance of generational stability, displays a statistically significant direct effect on loan officers' credit availability decision ($\beta = 0.2328$; $p < 0.1$). Thus, loan officers that place great importance on the SEW dimension of dynastic succession tend to rate loan applications more positively on an overall level. In addition, the importance of the dimension of generational stability is found to positively moderate the effect of family ownership on the loan officers' credit availability decision ($\beta = 0.1467$; $p < 0.1$). Put differently, the results suggest that the higher the loan officers' attitude regarding the importance of generational stability, the higher the likelihood that loan officer will prefer family firms with a higher degree of family involvement with respect to family ownership, i.e. firms that are more similar to themselves in that they display a similar attitude toward the relevance of the generational FIBER dimension.

Evaluation Criteria	Coefficient	Std.Error	t-ratio
Moderating effects			
Similarity effects			
Individual level			
FIBER1 - Control	-0.1387	0.1102	-1.2585
FIBER2 - Identification	-0.0313	0.1062	-0.2949
FIBER3 - Social Ties	0.1339	0.1155	1.1599
FIBER4 - Emotional Attachment	0.1566	0.1069	1.4655
FIBER5 - Generational Stability	0.2328	0.1257	1.8515 †
Family Ownership x FIBER1	0.0923	0.0704	1.3110
Family Ownership x FIBER2	-0.0207	0.0679	-0.3050
Family Ownership x FIBER3	0.1089	0.0738	1.4765
Family Ownership x FIBER4	0.0016	0.0683	0.0232
Family Ownership x FIBER5	0.1467	0.0803	1.8257 †
Family Management x FIBER1	0.1503	0.0704	2.1341 *
Family Management x FIBER2	0.0599	0.0679	0.8828
Family Management x FIBER3	-0.0525	0.0738	-0.7119
Family Management x FIBER4	-0.0161	0.0683	-0.2365
Family Management x FIBER5	-0.0797	0.0803	-0.9919
Family-Based Values x FIBER1	-0.0628	0.0704	-0.8916
Family-Based Values x FIBER2	0.0570	0.0679	0.8396
Family-Based Values x FIBER3	0.0530	0.0738	0.7191
Family-Based Values x FIBER4	0.0519	0.0683	0.7599
Family-Based Values x FIBER5	-0.0147	0.0803	-0.1831
Organizational level			
Private Non-Family Bank (dummy)	0.4624	0.1978	2.3373 *
Private Non-Family Bank x Family Ownership	-0.1829	0.1264	-1.4473
Private Non-Family Bank x Family Management	-0.2806	0.1264	-2.2203 *
Private Non-Family Bank x Family-Based Values	-0.0046	0.1264	-0.0363
Private Family-Controlled Bank (dummy)	-0.0026	0.2466	-0.0105
Private Family-Controlled Bank x Family Ownership	-0.0531	0.1575	-0.3370
Private Family-Controlled Bank x Family Management	-0.1426	0.1575	-0.9054
Private Family-Controlled Bank x Family-Based Values	0.1167	0.1575	0.7411
Framing Effects / Environmental Context Effect			
Szenario (dummy)	0.4492	0.1552	2.8938 **
Szenario (dummy) x Family Ownership	-0.0815	0.0992	-0.8215
Szenario (dummy) x Family Management	0.1126	0.0992	1.1351
Szenario (dummy) x Family-Based Values	-0.0679	0.0992	-0.6848
("†" if p < 0.1; "*" if p < 0.05; "**" if p < 0.01 and "***" if p < 0.001)			

Table 11: Results of the Moderating Effects

In addition, it was found that the first FIBER dimension which describes the importance of family control and influence moderates the effect of the degree of family involvement within the company's management on the loan officers' credit availability decisions ($\beta = 0.1503$; $p < 0.05$). In other words, the higher the loan officers' attitude regarding the importance of family control and influence under the hypothetical case that they are part of a family firm, the higher the likelihood that loan officer will prefer family firms with a higher degree of family involvement within the management of the company, i.e. firms that are more similar to themselves in that they display a similar attitude toward the relevance of family control and influence. All of the remaining FIBER dimensions did not significantly moderate any of the other family-related decision attributes ($p > 0.1$). Hence, hypothesis H9 can be only partially accepted. Only the two dimensions of family control and influence and generational stability have a significant moderating effect on the influence of the level of family ownership respectively family management on the loan officers' judgment and decision making.

Besides the impact of the perceived similarity on an individual level, it was hypothesized that loan officers' evaluation of family-related decision attributes will be moderated by the degree of perceived organizational level-similarity which was presumed to be low between firms with a high level of family influence and private non-family business banks in comparison to private family-controlled banks, public banks and cooperative banks. According to Table 11, the private non-family business bank dummy has a statistically significant positive direct effect on the loan officers' credit availability decision, stating that loan officers that work for private non-family business banks tend to evaluate loan applications in general more positively ($\beta = 0.4624$; $p < 0.05$). However, it was also found that the private non-family business bank dummy negatively moderates the effect of the level of family involvement within the company's management ($\beta = -0.2806$; $p < 0.05$), which means that loan officers that work for private non-family business banks assess an increase in the loan applicants degree of family involvement within the firm's management more negatively in comparison to loan officers who work at private family-controlled banks, public banks and/or cooperative banks. Both, the impact of the level of family ownership as well as the level of connection between the family's and company's value basis were not found to be significantly moderated by the private non-family business bank dummy.

In addition, an additional model was computed which assumes that the family-related decision attributes are assesses only in conjunction, i.e. as one variable. This is generally possible in conjoint analysis as it is a decompositional approach where part-worth utilities can be aggregated (Louviere, 1988). The aggregated value then basically equals the mean effect size of the level of family ownership, the level of family involvement within the management and the connection between the family and the business values. When concentrating the family-related decision attributes in the analysis, data shows that the impact of the level of family influence is negatively moderated by the private non-family business bank dummy on an overall level ($\beta = -0.1560$; $p < 0.05$), i.e. that loan officers working for private non-family business banks tend to assess any increase in the level of family influence negatively in comparison to loan officers who work for private family-controlled banks, public banks and/or cooperative banks.

The impact of the similarity between the borrower's and the lender's organization with respect to the family background did not have a significant effect on the evaluation of family-related decision attributes ($p > 0.1$), so that family-controlled banks do not differ from public or cooperative banks in their behavior. Thus, on an organizational level, it is the attitudinal similarity rather than the similarity of the family background that predicts loan officers' behavior toward family firms.

On the basis of these results, it can be noted that hypothesis H10b is reasonably supported by the gathered empirical material so that the bank loan officers' perceived similarity between the company they work for and loan applicants or their generic image of those with respect to SEW tends to be positively related to the loan officers willingness to support credit applications of firms with a higher degree of family involvement. Conversely, hypothesis H10a could not be supported by the empirical data, so that the similarity in the family background between the borrower and the lender's organization does not affect loan officers' behavior toward different types of family firms.

Finally, it was predicted that variations in the framing respectively environmental context of the loan officers' decision task will affect the outcome of the corresponding credit availability decisions. It was proposed that positive frames will cause loan officers to recall more positive associations with family influence and thus prefer firms with a higher degree of family involvement and vice versa. Alternatively, it was hypothesized that the influence of family-related decision attributes on the credit availability decision would be negatively affected by the environmental context, i.e. that loan officers would recall more positive associations with family influence in times of a weak economic environment and thus prefer firms with a higher degree of family involvement in such a context. The results that are presented in Table 11 show that the scenario dummy is positively related to the credit availability decision ($\beta = 0.4492$; $p < 0.01$). This means that loan officers that were presented with a positively framed experimental package (coded 0.5) were ceteris paribus generally more willing to support loan applicants in terms of granting loans. In contrast, loan officers that were presented with a negatively framed experimental package (coded -0.5) were ceteris paribus less willing to support loan applicants in terms of granting loans and rated loan applicants on average less favorable. However, when examining the interaction terms between the scenario dummy and the various family-related decision attributes, it can be observed that none of the coefficients is statistically significant ($p > 0.1$) which means that variations in the framing of the loan applications did not significantly affect the loan officers assessment of the family-related decision attributes within the context of this study's sample and its particular experimental approach. Hence, hypotheses H11a and H11b are not supported by the underlying empirical material.

5.3 Interaction Effects

The next set of hypotheses covered potential interaction effects by proposing that family-related decision attributes (family ownership, family management and the connection between the family and the company value basis) will influence the loan officers' assessment of the more general decision attributes (the monitoring board function, the CEO's experience, the level of transparency, the level of attestation and the independence of the additionally offered collateral) in the context of their loan availability decisions. The results regarding those interaction effects are presented in the following tables (Table 12 to Table 16).

Hypothesis H12a and H12b predicted an interaction effect between family-related decision attributes and the influence of the strength of the board in terms of the monitoring function. However, the empirical results do not support either of these hypotheses (p > 0.1), which is why they have to be rejected in regards to this particular sample (see Table 12).

Evaluation Criteria	**Coefficient**	**Std.Error**	**t-ratio**
Interaction effects			
Monitoring Board x Family Ownership	-0.0681	0.0875	-0.7773
Monitoring Board x Family Management	-0.0819	0.0875	-0.9360
Monitoring Board x Family-Based Values	0.0375	0.0875	0.4283
("†" if p < 0.1; "*" if p < 0.05; "**" if p < 0.01 and "***" if p < 0.001)			

Table 12: Interaction Effects between Family-Related Decision Attributes and the Monitoring Board

In addition, the hypotheses H13a and H13b, which proposed interaction effects between family-related decision attributes and the impact of the CEO's experience on the loan officers' credit availability decision, are not supported by the empirical material at hand (p > 0.1; see Table 13).

Evaluation Criteria	**Coefficient**	**Std.Error**	**t-ratio**
Interaction effects			
Experience of the CEO x Family Ownership	-0.0264	0.0876	-0.3014
Experience of the CEO x Family Management	0.0375	0.0876	0.4283
Experience of the CEO x Family-Based Values	-0.0819	0.0876	-0.9359
("†" if p < 0.1; "*" if p < 0.05; "**" if p < 0.01 and "***" if p < 0.001)			

Table 13: Interaction Effects between Family-Related Decision Attributes and the CEO's Experience

Similarly, the hypotheses H14a and H14b, which proposed interaction effects between family-related decision attributes and the impact of the level of transparency on the loan officers' credit availability decision, are not supported by the gathered data (p > 0.1; see Table 14).

Evaluation Criteria	**Coefficient**	**Std.Error**	**t-ratio**
Interaction effects			
Transparency x Family Ownership	0.0375	0.0876	0.4283
Transparency x Family Management	-0.0264	0.0876	-0.3014
Transparency x Family-Based Values	-0.0681	0.0876	-0.7772
("†" if p < 0.1; "*" if p < 0.05; "**" if p < 0.01 and "***" if p < 0.001)			

Table 14: Interaction Effects between Family-Related Decision Attributes and Transparency

However, the result of the econometric model suggest that the impact of the level of attestation on the loan officers' credit availability decisions is positively and significantly affected by the level of family influence within the company's top management team and the degree of overlap between the family's and the company's value basis (p < 0.001). In other words, the data revealed that the higher the level of family influence with respect to the company's management and the company's value basis, the higher the effect of audited information on the loan officers' credit availability decision. Nonetheless, no significant interaction effect between the level of family ownership and the degree of attestation could be found. Thus, hypothesis H15b is mainly supported by the empirical material, whereas its complement, i.e. hypothesis H15a, has to be rejected on the basis of the present sample (see Table 15).

Evaluation Criteria	Coefficient	Std.Error	t-ratio	
Interaction effects				
Level of Attestation x Family Ownership	0.0458	0.0871	0.5259	
Level of Attestation x Family Management	0.3319	0.0871	3.8091	***
Level of Attestation x Family-Based Values	0.3014	0.0871	3.4584	***
("†" if p < 0.1; "*" if p < 0.05; "**" if p < 0.01 and "***" if p < 0.001)				

Table 15: Interaction Effects between Family-Related Decision Attributes and Attestation

In addition, the analysis revealed that the hypotheses H16a and H16b, which proposed interaction effects between family-related decision attributes and the impact of the level of independence of the additionally offered collateral on the loan officers' credit availability decision, are not supported by the empirical material at hand ($p > 0.1$; see Table 16).

Evaluation Criteria	Coefficient	Std.Error	t-ratio
Interaction effects			
Independence of Collateral x Family Ownership	-0.0819	0.0876	-0.9360
Independence of Collateral x Family Management	-0.0681	0.0876	-0.7773
Independence of Collateral x Family-Based Values	-0.0264	0.0876	-0.3014
("†" if p < 0.1; "*" if p < 0.05; "**" if p < 0.01 and "***" if p < 0.001)			

Table 16: Interaction Effects between Family-Related Decision Attributes and Collateral

5.4 Controls

As mentioned earlier in this thesis, several controls have been included within the analysis. The results of the econometric model with respect to all of the control variables are presented in Table 17.

Most of these variables did not have a significant effect on the loan officers' judgment and decision making outcome. However, four controls did display a significant relationship. First, the average frequency of how often loan officers evaluate loan applications within their day-to-day job routine, has a highly significant positive direct impact on the loan officers credit availability decision ($p < 0.001$), i.e. that loan officer who usually handle a lot of loan applications tend to be more willing to grant a loan than loan officers who evaluate loan applications less frequently. Nevertheless, the effect size is rather small, which questions the relevance of this factor ($\beta = 0.0230$).

In addition, the data suggest a weakly significant negative moderating effect of age on the impact that the level of family ownership has on the loan officers' decision making policies ($p < 0.1$), i.e. the older loan officers are, the more likely they will prefer companies that display a lower level of family influence. But again, the effect size of this control variable is rather small ($\beta = -0.0177$).

Evaluation Criteria	Coefficient	Std.Error	t-ratio	
Controls				
Age	-0.0122	0.0160	-0.7597	
Sex (dummy)	-0.0909	0.2442	-0.3723	
Duration of Employment with Current Employer	-0.0058	0.0092	-0.6340	
Experience as Loan Officer	-0.0010	0.0175	-0.0557	
Avg. Frequency of Credit Application Evaluation	0.0230	0.0063	3.6682	***
Avg. Amount of Credit Application Evaluation	0.0000	0.0000	1.1805	
Higher Education (dummy)	0.1999	0.1630	1.2260	
Family status - married (dummy)	0.0878	0.2212	0.3971	
Children (dummy)	-0.3414	0.2382	-1.4332	
Grandchildren (dummy)	0.5067	0.7530	0.6730	
Prior Family Business Experience (dummy)	0.3129	0.2558	1.2231	
Member of Family Business (dummy)	0.0234	0.2856	0.0818	
Family Ownership x Age	-0.0177	0.0102	-1.7304	†
Family Ownership x Sex (dummy)	0.0632	0.1560	0.4053	
Family Ownership x Duration of Employment with Current Employer	-0.0085	0.0059	-1.4572	
Family Ownership x Experience as Loan Officer	0.0063	0.0112	0.5635	
Family Ownership x Avg. Frequency of Credit Application Evaluation	-0.0023	0.0040	-0.5765	
Family Ownership x Avg. Amount of Credit Application Evaluation	0.0000	0.0000	1.0597	
Family Ownership x Higher Education (dummy)	0.0288	0.1042	0.2761	
Family Ownership x Family status - married (dummy)	0.1447	0.1413	1.0237	
Family Ownership x Children (dummy)	-0.0046	0.1522	-0.0300	
Family Ownership x Grandchildren (dummy)	-0.1519	0.4810	-0.3158	
Family Ownership x Prior Family Business Experience (dummy)	-0.3801	0.1634	-2.3258	*
Family Ownership x Member of Family Business (dummy)	0.0597	0.1825	0.3270	
Family Management x Age	0.0032	0.0102	0.3137	
Family Management x Sex (dummy)	-0.1431	0.1560	-0.9168	
Family Management x Duration of Employment with Current Employer	0.0049	0.0059	0.8352	
Family Management x Experience as Loan Officer	-0.0148	0.0112	-1.3206	
Family Management x Avg. Frequency of Credit Application Evaluation	-0.0042	0.0040	-1.0515	
Family Management x Avg. Amount of Credit Application Evaluation	0.0000	0.0000	0.1397	
Family Management x Higher Education (dummy)	-0.1087	0.1042	-1.0434	
Family Management x Family status - married (dummy)	0.0346	0.1413	0.2448	
Family Management x Children (dummy)	0.0259	0.1522	0.1704	
Family Management x Grandchildren (dummy)	-0.1234	0.4810	-0.2565	
Family Management x Prior Family Business Experience (dummy)	0.2469	0.1634	1.5103	
Family Management x Member of Family Business (dummy)	-0.0107	0.1825	-0.0589	
Family-Based Values x Age	-0.0131	0.0102	-1.2820	
Family-Based Values x Sex (dummy)	-0.1058	0.1560	-0.6782	
Family-Based Values x Duration of Employment with Current Employer	0.0070	0.0059	1.1883	
Family-Based Values x Experience as Loan Officer	0.0095	0.0112	0.8495	
Family-Based Values x Avg. Frequency of Credit Application Evaluation	0.0059	0.0040	1.4630	
Family-Based Values x Avg. Amount of Credit Application Evaluation	0.0000	0.0000	-0.6010	
Family-Based Values x Higher Education (dummy)	-0.0666	0.1042	-0.6397	
Family-Based Values x Family status - married (dummy)	0.1626	0.1413	1.1507	
Family-Based Values x Children (dummy)	-0.1253	0.1522	-0.8233	
Family-Based Values x Grandchildren (dummy)	0.2323	0.4810	0.4829	
Family-Based Values x Prior Family Business Experience (dummy)	0.0190	0.1634	0.1161	
Family-Based Values x Member of Family Business (dummy)	-0.3034	0.1825	-1.6629	†

("†" if p < 0.1; "*" if p < 0.05; "**" if p < 0.01 and "***" if p < 0.001)

Table 17: Results of the Controls

A third control that had a significant effect on the loan officers decision making was the interaction term between the level of family ownership and the dummy for the loan officers' prior experience with family firms as an employer ($p < 0.05$). The direction of the effect is negative, which means that loan officers who had prior experience with family firms tend to disfavor loan applicants that are characterized by a high level of family ownership and vice versa. In addition, this effect is rather strong in comparison to the first two controls that had a significant effect on the loan officers' decision outcome ($\beta = -0.3801$). Finally, the study found a negative effect of the interaction term between the influence of the overlap between the family's and the company's value basis and the dummy that tests whether loan officers are part of a family firm. In other words, this result suggests that loan officers who are part of a family firm tend to favor family firms that are not strongly influenced by family values, i.e. do not display a strong overlap between the family's and the company's value basis. This effect is found to have a rather strong effect on loan officers' credit availability decisions ($\beta = -0.3034$; $p < 0.1$).

6 Discussion and Conclusion

6.1 Discussion and Interpretation of the Main Findings

The main goal of this research project was to find out whether and why lenders deal differently with various types of family firms within the context of their lending decisions and more specifically in the course of their credit availability decisions. From an overall level and with respect to the first part of the main research question, the empirical results of the underlying experimental study show that the level of family involvement has a positive direct effect on loan officers' credit availability decisions, indicating that lenders deal differently with family firms in that they tend to rather support family firms with higher levels of family influence in comparison to those where the family does not play such an integral role. The insight that family involvement has a significant effect on lenders' decisions is generally in line with the author's expectations. Nevertheless, it was not clear in which direction it would affect bank loan officers' decisions as on the one hand the extant theoretical frameworks were not able to make such specific predictions and on the other hand the currently available literature on this topic reported mixed empirical conclusions (see hypotheses H1a - H3b).

The present study provides empirical support for the notion that family involvement evokes positive associations in lenders which makes them more likely to benefit from advantageous lending policies. In particular, the results show that all of the three types of family involvement, i.e. family ownership, family participation within the top management team and the overlap between the family's and the company's value basis, exhibit a positive effect on loan officers' credit availability decisions. Thus, the present study was able to corroborate hypotheses H1a, H2a and H2b, which stated that the level of family influence within the business with respect to their ownership share (H1a), their participation in the management (H2a) and the overlap between the family's and the company's value basis (H3a) will be positively related to debt availability. Put differently, the results suggest that the higher the family ownership, the family's participation within the top management team of the company and the overlap between the family's and the company's value basis, the more positively bank loan officers will rate those companies in terms of the loan availability decision. Thus, the present study demonstrates that different types of family firms are treated heterogeneously by loan officers depending on the degree of family involvement within the prospective borrower's firm. In particular, it presents empirical evidence for the notion that family involvement evokes positive associations in lenders which makes family firms with a high level of family involvement more likely to benefit from advantageous lending policies. This finding integrates well with one part of the currently available literature which used only an agency theoretical perspective and based their findings on ex-post data sets. So, Anderson et al. (2003), Chua et al. (2011) and Bopaiah (1998) also conclude that family involvement has a positive effect on bank loan officers' decision making. Additionally, scholars from the field of marketing have as well generated evidence for the positive effect of family involvement within family firms on the perception of customers (see e.g. Craig et al., 2008; Carrigan & Buckley, 2008; Blombäck, 2009; Botero & Blombäck, 2010).

As mentioned, the level of family involvement was displayed in a differentiated way within the conjoint experiment, i.e. in terms of family ownership, family participation within the top management team and the overlap between family and business values. The results suggest that loan officers weight information regarding the level of family involvement differently depending on the type of family involvement. Information regarding the level of family ownership had the most profound effect on loan officers' credit availability decisions, followed by information regarding family management and then by information about the entanglement between the family's and the company's value basis. It is supposed that loan officers regard family ownership as the most important family-related decision attribute because it represents the original and primary source of power to exert influence on the business. The same holds true for the participation of the family within the top management team where the family can perform direct influence on the business. However, the influence of ownership is more critical as owners might decide to change the composition of the management team. Finally, it is assumed that loan officers place only minor importance to information regarding the overlap between the family's and the company's value basis, because (1) the nature of this type of family influence is rather indirect and might not be seen to be as relevant as the other types of family involvement and (2) is difficult to observe and assess in reality so that loan officers prefer to base their decisions on information they would also use in their day-to-day jobs, i.e. information about the company's ownership structure and about the composition of the management team. At this point, it has to be mentioned that the relative importance of the attributes always depends upon the specific design of a study and the chosen attribute variations (see e.g. Moskowitz et al., 2002 or Akaah & Korgaonkar, 1988). Therefore, further research is needed to confirm the presented findings regarding the relative importance of the family-related decision attributes.

Moreover, evidence was found that loan officers might be subject to the similarity bias, both with regards to the perceived similarity on an individual as well as on an organizational level. Originally, it was hypothesized that the higher the bank loan officers' perceived similarity between them and loan applicants or their generic image of those with respect to the FIBER dimensions, the more likely loan officers will prefer family firms with a higher degree of family involvement. The results suggest that loan officers who display a high attitudinal similarity with family firms regarding the importance of family control and generational stability within the company tend to favor loan applicants that are characterized by a high level of family involvement within the management of the firm or respectively by a high degree of family ownership. This finding supports our initial hypothesis. However, this effect could not be found with respect to the other dimension of the FIBER concept. It is assumed that the dimensions "family members' identification with the firm" and "emotional attachment to the firm" did not affect the loan officers' perceived similarity and thereby their credit availability decisions because of their strongly soft and complex nature which makes them hard to conceive and thereby though to include in the loan officers' judgment and decision making process. This aspect was confirmed in post-experimental conversations with some of the participating loan officer, who found it difficult to assess their attitude toward those dimensions. Furthermore, it has to be noted that loan officers are trained to focus on observable aspects and exclude emotions from business issues so that these dimensions were regarded to be irrelevant within an economic context. Thus, this might be another reason why those emotional-based similarity dimensions were not found to affect the loan officers' judgment and decision making process.

Besides the individual level-similarity, the results of the present study suggest that loan officers are susceptible to the perceived organizational-level similarity. In particular, it was hypothesized that the higher the bank loan officers' perceived similarity between the company they work for and loan applicants or their generic image of those with respect to the SEW, the more likely loan officers will prefer family firms with a higher degree of family involvement. On the basis of the assumption that private family-controlled banks, cooperative banks and public banks display a higher degree of similarity with firms that are strongly influenced by the family in comparison to private non-family banks, the present study was able to corroborate the hypothesis regarding the impact of organizational-level similarity. So, loan officers that work for banks that share important values with family firms like e.g. binding social ties or generational stability (family-controlled banks, cooperative banks and public banks), are more likely to perceive a higher level of similarity between them and prospective borrowers with a high level of family involvement and thus prefer those types of applicants.

Overall, the findings regarding the impact of the similarity bias integrate well with the currently available literature on investors' judgment and decision making processes. Bruns et al. (2008), for instance, found that loan officers' prefer borrowers that have a similar level of industry-specific experience. In addition, Murnieks et al. (2011) report that venture capitalists' decision making depends upon the cognitive similarity between investors and individual start-up teams.

A further behavioral aspect that has been investigated within this study is the impact of framing variations on the loan officers' judgment and decision making outcome. It was hypothesized that variations in the framing of a loan application would be positively related to the influence of family involvement on credit availability (H11a). Thus, when framed positively, bank loan officers were assumed to recall more positive associations with family influence and therefore prefer firms with a higher degree of family involvement. In contrast, when framed negatively, bank loan officers were supposed to recall more negative associations with family influence and thus prefer firms with a lower degree of family involvement. Supplementary, it was hypothesized that loan officers might also be inversely, i.e. negatively affected by the valence of the environmental context, which can be interpreted as a particular type of frame. Thereby, it was assumed that negative environmental contexts would cause loan officers to associate more positive characteristics with family influence and thus to prefer firms with higher degrees of family involvement (H11b). Unfortunately, none of the hypothesized effects could be supported on the basis of the underlying experimental study. Though loan officers assessed loan applications more positively on an overall level when being presented with a positive frame in comparison to a negative one, these framing variations did not affect loan officers' assessments of the different types and levels of family involvement, which means that the corresponding hypotheses could not be supported. In retrospect, it might be that loan officers were not affected by framing variations with respect to their evaluations regarding the influence of family involvement because of the type of frame that has been used. So, within the underlying conjoint experiment, the general economic environment was used as a framing instrument, which might not function as an appropriate frame to elicit positive or negative associations with different types of family firms or which causes loan officers' to associate positive or negative characteristics with all types of firms. A framing instrument that would be able to specifically elicit positive or negative associations in loan officers with respect to different types of family firms might be suitable to verify the initially stated hypothesis regarding the effect of framing variations on loan officers' assessments of alternative forms and levels of family involvement in the context of lending decisions.

Another line of investigation was focused on potential interaction effects between the family-related decision attributes and the other general decision attributes. The results of the corresponding analysis suggest that the loan officers' assessment of the level of attestation with respect to their credit availability decision will depend upon the level of family involvement. More specifically, the study found evidence that the influence of the level of attestation will increase with a higher degree of family involvement, i.e. the higher the family influence, the higher the effect on the loan officers' credit availability decision for loan applicants whose information are audited by an independent auditor. This finding is basically in line with hypothesis H15b, which predicted this effect. Thus, those results suggest that loan officer tend to require higher degrees of attestation from firms that display high levels of family involvement in comparison to firms with lower levels of family involvement. This finding is supported by existing literature that states that high family involvement is related to higher risks of moral hazard; partly as a consequence of the strong SEW orientation within these firms (see e.g. Stockmans et al., 2010 and Kellermanns et al., 2012). Stockmans et al. (2010), for instance, found that firms with a high level of family involvement will try to manipulate their earnings reports if firm performance is weak in order to communicate a better economic situation to external stakeholders and thereby protect their SEW. At this point, the present findings suggest that loan officers anticipate those upward earnings management policies by firms with high levels of family involvement and consequently tend to request audited information that verify the presented financials of these loan applicants. However, it has to be noted that the results corroborated this effect only with respect to family involvement within the company's top management team and the overlap between the family's and the company's value basis.

Family ownership did not have an impact on the loan officers' assessment of the level of attestation. This might be caused by the fact, that owners' per se are not able to e.g. manage earnings upward when firm performance is poor. Such actions can only be taken by the company's management team, which might be why loan officers did focus on this aspect of family involvement. In addition, the overlap between the family's and the company's value basis might have also been associated with a higher risk of moral hazard as the employees would tend to protect the owning family.

Besides the interaction effect between the level of attestation and the level of family involvement with regard to the top management team and the company's value basis, no other interaction effect between the three family-related (family ownership, family management and overlap between family and company values) and the further four general decision attributes (monitoring function of the board, experience of the CEO, level of transparency and the independence of the additionally offered collateral) could be identified within this particular experimental sample, which means that the hypotheses H12a, H12b, H13a, H13b, H14a, H14b, H16a and H16b could not be supported. As a consequence and based on the gathered data by this particular study, it can be concluded that the loan officers' evaluations of the monitoring function of the board, the experience of the CEO, the level of transparency and the independence of the additionally offered collateral are unlikely to depend upon the level of family involvement within the company of a potential borrower in the context of the credit availability decision. Put differently, loan officers' did not use information about the family's involvement within the company as a relevant cue to assess the value of the four general decision attributes (1) monitoring function of the board, (2) experience of the CEO, (3) level of transparency and (4) independence of the additionally offered collateral.

As seen in the literature review, the currently available literature on the topic of lending behavior toward family firms reports highly ambiguous empirical results; some scholars concluding that family involvement has a positive effect on lending decisions (Anderson et al., 2003; Chua et al., 2011; Bopaiah, 1998) while others indicating the opposite effect, i.e. a negative relationship between the level of family involvement and the loan officers' lending decisions (Niskanen et al., 2010; Bagnoli et al., 2011; Steijvers et al., 2010; Voordeckers & Steijvers, 2006; Boubakri & Ghouma, 2010; Steijvers & Voordeckers, 2009b). The present study might contribute to explain and harmonize these findings. So, the results suggest that the observed differences in the literature with respect to the conclusions about the effect of family involvement might stem from behavioral biases on the side of loan officers which have not been examined by currently available studies. In particular, the findings show that loan officers' evaluation of information about the level of family involvement within a company is subject to the similarity bias. Loan officers that display a high attitudinal similarity with family firms regarding the importance of family control and generational stability within the company, tend to favor loan applicants that are characterized by a high level of family involvement within the management of the firm or respectively by a high degree of family ownership.

Thus, the ambiguity of the results within the currently available literature might be partly explained by the similarity effect as some loan officers might evaluate the impact of family involvement positively whereas others will assess it negatively depending on the degree of attitudinal similarity between them and a particular family firm. In addition, the results suggest that an organizational level similarity bias affects the loan officers' judgment and decision making. So, loan officers that work for banks that share important values with family firms like e.g. binding social ties or generational stability, which was assumed to be the case in family-controlled banks, cooperative banks and public banks, are more likely to perceive a higher level of similarity between them and prospective borrowers with a high level of family involvement and thus prefer those types of applicants. Hence, the organizational level similarity bias might explain part of the ambiguity of empirical results within the available literature regarding the loan officers' decision making.

Figure 10 sums up the findings of the present research project with respect to the previously developed theoretical model.

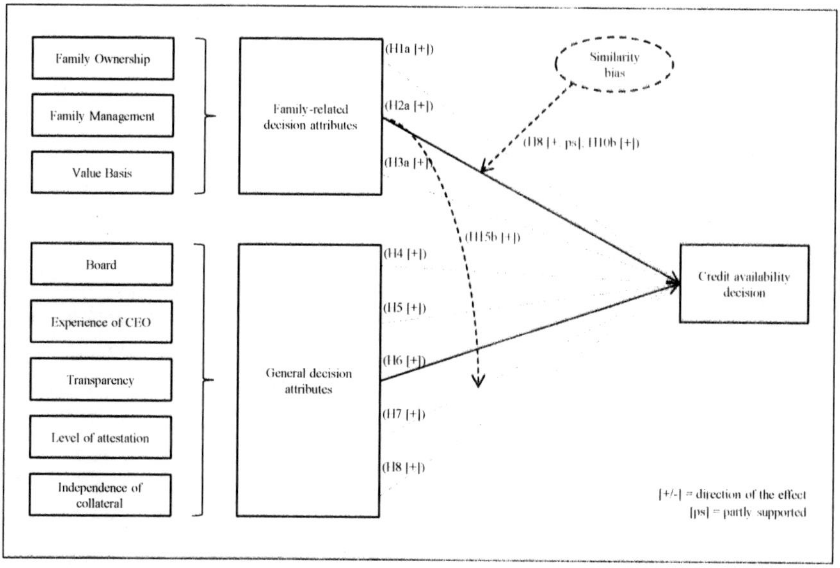

Figure 10: Visualization of Empirical Findings (Only Empirically Supported Effects)

With regards to the leading research question of whether and why lenders deal differently with distinct types of family firms it can be noted that loan officers tend to perceive family involvement as a positive factor from an overall perspective while at the same time indirectly accounting for the negative aspects that come with higher levels of family involvement in the context of their lending decisions (e.g. the threat of upward earnings management and thereby the misrepresentation of financial information). In addition, it was found that bank loan officers are susceptible to behavioral biases like the similarity bias which makes them prefer firms with a high level of family involvement more intensely when they share similar attitudes with them, especially in terms of attitudes toward the importance of control and generational stability. Thereby, the present study demonstrates on the basis of multiple theoretical concepts that and how lenders deal differently with family firms.

6.2 Contributions to Research

The findings of the present study contribute to the academic discussion within the currently available literature in several ways. In the following, the five primary contributions of this research project will be discussed.

First, this study extends the currently available literature on the topic of lending behavior toward family firms by applying new theoretical perspectives to the examination of the leading research question. Up until now, scholars that investigated the question of whether and why family involvement causes differences in lending behavior toward family firms relied solely on agency theoretical approaches while completely neglecting the value of other frameworks. However, by using this particular mono-theoretical approach, scholars implicitly assumed rational agents on the side of lenders which proved to be problematic when trying to investigate actual behavior or in this case lending behavior due to the fact that humans are not fully rational agents. Therefore, the present study adopts a behavioral economics perspective to the leading research question and focuses explicitly on the loan officers' judgment and decision making processes by applying concepts from the field of psychology. The related findings show that loan officers are not fully rational as proposed by neoclassical theories and agency theory, but rather vulnerable to systematic decision biases which explain part of the lending behavior toward family firms. In particular, the present research project found empirical evidence for the notion that loan officers are susceptible to the similarity bias, so that loan officer who perceive a higher degree of similarity between them and specific types of family firms are more likely to support those companies in the context of lending decisions. In addition, the currently available literature on the question of lending behavior toward family firms is characterized by highly ambiguous results and conclusions, so that one part of the literature argues that family involvement has a positive overall effect while the other part of the research community demonstrate the negative overall effect of family involvement on lending. Using a behavioral economics framework, the present study helps to explain part of the observed ambiguity in empirical data. According to this study, the decisions of loan officers are not fully rational as assumed by agency theory, so that not all loan officers make their lending decisions as prescribed by agency theory, but are rather vulnerable to a variety of biases, like e.g. the similarity bias that was examined within the present research project. This contribution should help scholars to better understand lending behavior toward family firms and motivate them to use distinct theoretical frameworks in order to describe loan officers' judgment and decision making more accurately as it is obviously not possible with a purely agency theoretical perspective. Besides the introduction of a behavioral orientated view, the present study complements the currently available literature on lending behavior toward family firms using insights from the SEW approach and the RBV - two important theoretical frameworks within family business research that are useful to answer the research question in focus. Moreover, it combined the SEW construct with the behavioral concept of the similarity bias to show that the higher the bank loan officers' perceived similarity between them and loan applicants or their generic image of those with respect to the FIBER dimensions, the more likely loan officers will prefer family firms with a higher degree of family involvement. To my knowledge, this is the first attempt in family business research that applied the SEW construct directly to the study of external stakeholders' behavior toward family firms. The results show that the SEW model might be more than just a way to explain family firm behavior. It might also be used to investigate the behavior of external stakeholders toward this type of business.

Second, the present study elaborated upon the topic of heterogeneity among family firms. A common approach within family business research is to treat family firms as a homogeneous group of organizations. However, scholars recently started to argue and to present evidence that the variations in behavior and performance among family firms might be even larger than those between family and non-family firms (Chua et al., 2012; Chrisman & Patel, 2012). A question that has not been addressed within the discussion about the heterogeneity of family firms is whether external stakeholders recognize variations and treat distinct types of family firms differently? As explained earlier, the answer to this question is of major importance to family firms' management, their communication with and behavior toward external stakeholders and thereby to all scholars that investigate the impact of family involvement on the behavior of stakeholders. The current findings are among the first to present empirical evidence toward this question supporting the notion that family firms are treated differently by lenders depending on the area and level of family involvement. According to the study's empirical data, loan officers favor family firms with high levels of family involvement in comparison to firms with lower levels of family influence. Additionally, the results show that all of the three examined types of family involvement, i.e. family ownership, family participation within the top management team and the overlap between family's and company's value basis, exhibit a positive effect on the loan officers credit availability decision. However, the data also suggests that loan officers weight information regarding the level of family involvement differently depending on the type of family involvement, which again emphasizes the heterogeneous nature of the impact of family involvement on external stakeholders' behavior and thus the necessity to acknowledge this aspect within future studies on this topic in order to ensure valid and useful research results.

Third, the study makes clear that not all frames are useful to elicit positive or negative associations with specific types of family firms. Initially, the authors aimed to explain part of the observed ambiguity of the empirical results within the currently available literature with the help of the concept of and the findings on the framing effect. As presented earlier, it was hypothesized that when framed positively, bank loan officers will recall more positive associations with family influence and thus prefer firms with a higher degree of family involvement and vice versa. In order to test the projection within the empirical part of the project, the general economic environment was utilized as a framing instrument. Unfortunately, it was not feasible to verify the corresponding hypothesis with this approach. Though unfortunate, it is not tragic as this non-finding also holds potentially important conclusions for researchers in that it shows that not all types of frames can be used to elicit positive or negative associations with family involvement or specific types of family firms. Future research should take this aspect into account and possibly investigate alternative frames.

Fourth, the current study expands the currently available literature by introducing alternative empirical methods to the study of lending behavior toward family firms. As seen earlier in this thesis, all of the currently available studies relied on historical data, mostly using regression analytical techniques to test the influence of family firms on lending behavior. However, the review of the empirical papers revealed potential methodological problems (especially the problem of endogeneity) that might have partly caused the high degree of ambiguity within the empirical results and might be due to the described methodological monotony within the currently available literature. As a consequence, the present research project applied a different methodology and thereby contributed to the methodological pluralism of research on the topic in focus in order to describe the loan officers' actual lending behavior more accurately, minimize the impact of methodological biases and thus increase the validity of research findings. In particular, the current study used an experimental approach to test the influence of family involvement on loan officers' judgment and decision making. As said before, endogeneity is one major threat within current research on the question in focus. In order to solve those issues, Antonakis et al. (2010) recommend the use of randomized experiments. They describe experiments as the "gold standard" or "the failsafe way to generate causal evidence". This study follows this recommendation and thereby complements the currently available empirical evidence and strengthens the argument for the positive overall effect of family involvement on loan officers' credit availability decisions.

Finally, the findings of the present study do not only contribute to the field of family business research but also to the extant literature on lending behavior in general. The findings suggest that family firm-related decision attributes are important cues for the bank loan officers' evaluation of prospective borrowers in the context of the credit availability decision. But the findings also show that information about the family's involvement within the company will most likely play a subordinate role in comparison to the traditional general decision attributes. Nevertheless, the data suggests that family-related decision attributes might play an integral role in loan officers' evaluation of general decision attributes and thereby be an important moderating variable for the traditionally discussed decision attributes. In addition, the present research project provides further empirical evidence for the impact and relevance of the humans' susceptibility to the similarity bias. Bruns et al. (2008) were the first to detect the existence of the similarity biases in the context of lending decisions. This study now strengthens these findings regarding the loan officers' vulnerability to this particular bias and additionally finds new dimensions that are relevant to the loan officers' perceived similarity between them and family firms (see selected FIBER dimensions).

Summing up, the current study contributes to the discussion regarding lending behavior toward family firms by (1) applying new theoretical perspectives to the research question, (2) starting to examine the differences in lending behavior toward varying types of family firms and thereby addressing the issue of heterogeneity of family firms, (3) analyzing the impact of two different contextual factors and (4) employing an experimental approach to generate empirical data in order to supplement the generated and currently available data sets. Thereby, it helps to close essential research gaps in the currently available literature on the question of lending behavior toward family firms. Besides those aspects, the study contributes to the literature on lending behavior in general as it (5) presents evidence for the relevance of family firm-related decision attributes and additionally strengthens the often discussed bank loan officers' susceptibility to the similarity bias.

6.3 Implications for Family Firms

Within the introduction of this thesis, it was pointed out how important bank debt is for family firms. According to pecking order theory, firms in general tend to prefer internal to external financing. However, in case of insufficient internal financial resources, firms favor debt over new external equity due to lower information costs (Myers, 1984). Authors like Coleman & Carsky (1999), Croci et al. (2011) or Poutziouris (2001) note that this relationship proves to be especially true for family firms as control is an important factor for this type of business. Additionally, Coleman & Carsky (1999) and Achleitner et al. (2011) found that family firms primarily use private bank debt, which emphasizes the importance of this source of financing. Despite its importance for family firms, little has been known about whether family involvement affects lending decisions of bank loan officers. Information about potential biases toward family firms or distinct types of family firms could help those companies to improve their chances of receiving funding by adopting appropriate actions. In the following, some specific practical implications of the present study's results will be discussed from the perspective of family firms.

Within this research project, the author found empirical evidence for the positive direct effect of the family's involvement within a company on the loan officers' judgment and decision making outcome in the context of lending decisions. So, loan officers tended to assess prospect borrowers more positively when family involvement was high in terms of family ownership, family management and the overlap between the family's and the company's value basis. Therefore, it can be assumed that loan officers tend to associate rather positive than negative characteristics with family influence. At this point, it is proposed that family firms could proactively leverage this relationship in order to enhance the chances of receiving the required funding. As mentioned previously, scholars from the field of marketing have shown that the term "family business" or "family firm" functions as category brand that can be used as a tool to communicate a company's image and thereby influence customers' perceptions of the business (see e.g. Blombäck, 2009). It was shown that this interdependency also holds true in the relationship between family firms and lenders. As a consequence, family firms are recommended to explicitly communicate the family's influence on the company in order to activate positive associations within loan officers and thereby enhance their chances of receiving funding. Numerous family firms try to separate family and business issues, concealing their roots and not mentioning the influence of the family on the company. This thesis advises family firms to highlight the family's involvement within the company in the context of loan applications, as loan officers will interpret this kind of information positively. However, it has to be noted that though those types of information enhance the overall chances of receiving loans, they do not compensate for unfavorable financials and other negative hard data. Furthermore it has to be kept in mind that the current public controversy about whether to trust in the economic system and its big corporations might have facilitated this study's findings about the positive effect of family involvement on the loan officers' credit availability decisions. Big anonymous corporations are currently seen rather critical by society. On the other hand, family firms are associated with tradition, trust, familiarity and ethical behavior – all of the things big widely held corporations are missing right now. So, maybe loan officers reacted positively to family influence in firms because of the current negative discussion about non-family firms, which made firms with strong family ties look better. However, this might change as soon as the public discussion shifts in a different direction. Therefore, family firms should be attentive to the current public image about family and non-family firms when deciding of whether or not and to what extent to communicate family involvement in the business.

In addition to this practical implication for family firms, the findings suggest that family firms should pay attention to attitudinal similarity between them and loan officers and/or the bank loan officers work for as this study found additional empirical support for the notion that loan officers are susceptible to their perceived similarity between them and loan applicants – both on an individual as well as organizational level. So, the results show that loan officers who display a high attitudinal similarity with family firms with respect to the importance of family control and generational stability tend to favor loan applicants that are characterized by a high level of family involvement within the management of the firm or the company's ownership. This observed relationship could again be used by family firms to enhance chances of receiving funding. So, family firms could try to find out about the loan officers' attitudes within conversations and use this information to choose the appropriate loan officer. However, family firms may face difficulties in observing the loan officers attitudes in reality, so that this type of information might probably only be acquired in the course of long-term relationships with lenders which would make it less relevant as in those situations other decision parameters would have become more relevant for the loan officers' decision making like e.g. relational trust that has been generated over time. Nevertheless, when family firms are able to gather information regarding the loan officers' attitudes, it could help them to either choose the appropriate loan officer or to adopt a proper communication strategy in the context of the loan application. Similarly and as mentioned previously, it was found that loan officers that work for banks that share important values with family firms like e.g. binding social ties or generational stability, which was assumed to be the case in family-controlled banks, cooperative banks and public banks, are more likely to perceive a higher level of similarity between them and prospective borrowers with a high level of family involvement and thus prefer those types of applicants. This finding holds essential implications for family firms. It can be argued that family firms should choose banks that share important attitudes and values with them as this could increase their chances of receiving funding. However, the present research does not propose that family firms should per se avoid private non-family banks, but rather approach the various potential lenders on the market differently depending on the type of bank and the degree of attitudinal similarity. Whereas highlighting the level of family involvement in negotiations with family-controlled banks, cooperative banks and public banks, family firms should carefully consider communicating strong family influence in conversations with private banks that are widely held.

Summing up the implications of the present study for family firms, family firms are recommended to proactively communicate the family's involvement within the business in the context of lending situations as lenders are likely to react positively to information regarding the level of family involvement. However, family firms should pay attention to the fact that loan officers' are susceptible to the similarity bias and thus adapt their communication strategy regarding the family's involvement depending on information regarding the attitudinal similarity between them and bank loan officers – both at an individual as well as an organizational level. If loan officers and/or the banks they work for are unlikely to share attitudes similar to those of family firms, family firms are recommended to avoid emphasizing strong family involvement. On the other hand, if loan officers and/or the bank they work for are likely to share attitudes similar to those of family firms, family firms are advised to emphasize strong family involvement.

6.4 Implications for Lenders

Besides the presented contributions to research and implications for family firms, this study also holds practical implications for lenders. In the following, some selected and specific implications of the present study's results will be discussed from the perspective of lenders.

On an overall level, the empirical results show that loan officers' judgment and decision making is influenced by the presence and degree of family involvement within the prospective borrower's company. In addition, this dissertation found evidence that this relationship can be partly attributed to decision biases or more specifically to the similarity bias which marked the focus of investigation in case of this research project. Hence, the results suggest that lending decisions are not made by computers or fully rational agents, but by human beings who are potentially susceptible to deviations from traditional neoclassical rationality and are therefore not able to always make objectively optimal decisions. However, lending organizations might not want their loan officers to be that vulnerable to decision biases as this might have negative consequences for the bank's profitability and/or their risk position (Larrick, 2007). Thus and under the assumption of a positive relationship between the level of rationality and the bank's performance, it is likely that lenders are concerned with minimizing the impact of decision biases on their employees' judgment and decision making outcome. So, in order to mitigate the impact of decision biases, literature asserts that loan officers first have to know about their vulnerability to these biases and understand them in order to make decisions more carefully and consciously and thereby reduce the risk of decision biases (Fischhoff, 1982; Bazerman, 1998). Fischhoff (1982), for instance, proposes four steps to minimize the effect of biases in general: (1) warn the decision maker about the possibility of decision biases, (2) describe the nature and direction of the decision bias, (3) provide individual feedback to decision makers and (4) train decision makers extensively. Therefore, this study provides the basis for tackling the risks of decision biases in the context of lending toward family firms as numerous behavioral biases that affect humans' judgment and decision making can be mitigated by detecting and creating awareness toward them. More specifically, the findings of the present study suggest that loan officers are susceptible to the similarity bias – both on an individual as well as organizational level, so that loan officers who display a high attitudinal similarity with family firms with respect to the importance of family control and generational stability tend to favor loan applicants that are characterized by a high level of family involvement within the management of the firm or the company's ownership. Similarly, loan officers that work for banks that share important values with family firms like e.g. binding social ties or generational stability, which was assumed to be the case in family-controlled banks, cooperative banks and public banks, are more likely to perceive a higher level of similarity between them and prospective borrowers with a high level of family involvement and thus prefer those types of applicants.

On the basis of these results, lending organizations are recommended to educate their employed loan officers about their potential vulnerability to the similarity bias in order to minimize the risks that are associated with biased judgment and decision making behavior as proposed by scholars like Fischhoff (1982). However, at this point it has to be noted that the attention toward and knowledge about potential decision biases is not a guarantee to mitigate the effect of the corresponding biases. Therefore, those attempts can rather be seen as enablers for a more rational behavior, which is why organizations should try to implement additional decision-making instruments that reduce the complexity of the specific decisions that have to be made, thereby reducing the cognitive load of decision makers which then will reduce the likelihood of behavioral biases (Bazerman, 1998). Nevertheless, the knowledge about the existence of those biases constitutes the basis for all further debiasing strategies and thus represents an essential piece of information from the lenders' perspective.

6.5 Limitations of Findings

Though the current research project used an experimental methodology which is seen as a solid way to generate causal evidence (see e.g. Antonakis et al., 2010), experiments in general and conjoint analysis in this particular case have also some limitations. And despite the fact that the study conducted the necessary attempts to address those limitations in order to minimize the impact of the related issues, the corresponding drawbacks are to be presented and discussed within this section.

First, the study relied on hypothetical cases to examine loan officers' judgment and decision making policies which might have reduced the external validity of the generated findings. However, research within the field of judgment and decision making found that hypothetical cases are a useful instrument for capturing and examining actual judgment and decision making policies (Chaput Saintonge & Hathaway, 1981; Riquelme & Rickards, 1992; Shepherd, 1999). Moreover, loan officers' judgment and decision making within their day-to-day business has a large paper component which should increase the congruence between real-world situations and the experimental setting within this study as it also used paper-based instructions and profiles (Brehmer & Brehmer, 1988; Phelps & Shanteau, 1978). In addition, the loan officers were asked about their behavioral intention with respect to the hypothetical cases which might not equal their actual behavior in real world situations and thus threaten the external validity of the study as well. At this point, Ajzen (1991) asserts that humans' behavioral intentions are the immediate antecedent of their behavior so that the related threats to external validity should not represent major problems within the present study. Please note that though the use of hypothetical cases in conjoint experiments always comes along with threats to external validity, it is still better suited to make valid inferences than those methods that have been used within the currently available literature (Shepherd, 1999; Stewart, 1993).

A further limitation of this study might lie in the presentation and design of the conjoint profiles. The conjoint profiles included only eight decision attributes and ignored other potentially relevant cues. By forcing loan officers to base their decision only upon the available information presented in the loan applications, this study might not have captured loan officers' actual decision making policies. So, bank loan officers might have attached importance to attributes only because they have been included in the profiles, which would have caused the study to pursue a self-fulfilling prophecy. In addition, the study's results might be biased because of the dichotomous presentation of the decision attributes, i.e. either high or low, as loan officers would have to first extract and clarify information regarding decision attributes in real-world situations which would cause the study to ignore perceptual requirements and processes from the loan officers' judgment and decision making. However, all those issues probably do not represent major threats and substantial problems for this study for the following reasons. First, the experiment controls for other potentially relevant decision cues within the instructions of the experiment as it lets the loan officers assume that all other potentially relevant variables are constant across the presented profiles. Second, the included decision attributes have been derived on the basis of different theories. In addition, the thereby resulting hypothetical loan applications have then been pilot tested by different experts in order to assure their appropriateness. The results confirmed the construct's face validity. Third, the potential limitation that loan officers placed importance to the decision attributes only because they have been included in the profiles is more likely to be present in conjoint experiments that examine novice decision makers and less likely with experts or experienced loan officers (Shepherd et al., 2000). As the present sample included majorly highly experienced bank loan officers, this limitation should not be of major concern for the findings of the present study. Thus, although the presented issues do represent limitations of the conjoint technique, the present study was able to mitigate any negative effect they might have by deriving the decision attributes on the basis of the theoretical literature and pilot testing the resulting hypothetical loan applications with experts from different fields.

Finally, there may also be concerns regarding the generalizability of the findings as the sample examined only judgment and decision making policies of German bank loan officers. So, Ellul et al. (2007) found that the institutional environment or the IPE, which is the way how market participants are disciplined, has a significant impact on loan officers' behavior and thus on family firms' loan availability. In addition, lending in Germany is strongly regulated and the decision power to grant loans is spread among two individuals (market and back-office). Therefore, the operations are characterized by a functional separation of trading, back-office processing and control as well as accounting and monitoring (see BaFin - Bundesanstalt für Finanzdienstleistungsaufsicht, 2010). Other countries have different regulatory laws, so that loan officers might employ different decision rules. However, as this dissertation examined only decision attributes that have a rather soft and not directly financial nature, it can be assumed that the institutional environment should not have a profound impact on loan officers' assessment regarding those informational cues. Nevertheless, replications of this study within other countries would be helpful to increase the generalizability of the present findings and rule out potential country effects.

6.6 Recommendations for Future Research

Despite the dissertation's contribution to the topic of lending behavior toward family firms, it also made clear that there is still a need for further research in order to better understand the impact of family involvement on the behavior of lenders who represent a crucially important group of stakeholders.

First, the present study examined the impact of eight specific decision attributes, three family-related and five general attributes. Though this approach was a useful starting point in the examination of loan officers' decision making toward family firms, research could benefit by examining alternative attributes and combinations of these. In particular, this study focused on the family ownership, family management and the overlap between the family's and the company's value basis, while keeping all other family-related variables constant (see section 3.2 and 4.3.4). However, the F-PEC scale defines further family-related decision attributes, like e.g. the generational stage of the family firm. In addition and due to its experimental design, the present study was only able to examine selected interaction effects between family-related and general decision attributes. Again, other potentially relevant interaction effects with alternative general decision variables might exist. More specifically, scholars are recommended to focus on general decision attributes that are related to trust or that are used to mitigate problems of distrust, just like external attestation that was used within this study which revealed a significant relationship with family-related decision attributes.

Second, future research is encouraged to study alternative frames that might elicit positive or negative associations with family involvement. This study was not able to empirically support the framing effect in the context of loan officers' decision making toward different types of family firms. The findings rather suggest that not all frames are appropriate to provoke positive or negative associations with specific types of family firms. Though unfortunate, these non-findings leave room for future research. Assuming that framing is a universal principle, it is reasonable to expect this effect to be also applicable to the study of lending behavior toward family firms. The remaining question is which frame is the appropriate one? Answering this question would hold important implication not only for practitioners but also for marketing scholars in the field of family business research.

Third, future research could replicate this study or this type of study in other countries in order to enhance the value and external validity of the related findings. As mentioned in the last section, the present thesis might be criticized with respect to the generalizability of the findings as the particular sample examined only judgment and decision making policies of German bank loan officers. Hence, scholars might improve the generalizability of the current findings by conducting this type of experiments with loan officers in other countries. This approach might also reveal differences between countries regarding the image of and external stakeholders' behavior toward different types of family firms. Research in this area might also contribute to our understanding of internal differences between family firms from distinct countries. With the underlying idea of firms adapting to their environment, this research avenue would open up the possibilities for evolutionary approaches and theories to explain differences between family and non-family firms as well as different types of family firms.

Fourth, the findings of the present study suggest that loan officers are susceptible to the similarity bias. Taking into account that the literature on behavioral economics defined numerous alternative potential biases, a wide field of research opportunities emerges. Scholars might examine the specific impact of behavioral biases in the context of lending behavior toward family firms which might help to contribute to our understanding of the topic and help to answer the question of why lenders deal differently with family firms in comparison to non-family firms and other types of family firms. In addition, scholars in the field of family business research are called to use behavioral theories in general more intensely as they provide promising paths for future research. They might help to explain external stakeholders' behavior toward family firms as well as family firm behavior. To date, only few studies in the field of family business research explicitly use concepts from behavioral economics. Recently, Chrisman & Patel (2012) used prospect theory to explain variations in R&D investments of family and non-family firms. Future research should follow this path.

Finally and as described previously, the current findings found that loan officers are influence by their perceived similarity between them and loan applicants on dimensions that are related to the SEW concept, or more specifically to the FIBER dimensions. Those findings are interesting as they reveal new perspectives of the SEW model. The results show that that the concept is applicable to the investigation of external stakeholders' attitudes and behaviors' toward family firms. Thereby they open up numerous research opportunities. Nevertheless, the study could not confirm the significant influence of all FIBER dimensions which might either be caused by the fact that loan officers do just not pay attention to them or by deficiencies in the measurement of the FIBER dimensions on the side of loan officers. Therefore, scholars are called to refine the empirical instrument to measure the FIBER dimensions – both on the level of family firms as well as on the level of external stakeholders. Advancements on this topic might also be useful for marketing scholars in the field of family business research as it would provide them with an additional tool to examine the impact of family brands on customers' behaviors, possibly arguing that people with a high FIBER measure are especially receptive to family brands.

6.7 Conclusion

This dissertation examined the impact of family firms on loan officers' judgment and decision making in the context of lending. Building upon a behavioral economics framework and complementing it with insights from the agency perspective, the SEW model and the RBV, the present study demonstrated that loan officers treat loan applicants with varying levels of family involvement differently because of the associations they make with family influence. Because it used a behavioral economics framework, this peace of research also examined the effect of family involvement on the impact of specific behavioral biases in the course of the bank loan officers' credit availability decisions. It found evidence for the existence of the similarity bias in that loan officers will prefer firms with higher levels of family involvement when they share similar attitudes that are related to the SEW concept. In addition, this dissertation showed that loan officers in Germany tend to associate positive characteristics with family involvement which is why firms with a higher level of family influence are privileged over other businesses.

Bank loans represent a primarily source of funding for firms in general, but in particular for family firms as control and the preservation of their SEW is an essential goal for these types of firms. This study makes an important contribution in that it investigates the underlying process of lending to family firms. Understanding the loan officers' judgment and decision making policies toward different types of family firms can help explain differences within this heterogeneous group of organizations. In addition, it might provide representatives of family firms with the required knowledge to enhance the chances of receiving funding and thereby increasing their economic viability.

Overall, this work extends the theoretical perspectives and empirical evidence of the currently available literature on the topic of lending behavior toward family firms (e.g., Anderson et al., 2003; Chua et al., 2011; Steijvers & Voordeckers, 2009b; Bagnoli et al., 2011). However, it has also to be noted that more research is needed to improve our understanding of the impact of family involvement on the side of a prospective borrowers on loan officers' judgment and decision making in the context of lending.

Appendix

universität Witten/Herdecke

Studie zum Thema „Entscheidungsverhalten von Firmenkundenbetreuern im Rahmen der Kreditvergabe"

Dipl. Kfm. Thomas Pijanowski (korrespondierender Autor)

Universität Witten/Herdecke (WIFU - Wittener Institut für Familienunternehmen)

Alfred-Herrhausen-Straße 50, 58448 Witten

Telefon: 02302 92 65 13, Mobil: 0163 73 41 117

E-Mail: thomas.pijanowski@uni-wh.de

Prof. Dr. Andreas Hack

WHU – Otto Beisheim School of Management (INTES Institut für Familienunternehmen)

Burgplatz 2, 56179 Vallendar, Germany

E-Mail: andreas.hack@whu.edu

Prof. Dr. Arist von Schlippe

Universität Witten/Herdecke (WIFU - Wittener Institut für Familienunternehmen)

Alfred-Herrhausen-Straße 50, 58448 Witten

E-Mail: schlippe@uni-wh.de

Fig. 1: Experimental Document - Front Page

Zweck der Studie

Die Studie untersucht, inwiefern sich **verschiedene Charakteristika von Familienunternehmen** auf die **Kreditvergabeentscheidungen von Firmenkundenbetreuern** auswirken.

Allgemeine Informationen zur Studie

Das Experiment besteht aus **zwei** Teilen. Im **ersten** Teil werden Sie gebeten, einige hypothetische Unternehmen zu bewerten. Im **zweiten** Teil werden wir Ihnen noch einige Fragen stellen, welche uns bei der Analyse der Ergebnisse helfen werden.

Das gesamte Experiment wird erfahrungsgemäß **ungefähr 30-40 Minuten dauern**. Ihre Antworten werden ausschließlich zu wissenschaftlichen Zwecken verwendet. Alle Angaben werden **streng vertraulich** und **anonym** behandelt. Bitte beantworten Sie **alle** Fragen. Wir können nur vollständig ausgefüllte Fragebogen verwenden. Setzen Sie bitte daher pro Frage immer nur ein Kreuz.

Bitte lesen Sie sich die folgende Anleitung sehr sorgfältig durch. Dies erleichtert den Ablauf und stellt die Basis für eine korrekte Analyse des Experiments dar.

VIELEN DANK FÜR IHRE TEILNAHME

AN DIESER STUDIE

Fig. 2: Experimental Document - General Information

TEIL 1 DER STUDIE

Fig. 3: Experimental Document - Separator Sheet for Part 1

Anleitung

Im Rahmen des ersten Teils dieser Studie sollen Sie eine Reihe von hypothetischen **Familienunternehmen** beurteilen, welche bei Ihnen einen Kredit beantragen. Die Familienunternehmen unterscheiden sich hierbei im Hinblick auf die folgenden acht Parameter:

- Anteil des Unternehmens in Familienbesitz
- Beteiligung der Familie im Management
- Verbindung der Unternehmenskultur mit familiären Werten
- Beirat
- Erfahrung des Geschäftsführers
- Transparenz
- Unabhängigkeit der Informationen
- Unabhängigkeit der Sicherheiten

Die einzelnen Parameter werden auf der nächsten Seite näher erläutert. Es werden Ihnen insgesamt **33 Kreditanträge** präsentiert, welche jeweils unterschiedliche Parameterkombinationen aufweisen. Sie werden gebeten je Kreditantrag zu beurteilen mit welcher Wahrscheinlichkeit Sie die Kreditanträge im Rahmen ihrer üblichen Tätigkeit unterstützen würden. Dabei antworten Sie, indem Sie auf einer Skala von 1 (Sehr gering) bis 9 (Sehr hoch) die Zahl ankreuzen, die Ihrer Einschätzung am nächsten kommt. Die 33 zu bewertenden Kreditanträge sehen grundsätzlich wie folgt aus:

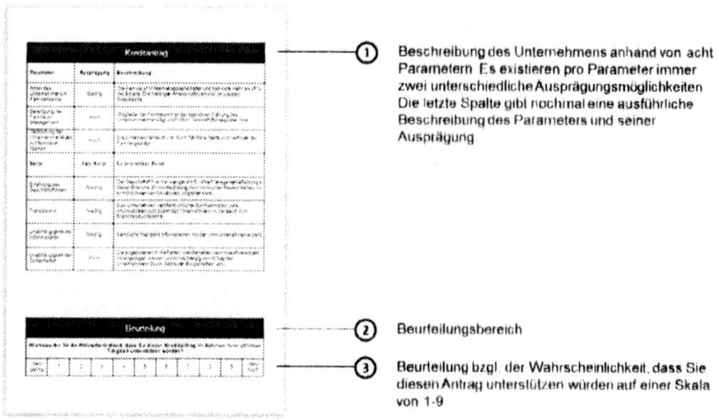

universität

Fig. 4: Experimental Document - Instructions

Variable Parameter

Wie bereits erwähnt, unterscheiden sich die Unternehmen im Hinblick auf acht Parameter. Im Folgenden finden Sie eine Übersicht über die möglichen Ausprägungen der Parameter inkl. einer kurzen Beschreibung. Die zu bearbeitenden Kreditanträge stellen unterschiedliche Kombinationen dieser Parameter dar.

Beschreibung aller variablen Parameter		
Parameter	**Ausprägung**	**Beschreibung**
Anteil des Unternehmens in Familienbesitz	Hoch	Die Familie ist Mehrheitsgesellschafter und hält mehr als 50% der Anteile. Die sonstigen Anteile befinden sich im privaten Streubesitz.
	Niedrig	Die Familie ist Minderheitsgesellschafter und hält nicht mehr als 25% der Anteile. Die sonstigen Anteile befinden sich im privaten Streubesitz.
Beteiligung der Familie im Management	Hoch	Mitglieder der Familie sind an der operativen Führung des Unternehmens beteiligt und haben Geschäftsführerposten inne.
	Niedrig	Das Unternehmen ist fremdgeführt. Geschäftsführer entstammen nicht der Familie.
Verbindung der Unternehmenskultur mit familiären Werten	Hoch	Die Unternehmenskultur ist durch familiäre Werte und Leitlinien der Familie geprägt.
	Niedrig	Die Unternehmenskultur ist unabhängig von familiären Werten und Leitlinien der Familie.
Beirat	Kontrollierender Beirat	Der Beirat überwacht die Entscheidungen der Geschäftsführung sowie die Erfüllung ihrer Aufgaben und nimmt die Interessen aller Kapitalgeber wahr.
	Kein Beirat	Es existiert kein Beirat.
Erfahrung des Geschäftsführers	Hoch	Der Geschäftsführer hat mehr als 5 Jahre Managementerfahrung in dieser Branche. Er hat gezeigt auch mit schwierigen Situationen umgehen zu können.
	Niedrig	Der Geschäftsführer hat weniger als 5 Jahre Managementerfahrung in dieser Branche. Er konnte bislang noch nicht unter Beweis stellen, ob er mit schwierigen Situationen umgehen kann.
Transparenz	Hoch	Das Unternehmen veröffentlicht überdurchschnittlich viele Informationen zum Stand des Unternehmens im Vergleich zum Branchendurchschnitt.
	Niedrig	Das Unternehmen veröffentlicht unterdurchschnittlich viele Informationen zum Stand des Unternehmens im Vergleich zum Branchendurchschnitt.
Unabhängigkeit der Informationen	Hoch	Sämtliche finanzielle Informationen wurden von unabhängigen Wirtschaftsprüfern erstellt und geprüft.
	Niedrig	Sämtliche finanzielle Informationen wurden vom Unternehmen erstellt.
Unabhängigkeit der Sicherheiten	Hoch	Die angebotenen Sicherheiten, welche neben dem Investitionsobjekt herangezogen werden, sind <u>unabhängig</u> vom Erfolg des Unternehmens (bspw. Gebäude, Bürgschaften, etc.).
	Niedrig	Die angebotenen Sicherheiten, welche neben dem Investitionsobjekt herangezogen werden, sind <u>abhängig</u> vom Erfolg des Unternehmens (bspw. Forderungen, etc.).

universität

Fig. 5: Experimental Document - Presentation of Variable Decision Attributes

Rahmenbedingungen, welche bei allen Anträgen identisch sind

Bei **allen** hier beschriebenen Unternehmen handelt es sich um mittelständische Familienunternehmen, welche sich bereits in der zweiten Generation befinden, einen **Umsatz von 10 Mio. EUR/Jahr** generieren und rund **80 Mitarbeiter** beschäftigen. Die Unternehmen fertigen grundsätzlich nicht mehr als **10 verschiedene Produkte** und haben einen **Marktanteil von 10%**. Dabei ist die **Wettbewerbssituation als normal** einzustufen. Es existiert weder ein außergewöhnlich schwacher noch intensiver Wettbewerb. Stellen Sie sich bitte bei der Beurteilung der Kreditanträge vor, dass die **gesamtwirtschaftliche Situation in Deutschland positiv** ist. Die **Wirtschaft wächst** und es wird prognostiziert, dass dies mindestens für die nächsten 24 Monate anhält. Die Arbeitslosenquote sinkt und die Anzahl der Insolvenzen befindet sich auf einem sehr niedrigen Stand.

Sämtliche Unternehmen beantragen einen Kredit für Erweiterungsinvestitionen (wie bspw. Maschinen oder Gebäude), um weiteres Wachstum zu finanzieren. Die zu erwartende Rendite des Investitionsprojekts ist dabei als branchenüblich anzusehen. Die beantragten **Kreditsummen belaufen sich allesamt jeweils auf 500 TEUR** und die Unternehmen streben eine **für solche Projekte übliche Kreditlaufzeit** an.

Die finanzielle Ausgangssituation (wie bspw. Liquidität, Ertragskraft und Eigenkapitalausstattung) ist bei allen Unternehmen ebenfalls identisch. Allerdings ist auf dieser Basis keine eindeutige Entscheidung ausmachen, d.h. die finanzielle Lage der Familienunternehmen ist weder so schlecht, dass der Kredit direkt abgelehnt werden muss noch so gut, dass der Kredit ohne weiteres genehmigt werden könnte.

Bitte gehen Sie ferner davon aus, dass **alle sonstigen Parameter, welche hier nicht erwähnt wurden,** allerdings für Ihre Kreditentscheidung von Relevanz sein könnten, ebenfalls **für alle Unternehmen konstant bzw. gleich sind**, so dass sich die nachfolgenden Kreditanträge **nur** im Hinblick auf die zuvor beschriebenen acht Parameter unterscheiden.

Bitte halten Sie sich von Augen, dass es sich stets um **mittelständische Familienunternehmen** handelt, **welche Sie typischerweise auch im Rahmen Ihrer üblichen beruflichen Tätigkeit betreuen**.

universität

Fig. 6: Experimental Document - Presentation of Fixed Decision Attributes - Positive Scenario

TEIL 1 DER STUDIE

Die **gesamtwirtschaftliche Situation** in Deutschland ist **POSITIV**. Die **Wirtschaft WÄCHST** und es wird prognostiziert, dass dies mindestens für die nächsten 24 Monate anhält. Die Arbeitslosenquote sinkt und die Anzahl der Insolvenzen befindet sich auf einem sehr niedrigen Stand.

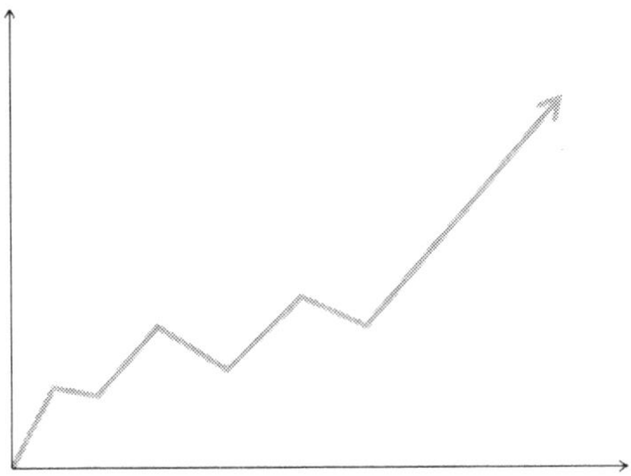

Fig. 7: Experimental Document - Frame Sheet - Positive Scenario

Rahmenbedingungen, welche bei allen Anträgen identisch sind

Bei **allen** hier beschriebenen Unternehmen handelt es sich um mittelständische Familienunternehmen, welche sich bereits in der zweiten Generation befinden, einen **Umsatz von 10 Mio. EUR/Jahr** generieren und rund **80 Mitarbeiter** beschäftigen. Die Unternehmen fertigen grundsätzlich nicht mehr als **10 verschiedene Produkte** und haben einen **Marktanteil von 10%**. Dabei ist die **Wettbewerbssituation als normal** einzustufen. Es existiert weder ein außergewöhnlich schwacher noch intensiver Wettbewerb. Stellen Sie sich bitte bei der Beurteilung der Kreditanträge vor, dass die **gesamtwirtschaftliche Situation in Deutschland negativ** ist. Die **Wirtschaft stagniert** und es wird prognostiziert, dass dies mindestens für die nächsten 24 Monate anhält. Die Arbeitslosenquote steigt und die Anzahl der Insolvenzen befindet sich auf einem relativ hohen Stand.

Sämtliche Unternehmen beantragen einen Kredit für Erweiterungsinvestitionen (wie bspw. Maschinen oder Gebäude), um weiteres Wachstum zu finanzieren. Die zu erwartende Rendite des Investitionsprojekts ist dabei als branchenüblich anzusehen. Die beantragten **Kreditsummen belaufen sich allesamt jeweils auf 500 TEUR** und die Unternehmen streben eine **für solche Projekte übliche Kreditlaufzeit** an.

Die finanzielle Ausgangssituation (wie bspw. Liquidität, Ertragskraft und Eigenkapitalausstattung) ist bei allen Unternehmen ebenfalls identisch. Allerdings ist auf dieser Basis keine eindeutige Entscheidung ausmachen, d.h. die finanzielle Lage der Familienunternehmen ist weder so schlecht, dass der Kredit direkt abgelehnt werden muss noch so gut, dass der Kredit ohne weiteres genehmigt werden könnte.

Bitte gehen Sie ferner davon aus, dass **alle sonstigen Parameter, welche hier nicht erwähnt wurden**, allerdings für Ihre Kreditentscheidung von Relevanz sein könnten, ebenfalls **für alle Unternehmen konstant bzw. gleich sind**, so dass sich die nachfolgenden Kreditanträge **nur** im Hinblick auf die zuvor beschriebenen acht Parameter unterscheiden.

Bitte halten Sie sich von Augen, dass es sich stets um **mittelständische Familienunternehmen** handelt, **welche Sie typischerweise auch im Rahmen Ihrer üblichen beruflichen Tätigkeit betreuen**.

universität

Fig. 8: Experimental Document - Presentation of Fixed Decision Attributes - Negative Scenario

TEIL 1 DER STUDIE

Die **gesamtwirtschaftliche Situation** in Deutschland ist **NEGATIV**. Die **Wirtschaft STAGNIERT** und es wird prognostiziert, dass dies mindestens für die nächsten 24 Monate anhält. Die Arbeitslosenquote steigt und die Anzahl der Insolvenzen befindet sich auf einem relativ hohen Stand.

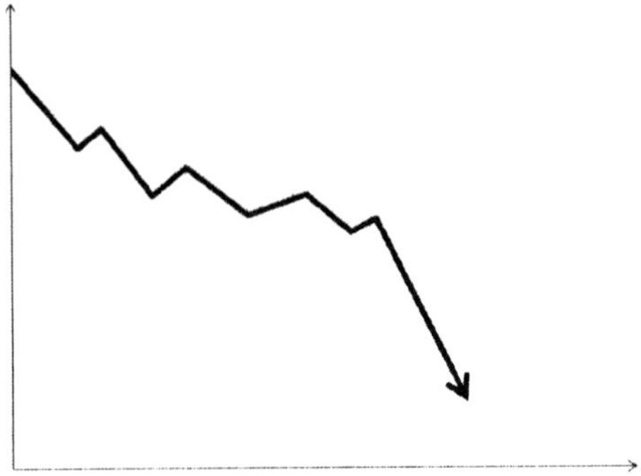

Fig. 9: Experimental Document - Frame Sheet - Negative Scenario

Kreditantrag

Parameter	Ausprägung	Beschreibung
Anteil des Unternehmens in Familienbesitz	Niedrig	Die Familie ist Minderheitsgesellschafter und hält nicht mehr als 25% der Anteile. Die sonstigen Anteile befinden sich im privaten Streubesitz.
Beteiligung der Familie im Management	Hoch	Mitglieder der Familie sind an der operativen Führung des Unternehmens beteiligt und haben Geschäftsführerposten inne.
Verbindung der Unternehmenskultur mit familiären Werten	Hoch	Die Unternehmenskultur ist durch familiäre Werte und Leitlinien der Familie geprägt.
Beirat	Kein Beirat	Es existiert kein Beirat.
Erfahrung des Geschäftsführers	Niedrig	Der Geschäftsführer hat weniger als 5 Jahre Managementerfahrung in dieser Branche. Er konnte bislang noch nicht unter Beweis stellen, ob er mit schwierigen Situationen umgehen kann.
Transparenz	Niedrig	Das Unternehmen veröffentlicht unterdurchschnittlich viele Informationen zum Stand des Unternehmens im Vergleich zum Branchendurchschnitt.
Unabhängigkeit der Informationen	Niedrig	Sämtliche finanzielle Informationen wurden vom Unternehmen erstellt.
Unabhängigkeit der Sicherheiten	Hoch	Die angebotenen Sicherheiten, welche neben dem Investitionsobjekt herangezogen werden, sind unabhängig vom Erfolg des Unternehmens (bspw. Gebäude, Bürgschaften, etc.).

Beurteilung

Wie bewerten Sie die Wahrscheinlichkeit, dass Sie diesen Kreditantrag im Rahmen ihrer üblichen Tätigkeit unterstützen würden?

Sehr gering	1	2	3	4	5	6	7	8	9	Sehr hoch

Kreditantrag 1 von 33

Fig. 10: Experimental Document - Sample of Complete Conjoint Profile and the Decision Task

TEIL 2 DER STUDIE

Auf den folgenden Seiten werden Sie gebeten einige Fragen zu beantworten, welche uns bei der Auswertung der Ergebnisse helfen werden. Bitte beantworten Sie auch hier unbedingt sämtliche Fragen. Zum Ablauf: Sie werden zunächst gebeten zu einigen Aussagen Stellung zu nehmen. Beachten Sie, dass es hier keine richtigen oder falschen Antworten gibt. Es kommt uns nur auf Ihre Meinung an. **Hier ist es äußerst wichtig, dass Sie absolut ehrlich antworten.** Abschließend sollen Sie noch Fragen zu Ihrer Person beantworten. Wir weisen darauf hin, dass all Ihre Antworten streng vertraulich und anonym behandelt werden.

universität

Fig. 11: Experimental Document - Separator Sheet for Part 2

Stellen Sie sich vor, SIE wären Familienunternehmer. Als wie wichtig würden Sie dann die folgenden Aussagen bewerten? *Kreuzen Sie dabei bitte jeweils eine Zahl von 1 (Überhaupt nicht wichtig) bis 6 (Sehr wichtig) an.*	*Überhaupt nicht wichtig*					*Sehr wichtig*
Die Mehrheit der Anteile meines Unternehmens ist im Besitz von Mitgliedern der Unternehmensfamilie.	1	2	3	4	5	6
Die Familienmitglieder üben einen maßgeblichen Einfluss auf strategische Unternehmensentscheidungen meines Familienunternehmens aus.	1	2	3	4	5	6
Die meisten leitenden Positionen in meinem Familienunternehmen werden mit Familienmitgliedern besetzt.	1	2	3	4	5	6
In meinem Familienunternehmen werden externe Manager durch die Familie ausgewählt und berufen.	1	2	3	4	5	6
Die Geschäftsführung ist überwiegend mit Mitgliedern der Familie besetzt.	1	2	3	4	5	6
Die Erhaltung der Familienkontrolle und Unabhängigkeit sind wichtige Ziele für mein Familienunternehmen.	1	2	3	4	5	6
Die Mitglieder der Familie haben ein starkes Zugehörigkeitsgefühl zu meinem Unternehmen.	1	2	3	4	5	6
Die Familienmitglieder haben das Gefühl, dass der Unternehmenserfolg auch Ihr persönlicher Erfolg ist.	1	2	3	4	5	6
Das Familienunternehmen hat eine große persönliche Bedeutung für die Familienmitglieder.	1	2	3	4	5	6
Teil des Familienunternehmens zu sein, hilft uns zu definieren, wer wir (als Individuen) sind.	1	2	3	4	5	6
Die Familienmitglieder sind stolz, wenn Sie anderen erzählen, dass wir ein Teil des Familienunternehmens sind.	1	2	3	4	5	6
Kunden verbinden oft unseren Familiennamen mit den Produkten und dem Service des Unternehmens.	1	2	3	4	5	6
Das Familienunternehmen ist sehr aktiv bei der sozialen Unterstützung von lokalen Gemeinden.	1	2	3	4	5	6
Nicht-Familienangehörige Mitarbeiter werden als Teil der Familie behandelt.	1	2	3	4	5	6
Die Geschäfte meines Familienunternehmens basieren meist auf Vertrauen und dem Grundsatz der Gegenseitigkeit.	1	2	3	4	5	6
Der Aufbau von engen und starken Beziehungen zu anderen Organisationen (anderen Unternehmen, Verbänden, etc.) ist wichtig für mein Unternehmen.	1	2	3	4	5	6
In meinem Familienunternehmen basieren Verträge mit Lieferanten auf langfristig beständigen Beziehungen.	1	2	3	4	5	6
Emotionen und Gefühle beeinflussen oft Entscheidungsfindungsprozesse in meinem Familienunternehmen.	1	2	3	4	5	6
Der Schutz des Wohlbefindens der Familienmitglieder ist neben dem Erfolg ein zentrales Ziel von unserem Familienunternehmen.	1	2	3	4	5	6
In meinem Familienunternehmen ist die emotionale Bindung zwischen den Familienmitgliedern sehr hoch.	1	2	3	4	5	6
In meinem Familienunternehmen sind gefühlsbezogene, emotionale Erwägungen ebenso wichtig wie ökonomische Faktoren.	1	2	3	4	5	6
Eine starke emotionale Bindung zwischen den Familienmitgliedern hilft uns ein positives Selbstbild aufrechtzuerhalten.	1	2	3	4	5	6
In meinem Familienunternehmen empfinden die Familienmitglieder Wärme und Zuneigung füreinander.	1	2	3	4	5	6

Fig. 12: Experimental Document - Post Experimental Questionnaire - Part 1 (FIBER)

Stellen Sie sich vor, SIE wären Familienunternehmer. Als wie wichtig würden Sie dann die folgenden Aussagen bewerten? *Kreuzen Sie dabei bitte jeweils eine Zahl von 1 (Überhaupt nicht wichtig) bis 6 (Sehr wichtig) an.*	*Überhaupt nicht wichtig*					*Sehr wichtig*
Die Fortführung des Familienerbes und des Tradition ist ein wichtiges Ziel für mein Familienunternehmen.	1	2	3	4	5	6
Die Familieneigner bewerten Investitionen nicht auf Basis von kurzfristigen Überlegungen.	1	2	3	4	5	6
Die Familienmitglieder werden einen Verkauf des Unternehmens wahrscheinlich nicht in Betracht ziehen.	1	2	3	4	5	6
Die erfolgreiche Übergabe des Unternehmens in die nächsten Generation ein wichtiges Unternehmensziel für die Familienmitglieder	1	2	3	4	5	6

Fig. 13: Experimental Document - Post Experimental Questionnaire - Part 2 (FIBER)

Wenn Sie einen neuen Job suchen müssten, wie attraktiv wäre für Sie ein Familienunternehmen als Arbeitgeber? *Kreuzen Sie dabei bitte jeweils eine Zahl von 1 (Überhaupt nicht attraktiv) bis 6 (Sehr attraktiv) an.*

Überhaupt nicht attraktiv	1	2	3	4	5	6	Sehr attraktiv

Wenn Sie einen neuen Job suchen müssten, wie attraktiv wäre für Sie eine Publikumsgesellschaft als Arbeitgeber? *Kreuzen Sie dabei bitte jeweils eine Zahl von 1 (Überhaupt nicht attraktiv) bis 6 (Sehr attraktiv) an.*

Überhaupt nicht attraktiv	1	2	3	4	5	6	Sehr attraktiv

Haben Sie schon mal für ein Familienunternehmen gearbeitet (ausgenommen ist der derzeitige Arbeitgeber)?

☐Ja	☐Nein

Sind Sie Mitglied einer Eigentümerfamilie?

☐Ja	☐Nein

Wie bewerten Sie Familienunternehmen grundsätzlich im Vergleich zu Publikumsgesellschaften?
Kreuzen Sie dabei bitte jeweils eine Zahl von 1 (Überhaupt nicht attraktiv) bis 6 (Sehr attraktiv) an.

Sehr negativ	1	2	3	4	5	6	Sehr positiv

Fig. 14: Experimental Document - Post Experimental Questionnaire - Part 3

Angaben zur Person

(1)	Geschlecht	☐weiblich ☐männlich
(2)	Alter	______ Jahre
(3)	Familienstand	☐Ledig ☐Verheiratet ☐Verwitwet ☐Geschieden
(4)	Haben Sie Kinder?	☐ja ☐nein
(5)	Haben Sie Enkel?	☐ja ☐nein
(6)	Was ist Ihr höchster Bildungsabschluss?	☐Mittlere Reife ☐Abitur ☐Hochschulabschluss ☐Promotion ☐Habilitation ☐sonstige, bitte angeben ______
(7)	Wie viele Jahre sind Sie bei Ihrem jetzigen Arbeitgeber tätig?	______ Jahre
(8)	Wie lange arbeiten Sie bereits im Firmenkundengeschäft?	______ Jahre
(9)	Wie viele Kreditanträge bearbeiten Sie im Durchschnitt pro Monat?	______ Anträge/Monat
(10)	Wie hoch sind die durchschnittlichen Kreditbeträge der Anträge, welche Sie im Rahmen Ihrer Tätigkeit üblicherweise betreuen?	______ EUR/Antrag
(11)	Für welche Art von Bank arbeiten Sie?	☐Privatbank ☐Sparkasse ☐Genossenschaftsbank
(12)	Ist Ihre Bank im Familienbesitz? (Nur beantworten, wenn Sie für eine Privatbank arbeiten)	☐ja ☐nein

universität

Fig. 15: Experimental Document - Post Experimental Questionnaire - Part 4

VIELEN DANK FÜR IHRE TEILNAHME

AN DIESER STUDIE

Fig. 16: Experimental Document - Back Page

References

Abelson, R. P., & Levi, A. (1985). Decision Making and Decision Theory. In G. Lindzey, & E. Aronson (Eds.), *Handbook of Social Psychology* (pp. 231–309). New York: Random House.

Achleitner, A.-K., Kaserer, C., Günther, N., & Volk, S. (2011). *Die Kapitalmarktfähigkeit von Familienunternehmen - Unternehmensfinanzierung über Schuldschein, Anleihe und Börsengang (Capital Market Financing of Family Firms)*. Working Paper.

Addelman, S. (1962). Symmetrical and Asymmetrical Fractional Factorial Plans. *Technometrics*, *4*, 47–58.

Ajzen, I. (1985). From Intentions to Actions: A Theory of Planned Behavior. In J. Kuhl, & J. Beckmann (Eds.), *Action Control: From Cognition to Behavior* (pp. 11–39). Berlin: Springer.

Ajzen, I. (1991). The Theory of Planned Behavior: Theories of Cognitive Self-Regulation. *Organizational Behavior and Human Decision Processes*, *50*, 179–211.

Akaah, I. P., & Korgaonkar, P. K. (1988). A Conjoint Investigation of the Relative Importance of Risk Relievers in Direct Marketing. *Journal of Advertising Research*, *28*, 38–44.

Akerlof, G. A. (1970). The Market for 'Lemons': Quality Uncertainty and the Market Mechanism. *The Quarterly Journal of Economics*, *84*, 488–500.

Alderfer, C. P. (1972). *Existence, Relatedness, and Growth: Human Needs in Organizational Settings*. New York: Free Press.

Ali, A., Chen, T.-Y., & Radhakrishnan, S. (2007). Corporate Disclosures by Family Firms: Conference Issue on Corporate Governance: Financial Reporting, Internal Control, and Auditing. *Journal of Accounting and Economics*, *44*, 238–286.

Amit, R., & Schoemaker, P. J. H. (1993). Strategic Assets and Organizational Rent. *Strategic Management Journal*, *14*, 33–46.

Anderson, R. C., Mansi, S. A., & Reeb, D. M. (2003). Founding Family Ownership and the Agency Cost of Debt. *Journal of Financial Economics*, *68*, 263–285.

Anderson, R. C., & Reeb, D. M. (2003). Founding-Family Ownership and Firm Performance: Evidence from the S&P 500. *The Journal of Finance*, *58*, 1301–1328.

Andersson, P. (2004). Does Experience Matter in Lending? A Process-Tracing Study on Experienced Loan Officers' and Novices' Decision Behavior. *Journal of Economic Psychology*, *25*, 471–492.

Antonakis, J., Bendahan, S., Jacquart, P., & Lalive, R. (2010). On Making Causal Claims: A Review and Recommendations. *The Leadership Quarterly*, *21*, 1086–1120.

Aristotle (1934). Nichomachean Ethics. In Aristotle (Ed.), *Aristotle in 23 Volumes*. Rackham transl. Cambridge: Harvard University Press.

Aronoff, C. E., & Ward, J. L. (1995). Family-Owned Businesses: A Thing of the Past or a Model for the Future? *Family Business Review*, *8*, 121–130.

Arregle, J.-L., Hitt, M. A., Sirmon, D. G., & Very, P. (2007). The Development of Organizational Social Capital: Attributes of Family Firms. *Journal of Management Studies*, *44*, 73–95.

Ashbaugh-Skaife, H., Collins, D. W., & LaFond, R. (2006). The Effects of Corporate Governance on Firms' Credit Ratings: Conference Issue on Implications of Changing Financial Reporting Standards. *Journal of Accounting and Economics*, *42*, 203–243.

Ashforth, B. E., & Humphrey, R. H. (1995). Emotion in the Workplace: A Reappraisal. *Human Relations*, *48*, 97–125.

Astrachan, J. H., Klein, S. B., & Smyrnios, K. X. (2002). The F-PEC Scale of Family Influence: A Proposal for Solving the Family Business Definition Problem. *Family Business Review*, *15*, 45–58.

BaFin - Bundesanstalt für Finanzdienstleistungsaufsicht (2010). *Mindestanforderungen an das Risikomanagement - MaRisk*. Rundschreiben 11/2010. Bonn.

Bagnoli, M., Liu, H.-T., & Watts, S. (2011). Family Firms, Debtholder–Shareholder Agency Costs and the Use of Covenants in Private Debt. *Annals of Finance*, *7*, 477–509.

Bain, J. S. (1968). *Industrial Organization*. (2nd ed.). New York: Wiley.

Bamber, M. E., & Stratton, R. A. (1997). The Information Content of the Uncertainty-Modified Audit Report: Evidence from Bank Loan Officers. *Accounting Horizons*, *11*, 1–11.

Bammens, Y., Voordeckers, W., & van Gils, A. (2011). Boards of Directors in Family Businesses: A Literature Review and Research Agenda. *International Journal of Management Reviews*, *13*, 134–152.

Banaji, M. R., & Hardin, C. D. (1996). Automatic Stereotyping. *Psychological Science*, *7*, 136–141.

Banaji, M. R., Hardin, C. D., & Rothman, A. J. (1993). Implicit Stereotyping in Person Judgment. *Journal of Personality and Social Psychology*, *65*, 272–281.

Bandyopadhyay, S. P., & Francis, J. R. (1995). The Economic Effect of Differing Levels of Auditor Assurance on Bankers' Lending Decisions. *Canadian Journal of Administrative Sciences / Revue Canadienne des Sciences de l'Administration*, *12*, 238–249.

Barney, J. B. (1991). Firm Resources and Sustained Competitive Advantage. *Journal of Management*, *17*, 99–120.

Barney, J. B. (1997). *Gaining and Sustaining Competitive Advantage*. Reading: Addison-Wesley.

Barney, J. B. (2005). Where Does Inequality Come From? The Personal and Intellectual Roots of Resource-Based Theory. In K. G. Smith, & M. A. Hitt (Eds.), *Great Minds in Management: The Process of Theory Development* (pp. 280–303). Oxford: Oxford University Press.

Barney, J. B., & Arikan, A. M. (2001). The Resource-Based View: Origins and Implications. In M. A. Hitt, R. E. Freeman, & J. S. Harrison (Eds.), *The Blackwell Handbook of Strategic Management* (pp. 124–188). Oxford: Blackwell Pub.

Baron, R. A. (2008). The Role of Affect in the Entrepreneurial Process. *Academy of Management Review, 33*, 328–340.

Bazerman, M. H. (1998). *Judgment in Managerial Decision Making.* (4th ed.). New York: John Wiley & Sons.

Beaulieu, P. R. (1994). Commercial Lenders' Use of Accounting Information in Interaction with Source Credibility. *Contemporary Accounting Research, 10*, 557–585.

Bellucci, A., Borisov, A., & Zazzaro, A. (2011). Do Male and Female Loan Officers Differ in Small Business Lending? A Review of the Literature. In G. Calcagnini, & I. Favaretto (Eds.), *The Economics of Small Businesses* (pp. 195-219). Heidelberg: Physica-Verlag HD.

Bennedsen, M., Perez-Gonzales, F., & Wolfenzon, D. (2010). The Governance of Family Firms. In H. K. Baker, & R. C. Anderson (Eds.), *Corporate Governance: A Synthesis of Theory, Research, and Practice* (pp. 371–389). Hoboken: Wiley.

Berger, A. N., & Udell, G. F. (1995). Relationship Lending and Lines of Credit in Small Firm Finance. *The Journal of Business, 68*, 351–381.

Berger, C. R. (1973). Task Performance and Attributional Communication as Determinants of Interpersonal Attraction. *Speech Monographs, 40*, 280–286.

Berger, H. S. (1997). One Risk Manager's Approach. *Commercial Lending Review, 13*, 72–74.

Berlin, M., & Mester, L. J. (1992). Debt Covenants and Renegotiation. *Journal of Financial Intermediation, 2*, 95–133.

Berrone, P., Cruz, C. C., & Gomez-Mejia, L. R. (2012). Socioemotional Wealth in Family Firms: Theoretical Dimensions, Assessment Approaches, and Agenda for Future Research. *Family Business Review, 25*, 258–279.

Berrone, P., Cruz, C. C., Gomez-Mejia, L. R., & Larraza-Kintana, M. (2010). Socioemotional Wealth and Corporate Responses to Institutional Pressures: Do Family-Controlled Firms Pollute Less? *Administrative Science Quarterly, 55*, 82–113.

Bester, H. (1985). Screening vs. Rationing in Credit Markets with Imperfect Information. *American Economic Review, 75*, 850–55.

Biggs, S. F., Bedard, J. C., Gaber, B. G., & Linsmeier, T. J. (1985). The Effects of Task Size and Similarity on the Decision Behavior of Bank Loan Officers. *Management Science, 31*, 970–987.

Bleda, P. R. (1974). Toward a Clarification of the Role of Cognitive and Affective Processes in the Similarity-Attraction Relationship. *Journal of Personality and Social Psychology, 29*, 368–373.

Blombäck, A. (2009). *Family Business: A Secondary Brand in Corporate Brand Management.* CeFEO Working Paper.

Boot, A. W. A. (2000). Relationship Banking: What Do We Know? *Journal of Financial Intermediation, 9*, 7–25.

Bopaiah, C. (1998). Availability of Credit to Family Businesses. *Small Business Economics, 11*, 75–86.

Botero, I. C., & Blombäck, A. (2010). *Leveraging the Family Brand: Using Brand Management to Highlight the Advantages of Family Firms.* Conference Paper. IFERA, Lancaster, 2010 book of proceedings. Lancaster.

Botosan, C. A. (1997). Disclosure Level and the Cost of Equity Capital. *The Accounting Review, 72*, 323–349.

Botosan, C. A., & Plumlee, M. A. (2002). A Re-examination of Disclosure Level and the Expected Cost of Equity Capital. *Journal of Accounting Research, 40*, 21–40.

Boubakri, N., & Ghouma, H. (2010). Control/Ownership Structure, Creditor Rights Protection, and the Cost of Debt Financing: International Evidence. *Journal of Banking & Finance, 34*, 2481–2499.

Box, G. E. P., Hunter, J. S., & Hunter, W. G. (2005). *Statistics for Experimenters: Design, Innovation, and Discovery.* (2nd ed.). Hoboken: Wiley.

Brehmer, A., & Brehmer, B. (1988). What Have We Learned about Human Judgment from Thirty Years of Policy Capturing? In B. Brehmer, & C. Joyce (Eds.), *Human Judgment: The SJT View* (pp. 75–114). Amsterdam: Elsevier.

Breidert, C., Hahsler, M., & Reutterer, T. (2006). A Review of Methods for Measuring Willingness-To-Pay. *Innovative Marketing, 2*, 8–32.

Brick, I. E., & Palia, D. (2007). Evidence of Jointness in the Terms of Relationship Lending. *Journal of Financial Intermediation, 16*, 452–476.

Brigham, E. F., & Ehrhardt, M. C. (2011). *Financial Management: Theory and Practice.* (13th ed.). Mason: South-Western Cengage Learning.

Brug, J., Ruiter, R. A. C., & van Assema, P. (2003). The (Ir)Relevance of Framing Nutrition Education Messages. *Nutrition and Health, 17*, 9–20.

Brunninge, O., & Melander, A. (2011). *Constructing Family Firm Identity Over Generations: The Case of the Swedish Pulp and Paper Firm MoDo 1872-1990.* JIBS Working Papers: Jönköping International Business School.

Bruns, V., & Fletcher, M. (2008). Banks' Risk Assessment of Swedish SMEs. *Venture Capital, 10*, 171–194.

Bruns, V., Holland, D. V., Shepherd, D. A., & Wiklund, J. (2008). The Role of Human Capital in Loan Officers' Decision Policies. *Entrepreneurship Theory and Practice, 32*, 485–506.

Bryman, A., & Bell, E. (2007). *Business Research Methods.* (2nd ed.). Oxford: Oxford University Press.

Burleson, B. R., & Denton, W. H. (1992). A New Look at Similarity and Attraction in Marriage: Similarities in Social-Cognitive and Communication Skills as Predictors of Attraction and Satisfaction. *Communication Monographs*, *59*, 268–287.

Buttner, E. H., & Rosen, B. (1989). Funding New Business Ventures: Are Decision Makers Biased Against Women Entrepreneurs? *Journal of Business Venturing*, *4*, 249–261.

Byrne, D. E. (1971). *The Attraction Paradigm*. New York: Academic Press.

Cabrera-Suárez, K., Saá-Pérez, P. de, & García-Almeida, D. (2001). The Succession Process from a Resource- and Knowledge-Based View of the Family Firm. *Family Business Review*, *14*, 37–48.

Camerer, C. F., & Johnson, E. J. (1991). The Process-Performance Paradox in Expert Judgment: How Can Experts Know So Much And Predict So Badly? In K. A. Ericsson, & J. Smith (Eds.), *Toward a General Theory of Expertise: Prospects and Limits* (pp. 195–217). Cambridge, New York: Cambridge University Press.

Campbell, D. T., Stanley, J. C., & Gage, N. L. (1963). *Experimental and Quasi-Experimental Designs for Research*. Boston: Houghton Mifflin.

Campbell, K. W., & Sedikides, C. (1999). Self-Threat Magnifies the Self-Serving Bias: A Meta-Analytic Integration. *Review of General Psychology*, *3*, 23–43.

Carrigan, M., & Buckley, J. (2008). 'What's so special about family business?' An exploratory study of UK and Irish consumer experiences of family businesses. *International Journal of Consumer Studies*, *32*, 656–666.

Carter, C. R., Kaufmann, L., & Michel, A. (2007a). Behavioral Supply Management: A Taxonomy of Judgment and Decision-Making Biases. *International Journal of Physical Distribution & Logistics Management*, *37*, 631–669.

Carter, S., Shaw, E., Lam, W., & Wilson, F. (2007b). Gender, Entrepreneurship, and Bank Lending: The Criteria and Processes Used by Bank Loan Officers in Assessing Applications. *Entrepreneurship Theory and Practice*, *31*, 427–444.

Cennamo, C., Berrone, P., Cruz, C. C., & Gomez-Mejia, L. R. (2012). Socioemotional Wealth and Proactive Stakeholder Engagement: Why Family-Controlled Firms Care More About Their Stakeholders. *Entrepreneurship Theory and Practice*, *36*, 1153–1173.

Chami, R. (1997). *What's Different About Family Businesses?* Working Paper.

Chaput Saintonge, D. M. de, & Hathaway, N. R. (1981). Antibiotic Use in Otitis Media: Patient Simulations as an Aid to Audit. *BMJ*, *283*, 883–884.

Chen, S., Chen, X., & Cheng, Q. (2008). Do Family Firms Provide More or Less Voluntary Disclosure? *Journal of Accounting Research*, *46*, 499–536.

Choi, Y. R., & Shepherd, D. A. (2004). Entrepreneurs' Decisions to Exploit Opportunities. *Journal of Management*, *30*, 377–395.

Chrisman, J. J., Chua, J. H., & Sharma, P. (2003). *Current Trends and Future Directions in Family Business Management Studies: Toward a Theory of the Family Firm*. Coleman Foundation White Paper Series.

Chrisman, J. J., Chua, J. H., & Sharma, P. (2005). Trends and Directions in the Development of a Strategic Management Theory of the Family Firm. *Entrepreneurship Theory and Practice, 29*, 555–576.

Chrisman, J. J., Kellermanns, F. W., Chan, K. C., & Kartono, L. (2010). Intellectual Foundations of Current Research in Family Business: An Identification and Review of 25 Influential Articles. *Family Business Review, 23*, 9–26.

Chrisman, J. J., & Patel, P. C. (2012). Variations in R&D Investments of Family and Nonfamily Firms: Behavioral Agency and Myopic Loss Aversion Perspectives. *Academy of Management Journal, 55*, 976–997.

Chrisman, J. J., Sharma, P., & Taggar, S. (2007). Family Influences on Firms: An Introduction. *Journal of Business Research, 60*, 1005–1011.

Chua, J. H., Chrisman, J. J., Kellermanns, F. W., & Wu, Z. (2011). Family Involvement and New Venture Debt Financing. *Journal of Business Venturing, 26*, 472–488.

Chua, J. H., Chrisman, J. J., & Sharma, P. (1999). Defining the Family Business by Behavior. *Entrepreneurship Theory and Practice, 23*, 19–39.

Chua, J. H., Chrisman, J. J., & Sharma, P. (2003). Succession and Nonsuccession Concerns of Family Firms and Agency Relationship with Nonfamily Managers. *Family Business Review, 16*, 89–107.

Chua, J. H., Chrisman, J. J., Steier, L. P., & Rau, S. B. (2012). Sources of Heterogeneity in Family Firms: An Introduction. *Entrepreneurship Theory and Practice, 36*, 1103–1113.

Claessens, S., Djankov, S., Fan, J. P. H., & Lang, L. H. P. (2002). Disentangling the Incentive and Entrenchment Effects of Large Shareholdings. *The Journal of Finance, 57*, 2741–2771.

Coco, G. (2000). On the Use of Collateral. *Journal of Economic Surveys, 14*, 191–214.

Cohen, J., & Cohen, P. (1983). *Applied Multiple Regression/Correlation Analysis for the Behavioral Sciences.* (2nd ed.). Hillsdale: Lawrence Erlbaum Associates.

Coleman, S., & Carsky, M. (1999). Sources of Capital for Small Family-Owned Businesses: Evidence from the National Survey of Small Business Finances. *Family Business Review, 12*, 73–85.

Comeig, I., Bediou, B., Jaramillo-Gutiérrez, A., & Sander, D. (2010). *Self-Selection in Risky Financial Decision-Making: An Experiment on Framing and "Perceived Loss" Aversion.* Working Paper.

Cooper, D. R., & Schindler, P. S. (2008). *Business Research Methods.* (10th ed.). Boston: McGraw-Hill Irwin.

Covin, T. J. (1994). Profiling Preference for Employment in Family-Owned Firms. *Family Business Review, 7*, 287–296.

Cozby, P. C. (2009). *Methods in Behavioral Research.* (10th ed.). Boston: McGraw-Hill Higher Education.

Craig, J. B., Dibrell, C., & Davis, P. S. (2008). Leveraging Family-Based Brand Identity to Enhance Firm Competitiveness and Performance in Family Businesses. *Journal of Small Business Management, 46*, 351–371.

Cressy, R., & Toivanen, O. (2001). Is There Adverse Selection in the Credit Market? *Venture Capital, 3*, 215–238.

Croci, E., Doukas, J. A., & Gonenc, H. (2011). Family Control and Financing Decisions. *European Financial Management, 17*, 860–897.

Cruz, C. C., Firfiray, S., & Gomez-Mejia, L. R. (2011). Socioemotional Wealth and Human Resource Management (HRM) in Family-Controlled Firms. In J. Martocchio, H. Liao, & A. Joshi (Eds.), *Research in Personnel and Human Resources Management* (pp. 159–217). Bingley: Emerald Group Publishing.

Cruz, C. C., Gomez-Mejia, L. R., & Becerra, M. (2010). Perceptions of Benevolence and the Design of Agency Contracts: CEO-TMT Relationships in Family Firms. *Academy of Management Journal, 53*, 69–89.

Cruz, C. C., Justo, R., & De Castro, J. O. (2012). Does Family Employment Enhance MSEs Performance? *Journal of Business Venturing, 27*, 62–76.

Cyert, R. M., & March, J. G. (1963). *A Behavioral Theory of the Firm*. Englewood Cliffs: Prentice Hall.

Daily, C. M., & Dollinger, M. J. (1991). Family Firms are Different. *Journal of Business Venturing, 13*, 3–5.

Daily, C. M., & Thompson, S. S. (1994). Ownership Structure, Strategic Posture, and Firm Growth: An Empirical Examination. *Family Business Review, 7*, 237–249.

Dalton, D. R., Daily, C. M., Ellstrand, A. E., & Johnson, J. L. (1998). Meta-Analytic Reviews of Board Composition, Leadership Structure, and Financial Performance. *Strategic Management Journal, 19*, 269–290.

Dalton, D. R., Daily, C. M., Johnson, J. L., & Ellstrand, A. E. (1999). Number of Directors and Financial Performance: A Meta-Analysis. *Academy of Management Journal, 42*, 674–686.

Damásio, A. R. (1995). *Descartes' Error: Emotion, Reason, and the Human Brain*. New York: Avon Books.

De Meza, D., & Webb, D. C. (1987). Too Much Investment: A Problem of Asymmetric Information. *The Quarterly Journal of Economics, 102*, 281–92.

de Visscher, F. M., Aronoff, C. E., & Ward, J. L. (1995). *Financing Transactions: Managing Capital and Liquidity in the Family Business*. Marietta: Business Owner Resources.

Debicki, B. J., Matherne, C. F., Kellermanns, F. W., & Chrisman, J. J. (2009). Family Business Research in the New Millennium. *Family Business Review, 22*, 151–166.

DeCarlo, J. F., & Lyons, P. R. (1979). A Comparison of Selected Personal Characteristics of Minority and Non-Minority Female Entrepreneurs. *Journal of Small Business Management, 17*, 22–28.

Degryse, H., & van Cayseele, P. (2000). Relationship Lending within a Bank-Based System: Evidence from European Small Business Data. *Journal of Financial Intermediation*, *9*, 90–109.

Dess, G. G., & Picken, J. C. (1999). *Beyond Productivity: How Leading Companies Achieve Superior Performance by Leveraging their Human Capital*. New York: American Management Association.

Devendorf, S. A., & Highhouse, S. (2008). Applicant–Employee Similarity and Attraction to an Employer. *Journal of Occupational and Organizational Psychology*, *81*, 607–617.

Distelberg, B., & Sorenson, R. L. (2009). Updating Systems Concepts in Family Businesses: A Focus on Values, Resource Flows, and Adaptability. *Family Business Review*, *22*, 65–81.

Donovan, R. J., & Jalleh, G. (1999). Positively Versus Negatively Framed Product Attributes: The Influence of Involvement. *Psychology and Marketing*, *16*, 613–630.

Drigotas, S. M. (1993). Similarity Revisited: A Comparison of Similarity-Attraction Versus Dissimilarity-Repulsion. *British Journal of Social Psychology*, *32*, 365–377.

Druckman, J. N. (2001). The Implications of Framing Effects for Citizen Competence. *Political Behavior*, *23*, 225-256.

Duck, S. W., & Craig, G. (1978). Personality Similarity and the Development of Friendship: A Longitudinal Study. *British Journal of Social and Clinical Psychology*, *17*, 237–242.

Dyer, G. W. (2006). Examining the "Family Effect" on Firm Performance. *Family Business Review*, *19*, 253–273.

Dyer, W. G., & Whetten, D. A. (2006). Family Firms and Social Responsibility: Preliminary Evidence from the S&P 500. *Entrepreneurship Theory and Practice*, *30*, 785–802.

Eddleston, K. A., & Kellermanns, F. W. (2007). Destructive and Productive Family Relationships: A Stewardship Theory Perspective. *Journal of Business Venturing*, *22*, 545–565.

Eddleston, K. A., Kellermanns, F. W., & Sarathy, R. (2008). Resource Configuration in Family Firms: Linking Resources, Strategic Planning and Technological Opportunities to Performance. *Journal of Management Studies*, *45*, 26–50.

Edwards, K. D. (1996). Prospect Theory: A Literature Review. *International Review of Financial Analysis*, *5*, 19–38.

Einhorn, H. J., & Hogarth, R. M. (1981). Behavioral Decision Theory: Processes of Judgement and Choice. *Annual Review of Psychology*, *32*, 53–88.

Einhorn, H. J., & Hogarth, R. M. (1986). Decision Making Under Ambiguity. *The Journal of Business*, *59*, S225-S250.

Eisenhardt, K. M. (1989). Agency Theory: An Assessment and Review. *The Academy of Management Review*, *14*, 57–74.

Ellul, A., Guntay, L., & Lel, U. (2007). *External Governance and Debt Agency Costs of Family Firms*. Discussion Paper. International Finance Discussion Papers: Board of Governors of the Federal Reserve System (U.S.).

Elsas, R., & Krahnen, J. P. (1998). Is Relationship Lending Special? Evidence from Credit-File Data in Germany. *Journal of Banking & Finance*, *22*, 1283–1316.

Enders, C. K., & Tofighi, D. (2007). Centering Predictor Variables in Cross-Sectional Multilevel Models: A New Look at an Old Issue. *Psychological Methods*, *12*, 121–138.

Erikson, T., Sørheim, R., & Reitan, B. (2003). Family Angels vs. Other Informal Investors. *Family Business Review*, *16*, 163–171.

Fabozzi, F. J. (2008). *Handbook of Finance*. Hoboken: John Wiley & Sons.

Fagley, N. S. (1993). A Note Concerning Reflection Effects Versus Framing Effects. *Psychological Bulletin*, *113*, 451–452.

Fahy, J., & Smithee, A. (1999). Strategic Marketing and the Resource Based View of the Firm. *Academy of Marketing Science Review*, 1–20.

Fama, E., & Jensen, M. C. (1983). Separation of Ownership and Control. *Journal of Law and Economics*, *26*, 301–325.

Fay, M., & Williams, L. (1993). Gender Bias and the Availability of Business loans. *Journal of Business Venturing*, *8*, 363–376.

Fiegener, M. K., Brown, B. M., Prince, R. A., & File, K. M. (1996). Passing on Strategic Vision: Favored Modes of Successor Preparation by CEOs of Family and Nonfamily Firms. *Journal of Small Business Management*, *34*, 15–26.

Field, A. P., Miles, J., & Field, Z. (2012). *Discovering Statistics Using R*. London, Thousand Oaks: Sage Pub.

Fink, A. (2010). *Conducting Research Literature Reviews*. (3rd ed.). Los Angeles: Sage Pub.

Fischhoff, B. (1982). Debiasing. In D. Kahneman, P. Slovic, & A. Tversky (Eds.), *Judgment Under Uncertainty: Heuristics and Biases* (pp. 422–444). Cambridge: Cambridge University Press.

Fishburn, P. C. (1970). *Utility Theory for Decision Making*. Publications in operations research. New York: Wiley.

Fletcher, M. (1995). Decision Making by Scottish Bank Managers. *International Journal of Entrepreneurial Behaviour and Research*, *1*, 37–53.

Forbes, D. P., & Milliken, F. J. (1999). Cognition and Corporate Governance: Understanding Boards of Directors as Strategic Decision-Making Groups. *Academy of Management Review*, *24*, 489–505.

Frank, L., & Hackman, R. (1975). Effects of Interviewer-Interviewee Similarity on Interviewer Objectivity in College Admissions Interviews. *Journal of Applied Psychology*, *60*, 356–360.

Franke, N., Gruber, M., Harhoff, D., & Henkel, J. (2006). What You Are Is What You Like - Similarity Biases in Venture Capitalists' Evaluations of Start-Up Teams. *Journal of Business Venturing*, *21*, 802–826.

Gamliel, E., & Peer, E. (2006). Positive versus Negative Framing Affects Justice Judgments. *Social Justice Research*, *19*, 307-322.

García-Álvarez, E., & López-Sintas, J. (2001). A Taxonomy of Founders Based on Values: The Root of Family Business Heterogeneity. *Family Business Review, 14*, 209–230.

Gedajlovic, E., Carney, M., Chrisman, J. J., & Kellermanns, F. W. (2012). The Adolescence of Family Firm Research: Taking Stock and Planning for the Future. *Journal of Management, 38*, 1010–1037.

Gilad, D., & Kliger, D. (2008). Priming the Risk Attitudes of Professionals in Financial Decision Making. *Review of Finance, 12*, 567–586.

Gilovich, T., Griffin, D., & Kahneman, D. (2002). *Heuristics and Biases: The Psychology of Intuitive Judgement*. Cambridge: Cambridge University Press.

Gomez-Mejia, L. R., Cruz, C. C., Berrone, P., & Castro, J. de (2011). The Bind that Ties: Socioemotional Wealth Preservation in Family Firms. *The Academy of Management Annals, 5*, 653–707.

Gomez-Mejia, L. R., Haynes, K. T., Nuñez-Nickel, M., Jacobson, K. J. L., & Moyano-Fuentes, J. (2007). Socioemotional Wealth and Business Risks in Family-controlled Firms: Evidence from Spanish Olive Oil Mills. *Administrative Science Quarterly, 52*, 106–137.

Gomez-Mejia, L. R., Hoskisson, R. E., Makri, M., Sirmon, D. G., & Campbell, J. (2010a). *Innovation and the Preservation of Socioemotional Wealth in Family Controlled High Technology Firms*. Unpublished Manuscript. Texas A&M University, College Station.

Gomez-Mejia, L. R., Larraza-Kintana, M., & Makri, M. (2003). The Determinants of Executive Compensation in Family-Controlled Public Corporations. *Academy of Management Journal, 46*, 226–237.

Gomez-Mejia, L. R., Makri, M., & Kintana, M. L. (2010b). Diversification Decisions in Family-Controlled Firms. *Journal of Management Studies, 47*, 223–252.

Gomez-Mejia, L. R., Nuñez-Nickel, M., & Gutierrez, I. (2001). The Role of Family Ties in Agency Contracts. *Academy of Management Journal, 44*, 81–95.

Grant, R. M. (1991). The Resource-Based Theory of Competitive Advantage: Implications for Strategy Formulation. *California Management Review, 33*, 114–135.

Graves, L. M., & Powell, G. M. (1995). The Effect of Sex Similarity on Recruiters' Evaluations of Actual Applicants: A Test of the Similarity-Attraction Paradigm. *Personnel Psychology, 48*, 85–98.

Green, P. E. (1974). On the Design of Choice Experiments Involving Multifactor Alternatives. *Journal of Consumer Research, 1*, 61–68.

Green, P. E., & Srinivasan, V. (1978). Conjoint Analysis in Consumer Research: Issues and Outlook. *Journal of Consumer Research, 5*, 103–123.

Green, P. E., & Srinivasan, V. (1990). Conjoint Analysis in Marketing: New Developments with Implications for Research and Practice. *Journal of Marketing Research, 54*, 3–19.

Greenbaum, S. I., & Thakor, A. V. (1995). *Contemporary Financial Intermediation*. Fort Worth: Dryden Press.

Guiral, A., Ruiz, E., & Choy, H. L. (2010). *Information Content of Going Concern Audit Reports and the Provision of Non-Audit Services in Credit Decisions: A Lending Knowledge Structures Approach.* Conference Paper: 33rd Annual Congress of the European Accounting Association. Istanbul.

Guiral-Contreras, A., Gonzalo-Angulo, J. A., & Rodgers, W. (2007). Information Content and Recency Effect of the Audit Report in Loan Rating Decisions. *Accounting & Finance*, *47*, 285–304.

Habbershon, T. G., Williams, M., & MacMillan, I. C. (2003). A Unified Systems Perspective of Family Firm Performance. *Journal of Business Venturing*, *18*, 451–465.

Habbershon, T. G., & Williams, M. L. (1999). A Resource-Based Framework for Assessing the Strategic Advantages of Family Firms. *Family Business Review*, *12*, 1–25.

Hahn, G., & Shapiro, S. (1966). *A Catalogue and Computer Program for the Design and Analysis of Orthogonal Symmetric and Asymmetric Fractional Factorial Designs.* Report Nr. 66-C-165. Schenectady: General Electric Corporation.

Hair, J. F., Anderson, R. E., Tatham, R. L., & Black, W. C. (1995). *Multivariate Data Analysis with Readings.* (4th ed.). Englewood Cliffs: Prentice Hall.

Haizlip, J., May, N., Schorling, J., Williams, A., & Plews-Ogan, M. (2012). Perspective: The Negativity Bias, Medical Education, and the Culture of Academic Medicine: Why Culture Change Is Hard. *Academic Medicine*, *87*.

Haslam, S. A. (2004). *Psychology in Organizations: The Social Identity Approach.* (2nd ed.). London, Thousand Oaks: Sage Pub.

Hau, H., & Thum, M. (2009). Subprime Crisis and Board (In-) Competence: Private Versus Public Banks in Germany. *Economic Policy*, *24*, 701–752.

Hauswald, H., & Hack, A. (in press). Impact of Family Control/Influence on Stakeholders' Perceptions of Benevolence. *Family Business Review.*

Hayton, J. C., Allen, D. G., & Scarpello, V. (2004). Factor Retention Decisions in Exploratory Factor Analysis: a Tutorial on Parallel Analysis. *Organizational Research Methods*, *7*, 191–205.

Healy, P. M., & Palepu, K. G. (2001). Information Asymmetry, Corporate Disclosure, and the Capital Markets: A Review of the Empirical Disclosure Literature. *Journal of Accounting and Economics*, *31*, 405–440.

Heider, F. (1958). *The Psychology of Interpersonal Relations.* Hillsdale: Erlbaum.

Henderson, R., & Cockburn, I. (1994). Measuring Competence? Exploring Firm Effects in Pharmaceutical Research. *Strategic Management Journal*, *15*, 63–84.

Hernández-Cánovas, G., & Martínez-Solano, P. (2006). Banking Relationships: Effects on Debt Terms for Small Spanish Firms. *Journal of Small Business Management*, *44*, 315–333.

Herr, P. M., Sherman, S. J., & Fazio, R. H. (1983). On the Consequences of Priming: Assimilation and Contrast Effects. *Journal of Experimental Social Psychology*, *19*, 323–340.

Herzenstein, M., Sonenshein, S., & Dholakia, U. M. (2011). Tell Me a Good Story and I May Lend You Money: The Role of Narratives in Peer-to-Peer Lending Decisions. *Journal of Marketing Research, 48*, S138.

Higgins, E. T., Bargh, J. A., & Lombardi, W. J. (1985). The Nature of Priming Effects on Categorization. *Journal of Experimental Psychology: Learning, Memory, and Cognition, 11*, 59–69.

Higgins, E. T., & King, G. (1981). Accessibility of Social Constructs: Information Processing Consequences of Individual and Contextual Variability. In N. Cantor, & J. F. Kihlstrom (Eds.), *Personality, Cognition, and Social Interaction* (pp. 69–121). Hillsdale: L. Erlbaum Associates.

Hofmann, D. A., & Gavin, M. B. (1998). Centering Decisions in Hierarchical Linear Models: Implications for Research in Organizations. *Journal of Management, 24*, 623–641.

Holder-Webb, L., & Sharma, D. S. (2010). The Effect of Governance on Credit Decisions and Perceptions of Reporting Reliability. *Behavioral Research in Accounting, 22*, 1–20.

Homburg, C., Schneider, J., & Fassnacht, M. (2002). Opposites Attract, but Similarity Works: A Study of Interorganizational Similarity in Marketing Channels. *Journal of Business-to-Business Marketing, 10*, 31–54.

Horn, J. L. (1965). A Rationale and Test for the Number of Factors in Factor Analysis. *Psychometrika, 30*, 179-185.

Howe, K. R. (2004). A Critique of Experimentalism. *Qualitative Inquiry, 10*, 42–61.

Hoyle, R. H. (1993). Interpersonal Attraction in the Absence of Explicit Attitudinal Information. *Social Cognition, 11*, 309–320.

Huber, J., & Hansen, D. (1986). Testing the Impact of Dimensional Complexity and Affective Differences of Paired Concepts in Adaptive Conjoint Analysis. In M. Wallendorf, & P. Anderson (Eds.), *Advances in Consumer Research* (pp. 159–163). Provo: Association for Consumer Research.

Hutcheson, G., & Sofroniou, N. (1999). *The Multivariate Social Scientist: Introductory Statistics Using Generalized Linear Models*. London, Thousand Oaks: Sage Pub.

Hutzschenreuter, J. (2009). *Management Control in Small and Medium-Sized Enterprises: Indirect Control Forms, Control Combinations and Their Effect on Company Performance*. Wiesbaden: Gabler.

Huybrechts, J., Voordeckers, W., Lybaert, N., & Vandemaele, S. (2011). The Distinctiveness of Family-Firm Intangibles: A Review and Suggestions for Future Research. *Journal of Management & Organization, 17*, 268–287.

Inglehart, R. (1971). The Silent Revolution in Europe: Intergenerational Change in Post-Industrial Societies. *American Political Science Review, 65*, 991–1017.

International Family Enterprise Research Academy (2003). Family Businesses Dominate: International Family Enterprise Research Academy (IFERA). *Family Business Review, 16*, 235–240.

Isen, A. M., Nygren, T. E., & Ashby, G. F. (1988). Influence of Positive Affect on the Subjective Utility of Gains and Losses: It Is Just Not Worth The Risk. *Journal of Personality and Social Psychology*, *55*, 710–717.

Jackson, S. E., Brett, J. F., Sessa, V. I., Cooper, D. M., Julin, J. A., & Peyronnin, K. (1991). Some Differences Make a Difference: Individual Dissimilarity and Group Heterogeneity as Correlates of Recruitment, Promotions, and Turnover. *Journal of Applied Psychology*, *76*, 675–689.

Jankowicz, A., & Hisrich, R. (1987). Intuition in Small Business Lending Decisions. *Journal of Small Business Management*, *25*, 45–52.

Jensen, M. C., & Meckling, W. H. (1976). Theory of the Firm: Managerial Behavior, Agency Costs and Ownership Structure. *Journal of Financial Economics*, *3*, 305–360.

Jiménez, G., Salas-Fumás, V., & Saurina, J. (2011). The Effects of Formal and Informal Contracting in Credit Availability. *Journal of Money, Credit and Banking*, *43*, 109–132.

Johnson, D. A., Pany, K., & White, R. (1983). Audit Reports and the Loan Decision: Actions and Perceptions. *Auditing: A Journal of Practice and Theory*, *2*, 38–51.

Johnson, J. L., Daily, C. M., & Ellstrand, A. E. (1996). Boards of Directors: A Review and Research Agenda. *Journal of Management*, *22*, 409–438.

Johnson, R. M. (1974). Trade-off Analysis of Consumer Values. *Journal of Marketing Research*, *11*, 121–127.

Johnson, R. M. (1987). Adaptive Conjoint Analysis. In Sawtooth Software Inc. (Ed.), *Proceedings' of the Sawtooth Software Conference on Perceptual Mapping, Conjoint Analysis and Computer Interview* (pp. 253–265). Ketchum: Sawtooth Software Inc.

Johnson-Laird, P. N. (1983). *Mental Models: Towards a Cognitive Science of Language, Inference, and Consciousness*. Cambridge: Harvard University Press.

Jones, C. D., Makri, M., & Gomez-Mejia, L. R. (2008). Affiliate Directors and Perceived Risk Bearing in Publicly Traded, Family-Controlled Firms: The Case of Diversification. *Entrepreneurship Theory and Practice*, *32*, 1007–1026.

Kahneman, D. (1991). Anomalies: The Endowment Effect, Loss Aversion, and Status Quo Bias. *The Journal of Economic Perspectives*, *5*, 193–206.

Kahneman, D. (2000). Preface to Choices, Values, Fames. In D. Kahneman, & A. Tversky (Eds.), *Choices, Values, and Frames* (pp. ix–xvii). New York, Cambridge: Russell sage Foundation; Cambridge University Press.

Kahneman, D., Slovic, P., & Tversky, A. (Eds.) (1982). *Judgment Under Uncertainty: Heuristics and Biases*. Cambridge: Cambridge University Press.

Kahneman, D., & Tversky, A. (1979). Prospect Theory: An Analysis of Decision under Risk. *Econometrica*, *47*, 263–292.

Kaiser, H. F. (1974). An Index of Factorial Simplicity. *Psychometrika*, *39*, 31-36.

Kang, D. (2000). *The Impact of Family Ownership on Performance in Public Organizations: A Study of the US Fortune 500, 1982-1994*. Working Paper.

Karra, N., Tracey, P., & Phillips, N. (2006). Altruism and Agency in the Family Firm: Exploring the Role of Family, Kinship, and Ethnicity. *Entrepreneurship Theory and Practice*, *30*, 861–877.

Keasey, K., & McGuinness, P. (1990). Small New Firms and the Return to Alternative Sources of Finance. *Small Business Economics*, *2*, 213-222.

Kellermanns, F. W., Eddleston, K. A., & Zellweger, T. M. (2012). Extending the Socioemotional Wealth Perspective: A Look at the Dark Side. *Entrepreneurship Theory and Practice*, *36*, 1175–1182.

Keren, G., & Teigen, K. K. (2007). Yet Another Look at the Heuristics and Biases Approach. In D. J. Koehler, & N. Harvey (Eds.), *Blackwell Handbook of Judgment and Decision Making* (pp. 89–109). Malden: Blackwell Pub.

Kets de Vries, M. F. (1993). The Dynamics of Family Controlled Firms: The Good and the Bad News. *Organizational Dynamics*, *21*, 59–71.

Kida, T. E., Moreno, K. K., & Smith, J. F. (2001). The Influence of Affect on Managers' Capital-Budgeting Decisions. *Contemporary Accounting Research*, *18*, 477–494.

Kim, N. J., & Elias, R. Z. (2007). Financial Statements, Attestation Level and Lending Decision by Small Banks. *Southwest Business and Economics Journal*, *16*, 63–72.

Kimhi, A. (1997). Intergenerational Succession in Small Family Businesses: Borrowing Constraints and Optimal Timing of Succession. *Small Business Economics*, *9*, 309–318.

Kirk, R. E. (1995). *Experimental Design: Procedures for the Behavioral Sciences.* (3rd ed.). Pacific Grove: Brooks/Cole.

Kitindi, E. G., Magembe, B. A. S., & Sethibe, A. (2007). Lending Decision Making and Financial Information: The Usefulness of Corporate Annual Reports to Lenders in Botswana. *International Journal of Applied Economics and Finance*, *1*, 55–66.

Kleine, S. S., Kleine, R. E., III, & Allen, C. T. (1995). How Is a Possession "Me" or "Not Me"? Characterizing Types and an Antecedent of Material Possession Attachment. *Journal of Consumer Research*, *22*, 327–43.

Kline, P. (1999). *The Handbook of Psychological Testing.* (2nd ed.). London, New York: Routledge.

Kornblum, S., Hasbroucq, T., & Osman, A. (1990). Dimensional Overlap: Cognitive Basis for Stimulus-Response Compatibility - A Model and Taxonomy. *Psychological Review*, *97*, 253–270.

Kreft, I. G. G., & Leeuw, J. de (1998). *Introducing Multilevel Modeling*. London, Thousand Oaks: Sage Pub.

Kreft, I. G. G., Leeuw, J. de, & Aiken, L. S. (1995). The Effect of Different Forms of Centering in Hierarchical Linear Models. *Multivariate Behavioral Research*, *30*, 1–21.

Kreps, D. M., & Wilson, R. (1982). Reputation and Imperfect Information. *Journal of Economic Theory*, *27*, 253–279.

Krosnick, J. A., & Alwin, D. F. (1988). A Test of the Form-Resistant Correlation Hypothesis: Ratings, Rankings, and the Measurement of Values. *The Public Opinion Quarterly, 52*, 526–538.

Kühberger, A. (1998). The Influence of Framing on Risky Decisions: A Meta-analysis. *Organizational Behavior and Human Decision Processes, 75*, 23–55.

Lado, A. A., Boyd, N. G., & Wright, P. (1992). A Competency-Based Model of Sustainable Competitive Advantage: Toward a Conceptual Integration. *Journal of Management, 18*, 77–91.

Lambrechts, F., Koiranen, M., Grieten, S., & Bouwen, R. (2009). *Co-Creating Psychological Ownership for Change. Applying a Relational Practice Perspective in Family Business.* Conference Paper: 5th EIASM Workshop on Family Firm Management Research. Hasselt.

Larrick, R. P. (2007). Debiasing. In D. J. Koehler, & N. Harvey (Eds.), *Blackwell Handbook of Judgment and Decision Making* (pp. 316–337). Malden: Blackwell Pub.

Laudan, L. (1984). *Science and Values: The Aims of Science and their Role in Scientific Debate*. Berkeley: University of California Press.

Lazarsfeld, P. F., & Merton, R. K. (1954). Friendship as a Social Process: A Substantive and Methodological Analysis. In M. Berger, T. Abel, & C. H. Page (Eds.), *Freedom and Control in Modern Society* (pp. 18–66). New York: Van Nostrand.

Le Breton-Miller, I., & Miller, D. (2006). Why Do Some Family Businesses Out-Compete? Governance, Long-Term Orientations, and Sustainable Capability. *Entrepreneurship Theory and Practice, 30*, 731–746.

Leeth, J. D., & Scott, J. A. (1989). The Incidence of Secured Debt: Evidence from the Small Business Community. *Journal of Financial and Quantitative Analysis, 24*, 379–394.

Lehmann, E., & Neuberger, D. (2001). Do Lending Relationships Matter?: Evidence from Bank Survey Data in Germany. *Journal of Economic Behavior & Organization, 45*, 339–359.

Leland, H. E., & Pyle, D. H. (1977). Informational Asymmetries, Financial Structure, and Financial Intermediation. *The Journal of Finance, 32*, 371–387.

Levie, J., & Lerner, M. (2009). Resource Mobilization and Performance in Family and Non-family Businesses in the United Kingdom. *Family Business Review, 22*, 25–38.

Levin, I. P., & Gaeth, G. J. (1988). How Consumers are Affected by the Framing of Attribute Information Before and After Consuming the Product. *Journal of Consumer Research, 15*, 374–378.

Levin, I. P., Gaeth, G. J., Schreiber, J., & Lauriola, M. (2002). A New Look at Framing Effects: Distribution of Effect Sizes, Individual Differences, and Independence of Types of Effects. *Organizational Behavior and Human Decision Processes, 88*, 411–429.

Levin, I. P., Johnson, R. D., Russo, C. P., & Deldin, P. J. (1985). Framing Effects in Judgment Tasks with Varying Amounts of Information. *Organizational Behavior and Human Decision Processes, 36*, 362–377.

Levin, I. P., Schneider, S. L., & Gaeth, G. J. (1998). All Frames Are Not Created Equal: A Typology and Critical Analysis of Framing Effects. *Organizational Behavior and Human Decision Processes, 76*, 149–188.

Lichtenthal, J. D., & Tellefsen, T. (2001). Toward a Theory of Business Buyer-Seller Similarity. *The Journal of Personal Selling and Sales Management, 21*, 1–14.

Lipshitz, R., & Shulimovitz, N. (2007). Intuition and Emotion in Bank Loan Officers' Credit Decisions. *Journal of Cognitive Engineering and Decision Making, 1*, 212–233.

Litz, R. A. (1995). The Family Business: Toward Definitional Clarity. *Family Business Review, 8*, 71–81.

Lohrke, F. T., Holloway, B. B., & Woolley, T. W. (2010). Conjoint Analysis in Entrepreneurship Research: A Review and Research Agenda. *Organizational Research Methods, 13*, 16–30.

Louviere, J. J. (1988). Conjoint Analysis Modelling of Stated Preferences: A Review of Theory, Methods, Recent Developments and External Validity. *Journal of Transport Economics and Policy, 22*, 93–119.

Louviere, J. J., Hensher, D. A., & Swait, J. D. (2000). *Stated Choice Methods: Analysis and Applications*. Cambridge: Cambridge University Press.

Lubatkin, M. H., Schulze, W. S., Ling, Y., & Dino, R. N. (2005). The Effects of Parental Altruism on the Governance of Family-Managed Firms. *Journal of Organizational Behavior, 26*, 313–330.

Luce, R. D., & Tukey, J. W. (1964). Simultaneous Conjoint Measurement: A New Type of Fundamental Measurement. *Journal of Mathematical Psychology, 1*, 1–27.

Machauer, A., & Weber, M. (1998). Bank Behavior Based on Internal Credit Ratings of Borrowers. *Journal of Banking & Finance, 22*, 1355–1383.

Mahoney, J. T., & Pandian, J. R. (1992). The Resource-Based View within the Conversation of Strategic Management. *Strategic Management Journal, 13*, 363–380.

Malhotra, N. K. (1982). Information Load and Consumer Decision Making. *Journal of Consumer Research, 8*, 419–30.

Maslow, A. H. (1954). *Motivation and Personality*. New York: Harper & Brothers.

Mason, C., & Stark, M. (2004). What do Investors Look for in a Business Plan? *International Small Business Journal, 22*, 227–248.

Maule, J., & Villejoubert, G. (2007). What Lies Beneath: Reframing Framing Effects. *Thinking & Reasoning, 13*, 25–44.

Mazumdar, S. C., & Sengupta, P. (2005). Disclosure and the Loan Spread on Private Debt. *Financial Analysts Journal, 61*, 83–95.

McConaugby, D. L., Matthews, C. H., & Fialko, A. S. (2001). Founding Family Controlled Firms: Performance, Risk, and Value. *Journal of Small Business Management, 39*, 31–49.

McKenzie, C. M., & Nelson, J. (2003). What a Speaker's Choice of Frame Reveals: Reference Points, Frame Selection, and Framing Effects. *Psychonomic Bulletin & Review, 10*, 596-602.

McNamara, G., & Bromiley, P. (1997). Decision Making in an Organizational Setting: Cognitive and Organizational Influences on Risk Assessment in Commercial Lending. *The Academy of Management Journal, 40*, 1063–1088.

Mellers, B. A., Schwartz, A., Ho, K., & Ritov, I. (1997). Decision Affect Theory: Emotional Reactions to the Outcomes of Risky Options. *Psychological Science, 8*, 423–429.

Menkhoff, L., Neuberger, D., & Suwanaporn, C. (2006). Collateral-Based Lending in Emerging Markets: Evidence from Thailand. *Journal of Banking & Finance, 30*, 1–21.

Meyerowitz, B. E., & Chaiken, S. (1987). The Effect of Message Framing on Breast Self-Examination Attitudes, Intentions, and Behavior. *Journal of Personality and Social Psychology, 52*, 500–510.

Micelotta, E. R., & Raynard, M. (2011). Concealing or Revealing the Family? Corporate Brand Identity Strategies in Family Firms. *Family Business Review, 24*, 197–216.

Miller, D., Le Breton-Miller, I., Lester, R. H., & Cannella, A. A., JR. (2007). Are Family Firms Really Superior Performers? *Journal of Corporate Finance, 13*, 829–858.

Minichilli, A., Corbetta, G., & MacMillan, I. C. (2010). Top Management Teams in Family-Controlled Companies: 'Familiness', 'Faultlines', and Their Impact on Financial Performance. *Journal of Management Studies, 47*, 205–222.

Minichilli, A., Zattoni, A., & Zona, F. (2009). Making Boards Effective: An Empirical Examination of Board Task Performance. *British Journal of Management, 20*, 55–74.

Monsen, E., Patzelt, H., & Saxton, T. (2010). Beyond Simple Utility: Incentive Design and Trade-Offs for Corporate Employee-Entrepreneurs. *Entrepreneurship Theory and Practice, 34*, 105–130.

Montgomery, D. C. (2009). *Design and Analysis of Experiments*. International Student Version. (7th ed.). Hoboken: Wiley.

Montoya, R. M., Horton, R. S., & Kirchner, J. (2008). Is Actual Similarity Necessary for Attraction? A Meta-Analysis of Actual and Perceived Similarity. *Journal of Social and Personal Relationships, 25*, 889–922.

Moore, D. S., & McCabe, G. P. (1993). *Introduction to the Practice of Statistics*. (2nd ed.). New York: Freeman.

Moore, W. L., & Holbrook, M. B. (1990). Conjoint Analysis on Objects with Environmentally Correlated Attributes: The Questionable Importance of Representative Design. *Journal of Consumer Research, 16*, 490–497.

Moores, K. (2009). Paradigms and Theory Building in the Domain of Business Families. *Family Business Review, 22*, 167–180.

Morck, R., & Yeung, B. (2003). Agency Problems in Large Family Business Groups. *Entrepreneurship Theory and Practice, 27*, 367–382.

Morck, R., & Yeung, B. (2004). Family Control and the Rent-Seeking Society. *Entrepreneurship Theory and Practice*, *28*, 391–409.

Moskowitz, H., Krieger, B., & Rabino, S. (2002). Element Category Importance in Conjoint Analysis: Evidence for Segment Differences. *Journal of Targeting, Measurement and Analysis for Marketing*, *10*, 366–384.

Mueller, H. M., & Inderst, R. (1999). *Ownership Concentration, Monitoring, and the Agency Cost of Debt*. Working Paper.

Mulrow, C. D. (1994). Systematic Reviews: Rationale for Systematic Reviews. *BMJ*, *309*, 597–599.

Murnieks, C. Y., Haynie, J. M., Wiltbank, R. E., & Harting, T. (2011). 'I Like How You Think': Similarity as an Interaction Bias in the Investor–Entrepreneur Dyad. *Journal of Management Studies*, *48*, 1533–1561.

Myers, S. C. (1977). Determinants of Corporate Borrowing. *Journal of Financial Economics*, *5*, 147–175.

Myers, S. C. (1984). The Capital Structure Puzzle. *The Journal of Finance*, *39*, 575–592.

Naldi, L., Nordqvist, M., Sjöberg, K., & Wiklund, J. (2007). Entrepreneurial Orientation, Risk Taking, and Performance in Family Firms. *Family Business Review*, *20*, 33–47.

Naldi, L., Nordqvist, M., & Zellweger, T. M. (2008). *Intangible Resources and Family Firm Performance: The Moderating Role Family Involvement in Strategy Making*. Conference Paper: Babson Kaufmann Entrepreneurship Research Conference. Chapel Hill.

Neubauer, G. (2003). An IRT-Approach for Conjoint Analysis. *Advances in Methodology and Statistics*, 35–47.

Newbert, S. L. (2007). Empirical Research on the Resource-Based View of the Firm: An Assessment and Suggestions for Future Research. *Strategic Management Journal*, *28*, 121–146.

Niskanen, M., Kaikkonen, V., & Niskanen, J. (2010). The Debt Agency Costs of Family Ownership: Firm Level Evidence on Small and Micro Firms. *International Journal of Entrepreneurship and Small Business*, *11*, 353–366.

Olson, P. D., Zuiker, V. S., Danes, S. M., Stafford, K., Heck, R. K. Z., & Duncan, K. A. (2003). The Impact of the Family and the Business on Family Business Sustainability. *Journal of Business Venturing*, *18*, 639–666.

Orme, B. K. (2010). *Getting Started with Conjoint Analysis: Strategies for Product Design and Pricing Research*. (2nd ed.). Madison: Research Publishers.

Orpen, C. (1984). Attitude Similarity, Attraction, and Decision-Making in the Employment Interview. *The Journal of Psychology*, *117*, 111–120.

Ortiz-Molina, H., & Penas, M. F. (2004). *Lending to Small Businesses: The Role of Loan Maturity in Adressing Information Problems*. Discussion Paper.

Ortiz-Molina, H., & Penas, M. F. (2008). Lending to Small Businesses: The Role of Loan Maturity in Addressing Information Problems. *Small Business Economics*, *30*, 361–383.

Padilla, A. (2002). *Property Economics of Agency Problems*. Working Paper.

Panagopoulos, Y., & Spiliotis, A. (1998). The Determinants of Commercial Banks' Lending Behavior: Some Evidence for Greece. *Journal of Post Keynesian Economics*, *20*, 649–672.

Park, C. (2000). Monitoring and Structure of Debt Contracts. *The Journal of Finance*, *55*, 2157–2195.

Patzelt, H., Lechner, C., & Klaukien, A. (2011). Networks and the Decision to Persist with Underperforming R&D Projects. *Journal of Product Innovation Management*, *28*, 801–815.

Patzelt, H., & Shepherd, D. A. (2008). The Decision to Persist with Underperforming Alliances: The Role of Trust and Control. *Journal of Management Studies*, *45*, 1217–1243.

Patzelt, H., & Shepherd, D. A. (2009). Strategic Entrepreneurship at Universities: Academic Entrepreneurs' Assessment of Policy Programs. *Entrepreneurship Theory and Practice*, *33*, 319–340.

Peeters, G., & Czapinski, J. (1990). Positive-Negative Asymmetry in Evaluations: The Distinction Between Affective and Informational Negativity Effects. *European Review of Social Psychology*, *1*, 33–60.

Penrose, E. T. (1959). *The Theory of the Growth of the Firm*. New York: Wiley.

Peteraf, M. A. (1993). The Cornerstones of Competitive Advantage: A Resource-Based View. *Strategic Management Journal*, *14*, 179–191.

Petersen, M. A., & Rajan, R. G. (1995). The Effect of Credit Market Competition on Lending Relationships. *The Quarterly Journal of Economics*, *110*, 407–443.

Pfeffer, J., & Salancik, G. R. (1978). *The External Control of Organizations*. New York: Harper & Row Publishers.

Phelps, R. H., & Shanteau, J. (1978). Livestock Judges: How Much Information Can an Expert Use? *Organizational Behavior and Human Performance*, *21*, 209–219.

Picot, A., Dietl, H., & Franck, E. (2005). *Organisation: Eine Ökonomische Perspektive*. (4th ed.). Stuttgart: Schäffer-Poeschel.

Piñon, A., & Gambara, H. (2005). A Meta-Analytic Review of Framing Effect: Risky, Attribute and Goal Framing. *Psicothema*, *17*, 325–331.

Pocock, S. J. (1984). *Clinical Trials: A Practical Approach*. New York: Wiley.

Porter, M. E. (1979). How Competitive Forces Shape Strategy. *Harvard Business Review*, *57*, 137–145.

Porter, M. E. (1985). *Competitive Advantage: Creating and Sustaining Superior Performance*. New York: Free Press.

Poutziouris, P. Z. (2001). The Views of Family Companies on Venture Capital: Empirical Evidence from the UK Small to Medium-Size Enterprising Economy. *Family Business Review*, *14*, 277–291.

Powell, T. C. (2001). Competitive Advantage: Logical and Philosophical Considerations. *Strategic Management Journal*, *22*, 875–888.

Prahalad, C. K., & Hamel, G. (1990). The Core Competence of the Corporation. *Harvard Business Review*, *68*, 375–405.

Presas, P., Muñoz, D., & Guia, J. (2011). Branding Familiness in Tourism Family Firms. *The Journal of Brand Management*, *18*, 274–284.

Preston, C. C., & Colman, A. M. (2000). Optimal Number of Response Categories in Rating Scales: Reliability, Validity, Discriminating Power, and Respondent Preferences. *Acta Psychologica*, *104*, 1–15.

Priem, R. L., & Butler, J. E. (2001). Is the Resource-Based "View" a Useful Perspective for Strategic Management Research? *Academy of Management Review*, *26*, 22–40.

Ptacek, J. T., & Dodge, K. L. (1995). Coping Strategies and Relationship Satisfaction in Couples. *Personality and Social Psychology Bulletin*, *21*, 76–84.

Quiry, P., Vernimmen, P., Le Fur, Y., Dallochio, M., & Salvi, A. (2011). *Corporate Finance: Theory and Practice*. (3rd ed.). Chicester: Wiley.

Raiffa, H. (1968). *Decision Analysis: Introductory Lectures on Choices Under Uncertainty*. Reading: Addison-Wesley.

Rajan, R. G., & Winton, A. (1995). Covenants and Collateral as Incentives to Monitor. *Journal of Finance*, *50*, 1113–1146.

Randøy, T., & Goel, S. (2003). Ownership Structure, Founder Leadership, and Performance in Norwegian SMEs: Implications for Financing Entrepreneurial Opportunities. *Journal of Business Venturing*, *18*, 619–637.

Raudenbush, S. W., & Bryk, A. S. (2002). *Hierarchical Linear Models: Applications and Data Analysis Methods*. (2nd ed.). Thousand Oaks: Sage Pub.

Ravina, E. (2012). *Love & Loans: The Effect of Beauty and Personal Characteristics in Credit Markets*. Working Paper.

Ray, G., Barney, J. B., & Muhanna, W. A. (2004). Capabilities, Business Processes, and Competitive Advantage: Choosing the Dependent Variable in Empirical Tests of the Resource-Based View. *Strategic Management Journal*, *25*, 23–37.

Reed, R., & Defillippi, R. J. (1990). Causal Ambiguity, Barriers to Imitation, and Sustainable Competitive Advantage. *The Academy of Management Review*, *15*, 88–102.

Reutterer, T., & Kotzab, H. W. (2000). The Use of Conjoint-Analysis for Measuring Preferences in Supply Chain Design. *Industrial Marketing Management*, *29*, 27–35.

Riquelme, H., & Rickards, T. (1992). Hybrid Conjoint Analysis: An Estimation Probe in New Venture Decisions. *Journal of Business Venturing*, *7*, 505–518.

Robberson, M. R., & Rogers, R. W. (1988). Beyond Fear Appeals: Negative and Positive Persuasive Appeals to Health and Self-Esteem. *Journal of Applied Social Psychology*, *18*, 277–287.

Roberts, M. R., & Whited, T. M. (2012). *Endogeneity in Empirical Corporate Finance*. Working Paper.

Rodgers, W. (1999). The Influences of Conflicting Information on Novices and Loan Officers' Actions. *Journal of Economic Psychology*, *20*, 123–145.

Romano, C. A., Tanewski, G. A., & Smyrnios, K. X. (2001). Capital Structure Decision Making: A Model for Family Business. *Journal of Business Venturing*, *16*, 285–310.

Rosenbaum, M. E. (1986). The Repulsion Hypothesis: On the Nondevelopment of Relationships. *Journal of Personality and Social Psychology*, *51*, 1156–1166.

Rosman, A. J., & O'Neill, H. M. (1993). Comparing the Information Acquisition Strategies of Venture Capital and Commercial Lenders: A Computer-Based Experiment. *Journal of Business Venturing*, *8*, 443–460.

Ross, J. W., Beath, C. M., & Goodhue, D. L. (1996). Develop Long-Term Competitiveness Through IT Assets. *Sloan Management Review*, *38*, 31–42.

Ross, S. A. (1973). The Economic Theory of Agency: The Principal's Problem. *American Economic Review*, *63*, 134–39.

Roszkowski, M. J., & Snelbecker, G. E. (1990). Effects of "Framing" on Measures of Risk Tolerance: Financial Planners are Not Immune. *Journal of Behavioral Economics*, *19*, 237–246.

Rothman, A. J., Salovey, P., Antone, C., Keough, K., & Martin, C. D. (1993). The Influence of Message Framing on Intentions to Perform Health Behaviors. *Journal of Experimental Social Psychology*, *29*, 408–433.

Rottenstreich, Y., & Shu, S. (2007). The Connections Between Affect and Decision Making: Nine Resulting Phenomena. In D. J. Koehler, & N. Harvey (Eds.), *Blackwell Handbook of Judgment and Decision Making* (pp. 444–463). Malden: Blackwell Pub.

Rozin, P., & Royzman, E. B. (2001). Negativity Bias, Negativity Dominance, and Contagion. *Personality and Social Psychology Review*, *5*, 296–320.

Rubin, P. H. (1973). The Expansion of Firms. *Journal of Political Economy*, *81*, 936–949.

Rüsen, T. A., & Schlippe, A. von (2007). Krisen in Familienunternehmen und Unternehmensfamilien: Über parallele, interdependente Dynamiken in Familie und Unternehmen. *Organisationsberatung, Supervision, Coaching*, *14*, 309–330.

Russell, P. A., & Gray, C. D. (1994). Ranking or Rating? Some Data and their Implications for the Measurement of Evaluative Response. *British Journal of Psychology*, *85*, 79–92.

Russo, J., Medvec, V. H., & Meloy, M. G. (1996). The Distortion of Information during Decisions. *Organizational Behavior and Human Decision Processes*, *66*, 102–110.

Rutte, C. G., Wilke, H. A. M., & Messick, D. M. (1987). The Effects of Framing Social Dilemmas as Give-Some or Take-Some Games. *British Journal of Social Psychology*, *26*, 103–108.

Ryan, M., & Farrar, S. (2000). Using Conjoint Analysis to Elicit Preferences for Health Care. *BMJ*, *320*, 1530–1533.

Salvato, C., & Moores, K. (2010). Research on Accounting in Family Firms: Past Accomplishments and Future Challenges. *Family Business Review, 23*, 193–215.

Schein, E. H. (1984). Coming to a New Awareness of Organizational Culture. *Sloan Management Review, 25*, 2–15.

Schlippe, A. von, Nischak, A., & El Hachimi, M. (2008). Familienunternehmen verstehen. In A. von Schlippe, A. Nischak, & M. El Hachimi (Eds.), *Familienunternehmen verstehen: Gründer, Gesellschafter und Generationen* (pp. 19–29). Göttingen: Vandenhoeck & Ruprecht.

Schneider, A., & Church, B. K. (2008). The Effect of Auditors' Internal Control Opinions on Loan Decisions. *Journal of Accounting and Public Policy, 27*, 1–18.

Schulze, W. S., Lubatkin, M. H., & Dino, R. N. (2003). Toward a Theory of Agency and Altruism in Family Firms. *Journal of Business Venturing, 18*, 473–490.

Schulze, W. S., Lubatkin, M. H., Dino, R. N., & Buchholtz, A. K. (2001). Agency Relationships in Family Firms: Theory and Evidence. *Organization Science, 12*, 99–116.

Schwartz, A., Goldberg, J., & Hazen, G. (2008). Prospect Theory, Reference Points, and Health Decisions. *Judgment and Decision Making, 3*, 174–180.

Schwarz, N. (2000). Emotion, Cognition, and Decision Making. *Cognition and Emotion, 14*, 433–440.

Selznick, P. (1957). *Leadership in Administration: A Sociological Interpretation*. New York: Harper & Row Publishers.

Sengupta, P. (1998). Corporate Disclosure Quality and the Cost of Debt. *The Accounting Review, 73*, 459–474.

Sharma, P. (2003). *Stakeholder Mapping Technique: Toward the Development of a Family Firm Typology*. Working Paper. Waterloo.

Sharma, P. (2004). An Overview of the Field of Family Business Studies: Current Status and Directions for the Future. *Family Business Review, 17*, 1–36.

Sharma, P. (2008). Commentary: Familiness: Capital Stocks and Flows Between Family and Business. *Entrepreneurship Theory and Practice, 32*, 971–977.

Shaver, J. M. (1998). Accounting for Endogeneity When Assessing Strategy Performance: Does Entry Mode Choice Affect FDI Survival? *Management Science, 44*, 571–585.

Shepherd, D. A. (1999). Venture Capitalists' Assessment of New Venture Survival. *Management Science, 45*, 621–632.

Shepherd, D. A., Ettenson, R., & Crouch, A. (2000). New Venture Strategy and Profitability: A Venture Capitalist's Assessment. *Journal of Business Venturing, 15*, 449–467.

Shepherd, D. A., & Zacharakis, A. (1999). Conjoint Analysis: A New Methodological Approach for Researching the Decision Policies of Venture Capitalists. *Venture Capital, 1*, 197–217.

Sherman, S. J., Mackie, D. M., & Driscoll, D. M. (1990). Priming and the Differential Use of Dimensions in Evaluation. *Personality and Social Psychology Bulletin, 16*, 405–418.

Shiller, R. J. (1984). Stock Prices and Social Dynamics. *Brookings Papers on Economic Activity, 1984*, 457–510.

Shuto, A., & Kitagawa, N. (2011). The Effect of Managerial Ownership on the Cost of Debt. *Journal of Accounting, Auditing & Finance, 26*, 590–620.

Siebels, J.-F., & Knyphausen-Aufseß, D. zu (2012). A Review of Theory in Family Business Research: The Implications for Corporate Governance. *International Journal of Management Reviews, 14*, 280–304.

Simon, H. (1991). Organizations and Markets. *The Journal of Economic Perspectives, 5*, 25–44.

Sinkey, J. F. (2002). *Commercial Bank Financial Management in the Financial-Services Industry.* (6th ed.). Upper Saddle River: Prentice Hall.

Sirmon, D. G., & Hitt, M. A. (2003). Managing Resources: Linking Unique Resources, Management, and Wealth Creation in Family Firms. *Entrepreneurship Theory and Practice, 27*, 339–358.

Slovic, P., Fischhoff, B., & Lichtenstein, S. (1977). Behavioral Decision Theory. *Annual Review of Psychology, 28*, 1–39.

Smith, C. J. W., & Jensen, M. C. (2000). *Stockholder, Manager, and Creditor Interests: Applications of Agency Theory.*

Smith, C. J. W., & Warner, J. B. (1979). On Financial Contracting: An Analysis of Bond Covenants. *Journal of Financial Economics, 7*, 117–161.

Smith, J. B. (1998). Buyer–Seller Relationships: Similarity, Relationship Management, and Quality. *Psychology and Marketing, 15*, 3–21.

Soman, D. (2007). Framing, Loss Aversion, and Mental Accounting. In D. J. Koehler, & N. Harvey (Eds.), *Blackwell Handbook of Judgment and Decision Making* (pp. 379–398). Malden: Blackwell Pub.

Spence, M. (1973). Job Market Signaling. *The Quarterly Journal of Economics, 87*, 355–374.

Steijvers, T., & Voordeckers, W. (2009a). Collateral and Credit Rationing: A Review of Recent Empirical Studies as a Guide for Future Research. *Journal of Economic Surveys, 23*, 924–946.

Steijvers, T., & Voordeckers, W. (2009b). Private Family Ownership and the Agency Costs of Debt. *Family Business Review, 22*, 333–346.

Steijvers, T., Voordeckers, W., & Vanhoof, K. (2010). Collateral, Relationship Lending and Family Firms. *Small Business Economics, 34*, 243–259.

Stewart, T. R. (1993). *Notes on the Validity in Judgment Analysis.* Working Paper. Albany.

Stiglitz, J. E., & Weiss, A. (1981). Credit Rationing in Markets with Imperfect Information. *American Economic Review, 71*, 393–410.

Stockmans, A., Lybaert, N., & Voordeckers, W. (2010). Socioemotional Wealth and Earnings Management in Private Family Firms. *Family Business Review, 23*, 280–294.

Strauss, J. P., Barrick, M. R., & Connerley, M. L. (2001). An Investigation of Personality Similarity Effects (Relational and Perceived) on Peer and Supervisor Ratings and the Role of Familiarity and Liking. *Journal of Occupational and Organizational Psychology*, *74*, 637–657.

Tagiuri, R., & Davis, J. (1996). Bivalent Attributes of the Family Firm. *Family Business Review*, *9*, 199–208.

Tajfel, H., & Turner, J. C. (1986). The Social Identity Theory of Intergroup Behavior. In S. Worchel, & W. G. Austin (Eds.), *Psychology of Intergroup Relations* (pp. 7–24). Chicago: Nelson-Hall Publishers.

Taylor, S. E. (1991). Asymmetrical Effects of Positive and Negative Events: The Mobilization-Minimization Hypothesis. *Psychological Bulletin*, *110*, 67–85.

Tenenbaum, G., & Land, W. M. (2009). Mental Representations as an Underlying Mechanism for Human Performance. In M. Raab, J. G. Johnson, & H. R. Heekeren (Eds.), *Progress in Brain Research: The Bidirectional Link between Thought and Action* (pp. 251–266). Amsterdam, Boston: Elsevier.

Tokarczyk, J., Hansen, E., Green, M., & Down, J. (2007). A Resource-Based View and Market Orientation Theory Examination of the Role of "Familiness" in Family Business Success. *Family Business Review*, *20*, 17–31.

Tranfield, D., Denyer, D., & Smart, P. (2003). Towards a Methodology for Developing Evidence-Informed Management Knowledge by Means of Systematic Review. *British Journal of Management*, *14*, 207–222.

Trevino, L. K. (1986). Ethical Decision Making in Organizations: A Person–Situation Interactionist Model. *The Academy of Management Review*, *11*, 601–617.

Trotman, A. J., & Trotman, K. T. (2010). The Intersection of Family Business and Audit Research: Potential Opportunities. *Family Business Review*, *23*, 216–229.

Tsui, A. S., Egan, T. D., & O'Reilly, C. A., III (1992). Being Different: Relational Demography and Organizational Attachment. *Administrative Science Quarterly*, *37*, 549–579.

Tuckman, B. W. (1999). *Conducting Educational Research.* (5th ed.). Fort Worth: Harcourt Brace College Publishers.

Turner, J. C. (1988). *Rediscovering the Social Group: A Self-Categorization Theory*. Oxford: Blackwell Pub.

Tversky, A., & Kahneman, D. (1974). Judgment under Uncertainty: Heuristics and Biases. *Science*, *185*, 1124–1131.

Tversky, A., & Kahneman, D. (1981). The Framing of Decisions and the Psychology of Choice. *Science*, *211*, 453–458.

Uhlaner, L. M., van Goor-Balk, H., & Masurel, E. (2004). Family Business and Corporate Social Responsibility in a Sample of Dutch Firms. *Journal of Small Business and Enterprise Development*, *11*, 186–194.

Ulrich, T. A., & Arlow, P. (1981). A Multivariate Analysis Of Commercial Bank Lending To Small Business. *American Journal of Small Business, 6*, 47–57.

Voordeckers, W., & Steijvers, T. (2006). Business Collateral and Personal Commitments in SME Lending. *Journal of Banking & Finance, 30*, 3067–3086.

Ward, J. L. (1987). *Keeping the Family Business Healthy: How to Plan for Continuing Growth, Profitability, and Family Leadership*. San Francisco: Jossey-Bass.

Waterston, J. (1979). Compilation, Reviews and the Division for CPA Firms: A Bankers Perspective. *The Journal of Commercial Bank Lending, 4*, 11–18.

Webster, J., & Watson, R. (2002). Analyzing the Past to Prepare for the Future: Writing a Literature Review. *MIS Quarterly, 26*, xiii.

Werner, C., & Parmelee, P. (1979). Similarity of Activity Preferences among Friends: Those Who Play Together Stay Together. *Social Psychology Quarterly, 42*, 62–66.

Wernerfelt, B. (1984). A Resource-Based View of the Firm. *Strategic Management Journal, 5*, 171–180.

Wernick, C. (2007). *Strategic Investment Decisions in Regulated Markets: The Relationship Between Infrastructure Investments and Regulation in European Broadband*. Wiesbaden: Deutscher Universitätsverlag.

Wilson, F., Carter, S., Tagg, S., Shaw, E., & Lam, W. (2007). Bank Loan Officers' Perceptions of Business Owners: The Role of Gender. *British Journal of Management, 18*, 154–171.

Wiseman, R. M., & Gomez-Mejia, L. R. (1998). A Behavioral Agency Model of Managerial Risk Taking. *Academy of Management Review, 23*, 133–153.

Wittink, D. R., & Cattin, P. (1989). Commercial Use of Conjoint Analysis: An Update. *Journal of Marketing Research, 53*, 91–96.

Wittink, D. R., Vriens, M., & Burhenne, W. (1994). Commercial Use of Conjoint Analysis in Europe: Results and Critical Reflections. *International Journal of Research in Marketing, 11*, 41–52.

Wright, M., & Davidson, R. (2000). The Affect of Auditor Attestation and Tolerance for Ambiguity on Commercial Lending Decisions. *Auditing: A Journal of Practice and Theory, 19*, 67–81.

Yeong Tan, D. T., & Singh, R. (1995). Attitudes and Attraction: A Developmental Study of the Similarity-Attraction and Dissimilarity-Repulsion Hypotheses. *Personality and Social Psychology Bulletin, 21*, 975–986.

Yu, F. (2005). Accounting Transparency and the Term Structure of Credit Spreads. *Journal of Financial Economics, 75*, 53–84.

Zahra, S. A., Hayton, J. C., & Salvato, C. (2004). Entrepreneurship in Family vs. Non-Family Firms: A Resource-Based Analysis of the Effect of Organizational Culture. *Entrepreneurship Theory and Practice, 28*, 363–381.

Zellweger, T. M. (2006). *Risk, Return and Value in the Family Firm*. Dissertation at the University St. Gallen. Bamberg: Difo-Druck GmbH.

Zellweger, T. M., & Astrachan, J. H. (2008). On the Emotional Value of Owning a Firm. *Family Business Review, 21*, 347–363.

Zellweger, T. M., Eddleston, K. A., & Kellermanns, F. W. (2010). Exploring the Concept of Familiness: Introducing Family Firm Identity. *Journal of Family Business Strategy, 1*, 54–63.

Zellweger, T. M., Kellermanns, F. W., Chrisman, J. J., & Chua, J. H. (2012). Family Control and Family Firm Valuation by Family CEOs: The Importance of Intentions for Transgenerational Control. *Organization Science, 23*, 851–868.

Zellweger, T. M., Nason, R. S., Nordqvist, M., & Brush, C. G. (2011). Why Do Family Firms Strive for Nonfinancial Goals? An Organizational Identity Perspective. *Entrepreneurship Theory and Practice, 37*, 229–248.

CPSIA information can be obtained at www.ICGtesting.com
Printed in the USA
LVOW11s1618290714

396540LV00002B/229/P

9 783658 066826